IMAGES
of America

EARLY MARICOPA COUNTY 1871–1920

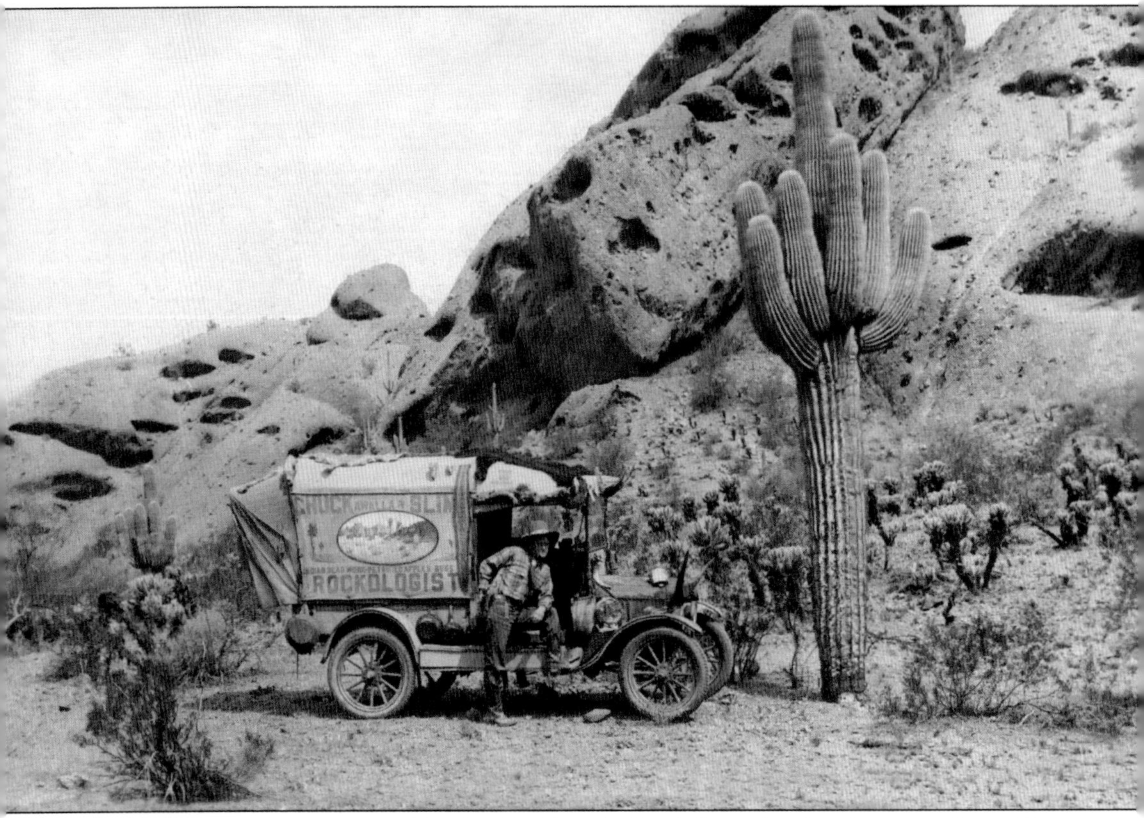

Edmund Ross, also known as "Chuckwalla Slim, the Rockologist," sold rocks, minerals, and Native American artifacts to tourists for over 30 years. He operated out of Los Angeles but traveled as an itinerant throughout the West. Here he poses with his truck with a Western diorama in the bed. (Real photographic postcard, photographer unknown, c. 1923. Collection of the author © vintagephoto.com.)

ON THE COVER: Watermelon was a popular crop in the Salt River Valley. This harvesting tableau shows several generations harvesting watermelon at E. F. Brusheur's ranch 4 miles north of downtown Phoenix. (Silver print, A. F. Messinger photographer, c. 1901. Collection of the author © vintagephoto.com.)

IMAGES
of America

EARLY MARICOPA COUNTY 1871–1920

Jeremy Rowe

ARCADIA PUBLISHING

ISBN 978-0-7385-7416-5

Published by Arcadia Publishing
Charleston, South Carolina

Printed in the United States of America

Library of Congress Control Number: 2010934683

For all general information, please contact Arcadia Publishing:
Telephone 843-853-2070
Fax 843-853-0044
E-mail sales@arcadiapublishing.com
For customer service and orders:
Toll-Free 1-888-313-2665

Visit us on the Internet at www.arcadiapublishing.com

The photographers that braved toxic chemistry, heavy equipment, glass plate negatives, and primitive, often dangerous travel and working conditions to create their images make our understanding and appreciation of Arizona's history possible. Collectors, libraries, and archives have acquired and preserved the images that have not been lost to careless handling or lack of recognition of the importance of the images through the years. This book is dedicated to these pioneers, be they amateurs or professionals, that took the time to capture these images for posterity, and to my grandsons Brendan and Ethan, in hopes that they will help preserve and interpret this visual legacy.

Contents

Acknowledgments

The author would like to than the fellow collectors and dealers that have helped build the collection that appears in this book over the past 30 years. Libraries and archives have assisted in providing the background information to help understand and interpret these images. Pioneers like Herb and Dorothy McLaughlin helped build initial awareness of historic images of Phoenix and seeded countless projects that share these priceless images. Organizations like the Daguerreian Society, Ephemera Society, and National Stereoscopic Association have helped link collectors and researchers to share information.

The author would also like to thank editor Jared Jackson, Kristie Kelley, David Mandel, and the staff at Arcadia Publishing for their guidance and assistance in preparing this book.

Unless otherwise noted, images are from the author's collection; more information is available at www.vintagephoto.com.

INTRODUCTION

Four major rivers joined together in central Arizona in what is now Maricopa County. The Verde and Salt Rivers merge at the Eastern edge of the county. The Salt and Agua Fria merge with the Gila River near the center of the county on its way to the Colorado. Long before Arizona was recognized for its mineral wealth, its native population knew central Arizona for the rivers that fed the irrigation canals that watered their crops.

Spanish explorers in the 16th and 17th centuries became the first European visitors to Arizona. They explored, established missions in the South, and sought mineral wealth as they traveled through, but left little impact in central Arizona.

Mountain men and trappers began to explore Arizona in the second decade of the 19th century. After leaving Missouri, 15-year-old Kit Carson moved to Santa Fe, New Mexico, and began exploring the West as a trapper. Carson first came to Arizona in 1826 and found Maricopa Indians living along the Gila River in central Arizona. In 1831, another party of trappers led by Pauline Weaver explored along the Salt and Gila Rivers in central Arizona as they traveled from Santa Fe to California.

The Treaty of Guadalupe Hidalgo brought the New Mexico Territory and the portion of Arizona north of the Gila River into the United States in 1848. The modern southern border of Arizona below the Gila River was finally defined by the Gadsden Purchase in 1853.

After the Mexican War, Arizona found itself on the southern route to California during the gold rush. Though an estimated 60,000 people crossed Arizona en route to California, their focus was on the gold fields and the travelers left little lasting impact. In 1850, along the Gila River east of Yuma and near the western edge of today's Maricopa county, the Oatman family wagon train was attacked, and young daughters Olive and Mary Ann abducted by Apaches. The tale of the Oatman girls and Olive's ordeal with the Apache and Mohave captivated the country. Her eventual rescue by a party led by her brother made headlines, generated books, and introduced Arizona to readers worldwide.

The Bartlett Survey was created to explore the geographic boundary of the United States prior to the Gadsden Purchase in 1852. John Russell Bartlett was an eastern intellectual and a political appointee to the Commission for the Mexican Boundary. Bartlett led the survey party that traveled from San Diego to Yuma, then followed the Gila River to the Pima Villages, and eventually into what is now Maricopa County on their route back to Texas. The sketches of Native Americans, and Arizona landscapes made by John Bartlett and expedition artist Henry Cheever Pratt are probably the earliest images of Maricopa County.

Arizona grew slowly before the Civil War. The 1860 Arizona census included only 2,421 "white," in a total of 6,482. Most of the "white" population lived in one of Arizona's two major settlements—Tucson and Yuma. The natives on the Gila Indian reservation, created on the Gila River in central Arizona on February 12, 1859, represented most of the population of central Arizona.

In 1862, the Confederate Congress passed the Arizona Enabling Act, proclaiming Arizona a Confederate territory. The Texas Confederate Cavalry were sent to bivouac in Tucson to strengthen the claim. The few skirmishes in Arizona, including one at Picacho Peak on April 15, 1862, occurred outside of what is now Maricopa County.

When the Arizona Organic Act officially created Arizona as a U.S. Territory on December 29, 1863, it was composed of four counties, Mohave, Pima, Yavapai, and Yuma. There would be no Maricopa County until eight years later.

Henry Wickenburg was an Arizona pioneer drawn west by California Gold Rush, arriving by boat from New York via Cape Horn. Wickenburg had apparently seen ore that explorer King Woolsey had picked up in Arizona's Harquahala Mountains. Henry came to explore and prospect in central Arizona in 1863 and discovered gold. Wickenburg developed the Vulture mine, initially building an arastra to process the ore with Charles E. Genung. Though Wickenburg sold the mine two years later to New York investors, he remained active and a significant figure early Maricopa County.

One of the first military outposts in Central Arizona was established by California Volunteers serving under Brig. Gen. John S. Mason about 7 miles above the confluence of the Salt and Verde rivers in central Arizona on September 7, 1865. The post was originally called Camp Verde (not to be confused with another Camp Verde established a few years later in Yavapai County). Fort McDowell, named for Civil War general Irwin McDowell, was built at the old Camp Verde site, and became a linchpin of military efforts to protect the emerging mines and settlements in central Arizona.

Jack Swilling, another important figure in early Maricopa County, arrived in Arizona in 1858, but quickly moved on to California. Discovery of Gold near Gila City drew Jack back to Arizona where he hired on with the Butterfield Overland Mail Company. A jack-of-all-trades, he appears throughout many events that shaped Central Arizona during this era. He was elected captain of a militia, the Gila Rangers, formed to protect miners from raiding Apache. Later he joined the Arizona Guards, which was first absorbed into the Confederate Army, then the Union Army after it captured Tucson and returned Arizona to the Union.

Swilling became part of the famous Walker party that explored Yavapai County for gold in 1863. Jack left the Walker Party and traveled throughout Central Arizona including exploration along the Salt and Gila Rivers looking for gold. After a brief stint in Tucson where he operated a business with Carl T. Hayden and married Trinidad Escalante, Swilling moved to Wickenburg and established the Swilling Irrigating and Canal Company to provide water for crops of wheat, barley, and corn in 1867.

Swilling moved his operations into the Salt River Valley in 1868, digging a canal from the Salt River east of what later became Phoenix. The settlement along the Salt River that began as Swillings Mill grew slowly progressing through several name changes including Helling Mill, Mill City, and finally Phoenix. The first post office was established in Phoenix on June 15, 1868. By 1870, the population of the territory had grown to 9,658. The 1870 Census of the Salt River Valley listed 124 Mexican and 116 Anglos—a total population of 240. One of the largest settlements in central Arizona was Wickenburg with a population of 174. For comparison: the population of Pima County was 5,716 with 3,224 in Tucson and 400 in Adamsville; 1,144 lived at Arizona City in Yuma County; and Prescott in Yavapai County had 668 residents.

Maricopa became the fifth county in the territory when it was created from portions of Yavapai and Pima counties on February 12, 1871. Located in the Center of the Territory along the Salt and Gila rivers, Maricopa County covers approximately 5,904,640 acres or 9,222 square miles.

The year 1872 saw a number of "firsts" in the Salt River Valley. A connection to the military telegraph line from Maricopa Station was installed in Morris Goldwater's new Phoenix store. Three enterprising Chinese businessmen opened the first laundry in Phoenix. Other businesses established in the boom that year included; James Grant's Harness Shop; J. Mitchell's Carriage Factory; Edward Irvine's bookstore and news depot; and the James Monihan and Starar brothers' Phoenix Livery, Feed, and Stables. The first public school opened in Phoenix in September with

20 students. J. C. Chamberlain sold his first crop of local honey, and George Buck and Mathilda Walters became the first couple to marry in Phoenix. The first newspaper in Phoenix, the *Salt River Valley Herald*, would not begin publication until 1877. In the East Valley, a small Mexican settlement, San Pablo, was founded at the base of the Tempe Buttes in 1872.

The earliest photographs taken in Maricopa County discovered to date are stereographs made by Dudley P. Flanders on his trip to Arizona that began in fall 1873. Stereographs were popular in the late 19th century and provide the best documentation of 19th-century Arizona. Stereographs were made with a camera with two lenses separated the same distance as human eyes. The camera took simultaneous images from the two perspectives, which were later printed and mounted on cardstock. An incredibly realistic presentation is created when the two images are seen in a viewer with the appropriate eye viewing each image.

During spring 1874, Flanders traveled to the oldest city in Maricopa County, Wickenburg, and photographed the stagecoach stop—Grant's Station. Flanders also photographed primitive mine works along the Hassayampa River. Later Flanders passed through what is now Phoenix to Maricopa Wells on his way to Tucson. Flanders apparently found little worth photographing in central Maricopa County during his tour of Arizona. The series of approximately 125 stereographs that Flanders published as *Scenes in Arizona* provide an incredible insight to the life and times of Territorial Arizona in 1874.

Just two years after Flanders passed through the area, George C. Rothrock established the first photographic studio in Maricopa County in 1876. Over the next 25 years, Rothrock's Phoenix studio produced hundreds of stereographs and photographs of Territorial Arizona. Rothrock created early documentation of Phoenix and traveled extensively throughout the Territory during the height of the Apache unrest. In Maricopa County, Rothrock made images of Native Americans, the troops in and around Camp McDowell, and canyons along the Hassayampa, Gila, and Salt Rivers.

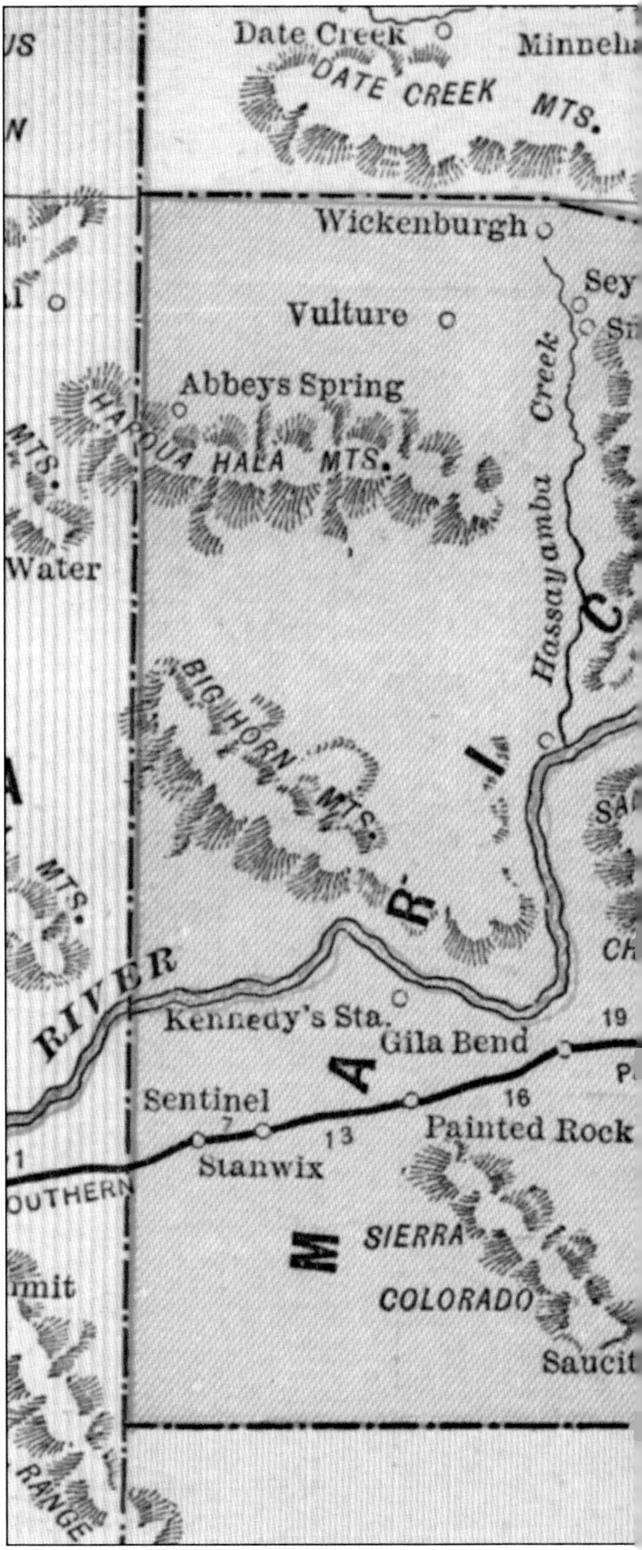

The c. 1885 map of Maricopa County shows features and settlements during the early development of the county. (Collection of the author © vintagephoto.com.)

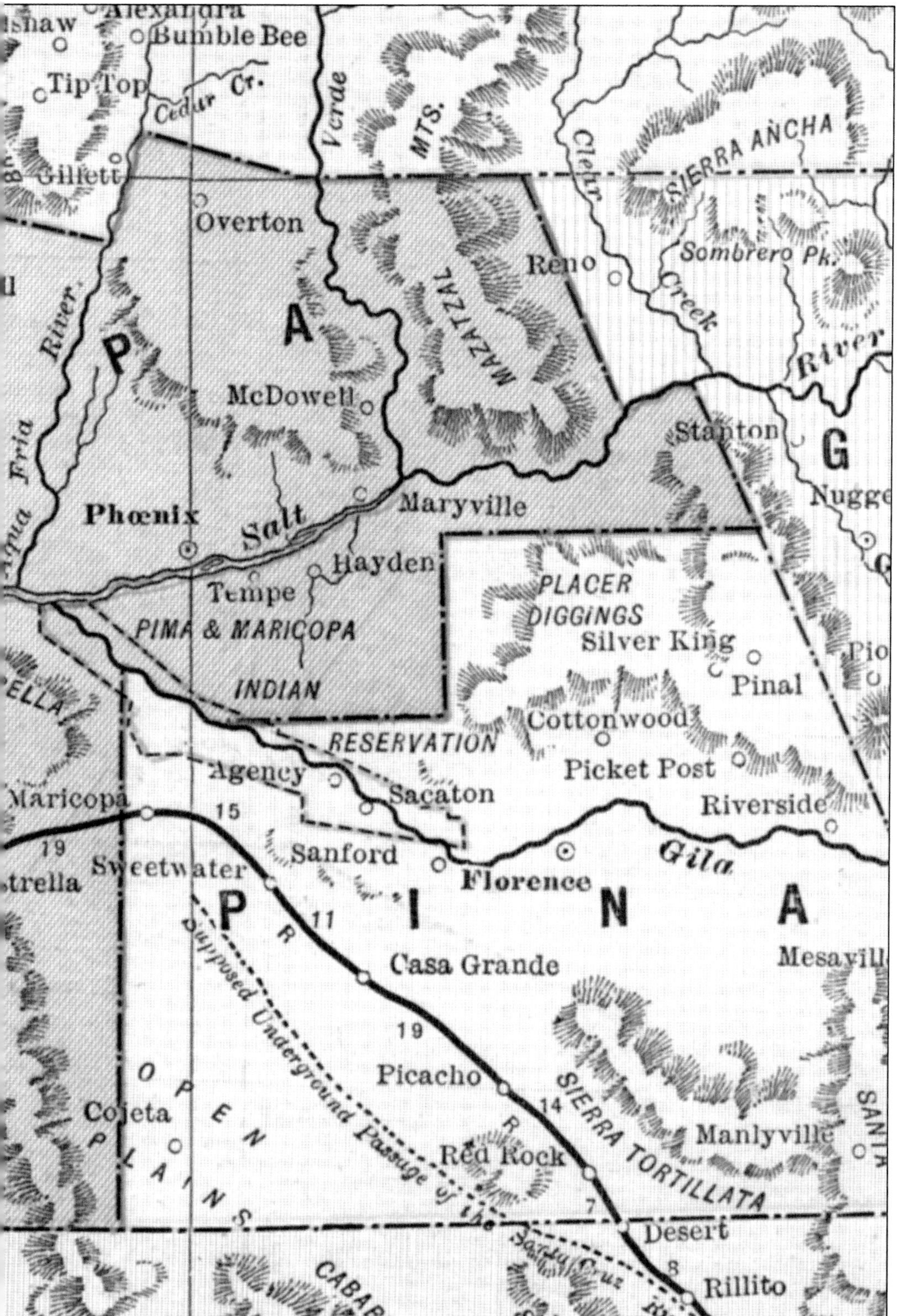
Bumble Bee
Tip Top
Cedar Cr.
Gillett
Verde
MTS.
Clear
SIERRA ANCHA
Overton
Sombrero Pk.
Reno
MAZATZAL
Creek
River
River
Agua Fria
P
A
McDowell
Stanton
G
Phœnix
Salt
Maryville
Hayden
Tempe
PLACER
DIGGINGS
Silver King
PIMA & MARICOPA
INDIAN
Pinal
Cottonwood
RESERVATION
Agency
Picket Post
Maricopa
Sacaton
Riverside
Sanford
Gila
Sweetwater
Florence
P
I
N
A
Casa Grande
Supposed Underground Passage of the Santa Cruz River
Picacho
SIERRA TORTILLATA
OPEN PLAINS
Manlyville
Cojeta
Red Rock
Desert
CABABI
Rillito

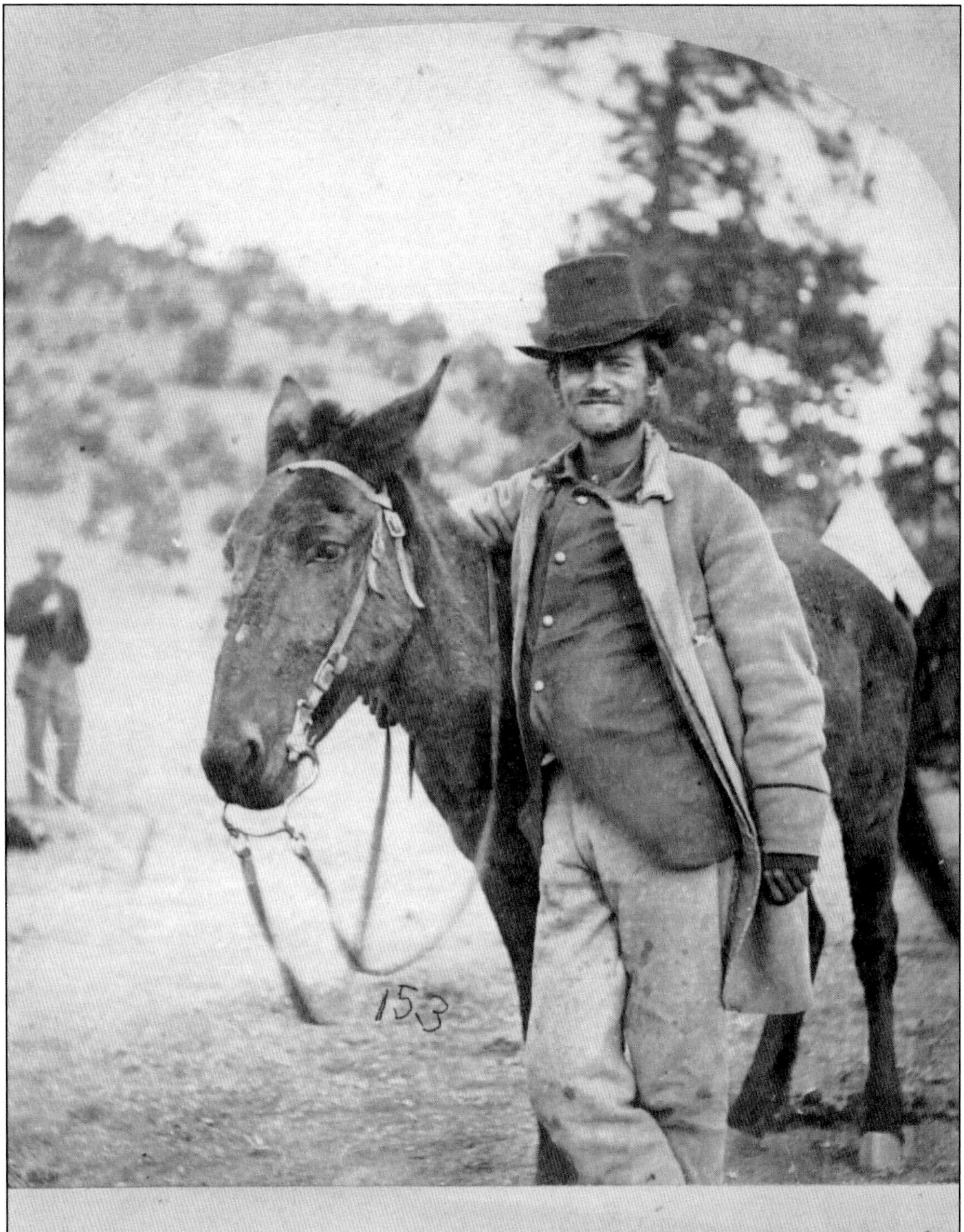

Fred Loring was an illustrator and correspondent for *Appleton's Journal*, following George Wheeler on his Grand Canyon expedition. Loring was one of the six stagecoach passengers killed just west of Wickenburg. The event drew national attention to Central Arizona as the site of the "Wickenburg Massacre." Stereographs were popular formats in the late 19th century and

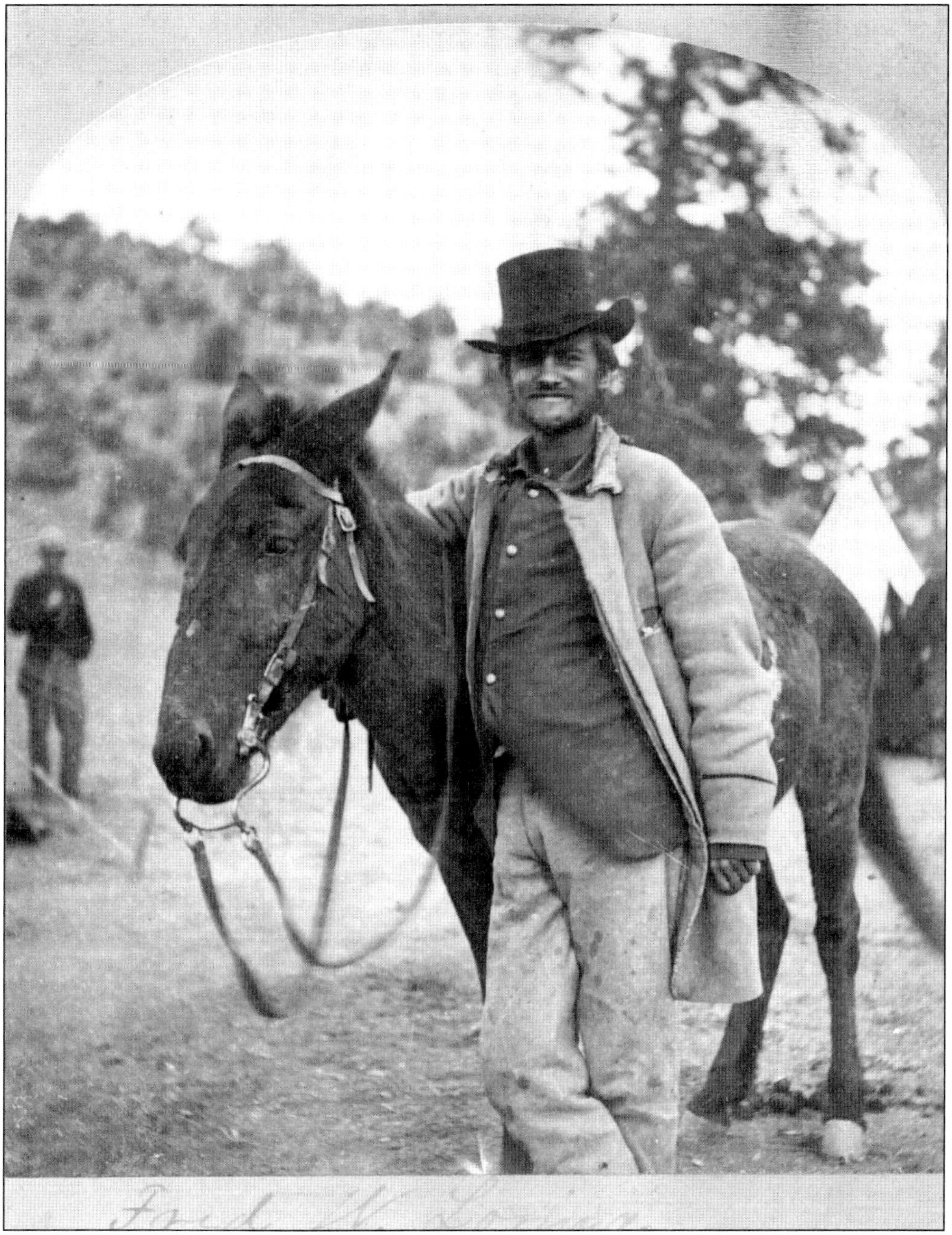

provide the best documentation of Arizona during this era. Made with a camera with two lenses separated similar to human eyes. An incredibly realistic view is created when the two images are viewed so each eye sees the appropriate image. (Stereograph by Timothy O'Sullivan for the Wheeler Expedition, November 1871. Collection of the author © vintagephoto.com.)

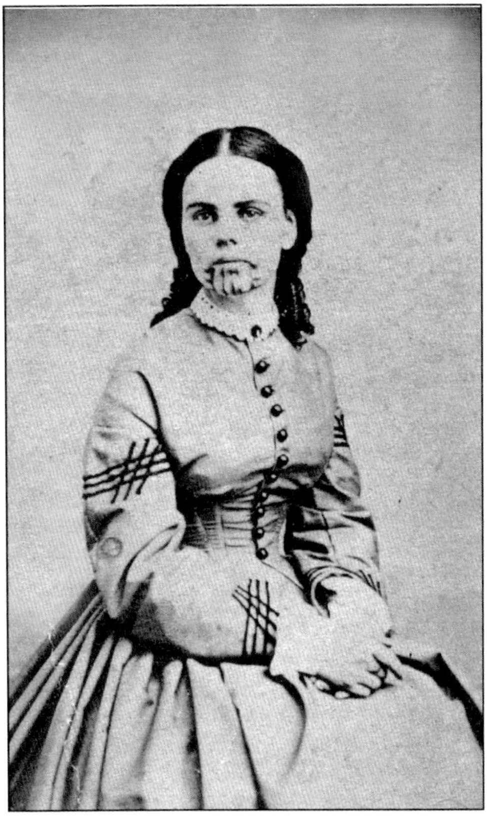

Cartes-de-visite photographs were albumen photographs mounted on 2.25-inch-by-4-inch card stock and were popular from around 1855 to 1900. This image is a portrait of Olive Oatman, who with her sister Mary Ann, were captured by Native Americans in 1850 and rescued by a party led by her brother in 1853. Olive became an iconic figure representing the dangers of Arizona. (Carte-de-visite, photographer unknown, c. 1856. Collection of the author © vintagephoto.com.)

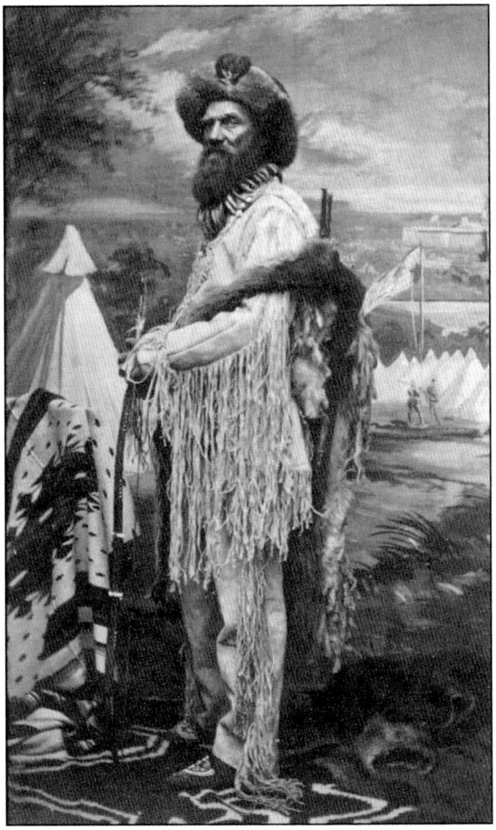

William F. M. Arney was appointed the secretary of the New Mexico Territory (which included Arizona) in July 1862. Originally from Kansas, Arney was active in Illinois politics before the Civil War and served as secretary and acting governor of the territory until 1867. Here Arney is photographed in Alexander Gardner's Washington, D.C., studio in buckskins with Navajo blankets as props. (Carte-de-visite photograph by Alexander Gardner, c. 1865. Collection of the author © vintagephoto.com.)

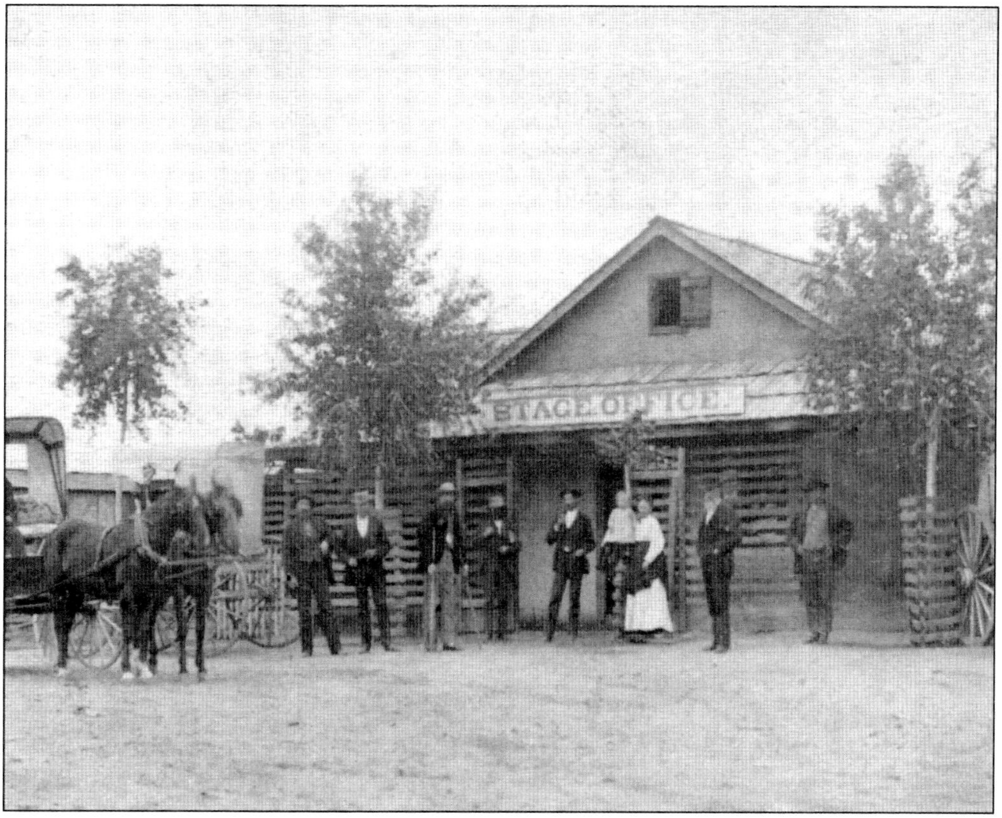

Wickenburg was founded by Henry Wickenburg in 1863 and began as a farming and mining settlement on the banks of the Hassayampa. Grant's Station was the stagecoach station on the route across the center of the territory. (Stereograph by Dudley P. Flanders, spring 1874. Collection of the author © vintagephoto.com.)

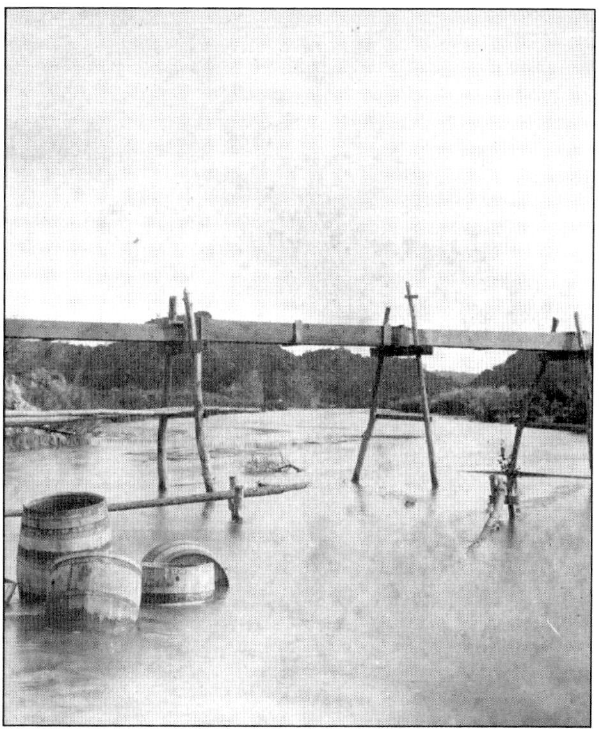

Prospectors discovered gold in the Hassayampa River in the 1860s. Soon placer mining works were operating along the river east of Wickenburg. The crude flume in this spring 1874 stereograph by Dudley P. Flanders illustrates the primitive construction and working conditions. (Stereograph, Dudley P. Flanders photographer, spring 1874 Collection of the author © vintagephoto.com.)

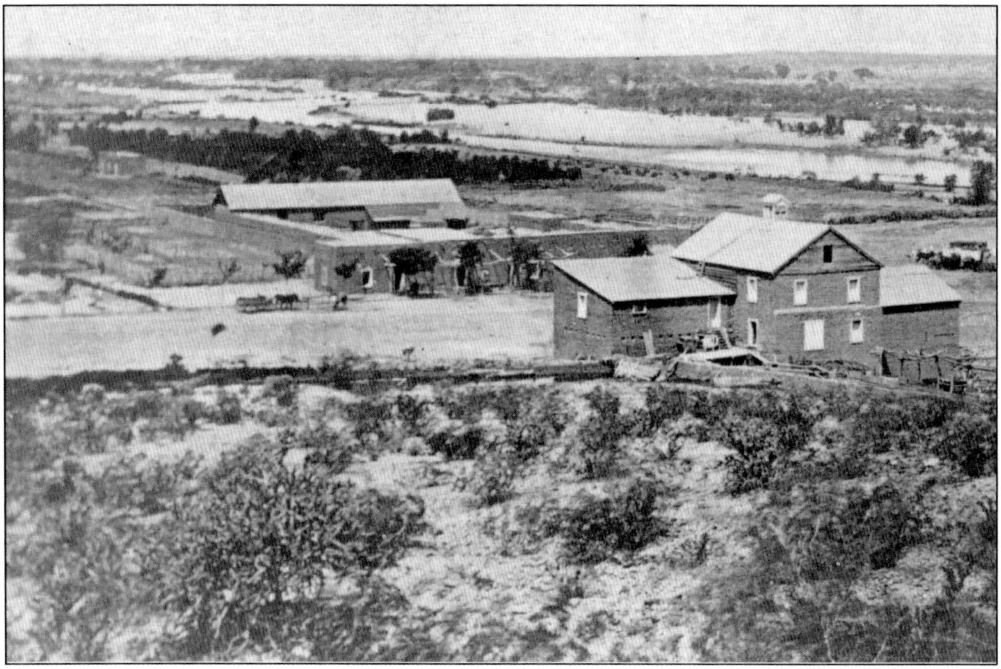

Charles Trumbull Hayden operated a mercantile and freight business that supplied mines and forts out of Tucson beginning about 1858. In 1866, while en route to Fort Whipple, he was delayed when trying to ford the Salt River near what became Tempe. After an initial move to Wickenburg in 1867, he relocated to Tempe and built a water-powered flourmill on the south side of the Salt River at the base of what is now Tempe Butte in 1874. The top view looks west from the Butte and shows the new Mill and the irrigation ditch that provided its power. The bottom view shows the west side of the new Mill with Tempe Butte framed behind. (Stereograph, S. Parmalee publisher, c. 1874. Collection of the author © vintagephoto.com.)

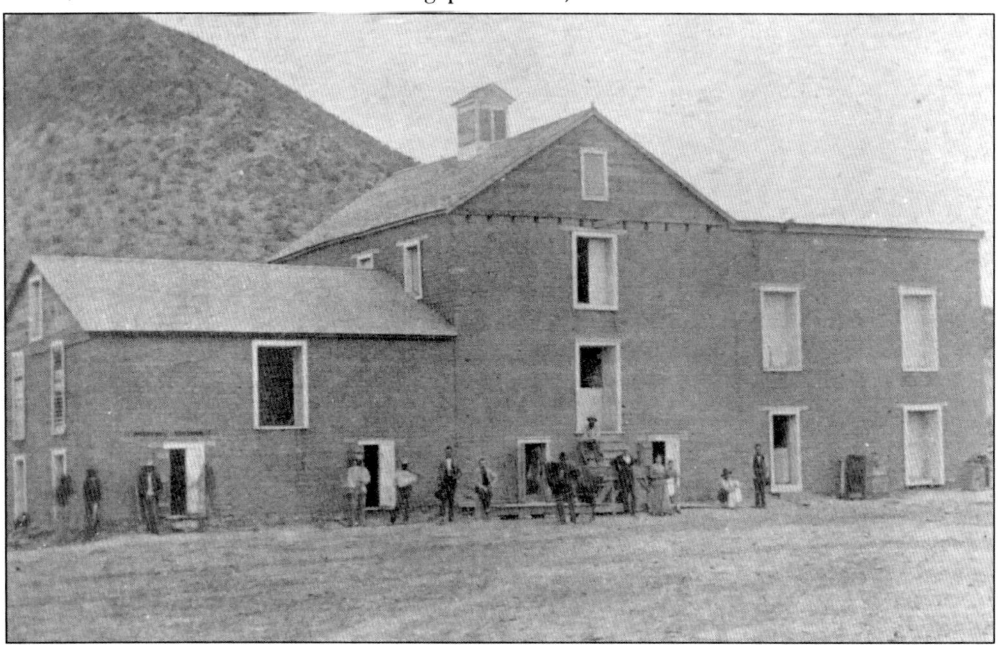

One

1874–1880

Many early Arizona photographers made images of Maricopa County during this era. Prescott photographer Daniel F. Mitchell took over the photographic studio in Prescott in 1877 and soon traveled south to document the emerging Phoenix streets and businesses. Henry Buehman of Tucson made cabinet card and stereographic portraits of the Maricopa, Pima and Apache of Maricopa County, and briefly operated a branch studio in Phoenix. Enoch Conklin of the Continent Stereograph Company came to Yuma to photograph the new railroad across Arizona and visited the Pima Villages along the Gila River in Maricopa County.

Charles Trumbull Hayden founded the city of Tempe just south of Hayden's Flour Mill in 1879. Beginning about 1858, Hayden operated a mercantile and freight business that supplied mines and forts out of Tucson. In 1866, he first saw the area while en route to Fort Whipple trying to ford the Salt River. After an initial move to Wickenburg in 1867, he relocated and built a water-powered flourmill on the south side of the Salt River at the base of the Tempe Butte in 1874. Five years later, Hayden established the town of Tempe.

By 1880 just down the Salt River, Phoenix had grown to a population of 1,708. It was now site of the Phoenix Flour Mill started in 1878 by King Woolsey, a National Bank, and an ice plant. Phoenix had eight restaurants, three operated by Chinese businessmen. Following a popular trend of the time, a 12–piece brass band was formed to participate in parades and public events. In central Maricopa County, 10,000 acres were under cultivation.

The 1880 census counted just over 41,000 Arizona residents. Men outnumbered women more than two-to-one. Pima County had the largest population. Only 5,689, about 13 percent of Arizona residents, lived in Maricopa County, with Phoenix accounting for only about one third.

Only 60 businesses qualified as "establishments" under the 1880 census definition were identified in the Arizona Territory, 18 of these were listed as manufacturers. The census documents list these businesses as having $272,600 in capital, and employing 210 males, two females, and two children and youths. The census noted the businesses as paying $111,180 in wages, using $390,028 in materials, and generating $618,355 in retail value products.

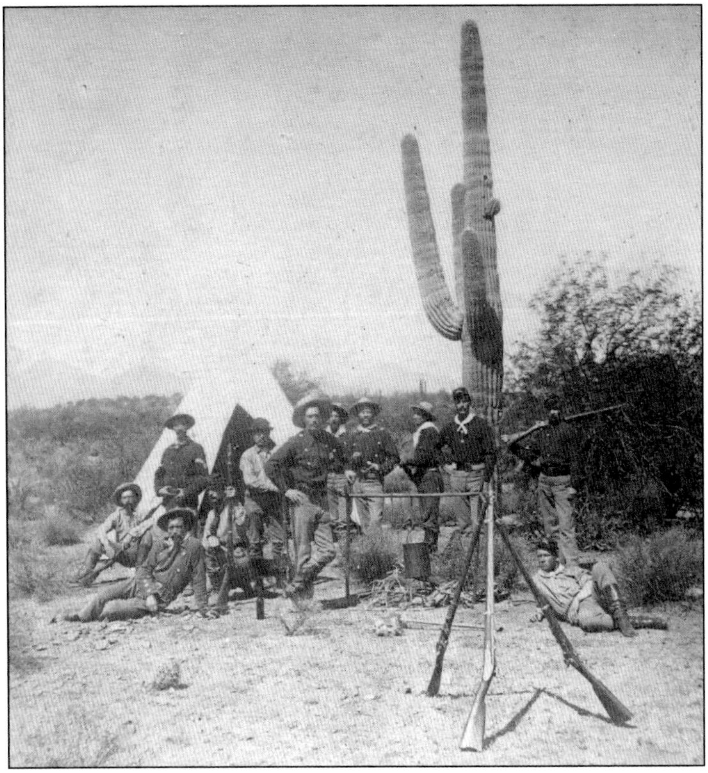

Camp Verde was established just after the Civil War to protect central Arizona from raiding apache along the Salt and Gila rivers. It was renamed Camp McDowell, after Maj. Gen. Irwin McDowell, became the base for Gen. George Crook's Apache campaign in the 1870s. This scene shows a group of soldiers from the Camp bivouacked in central Arizona. (Stereograph by George Rothrock, c. 1877. Collection of the author © vintagephoto.com.)

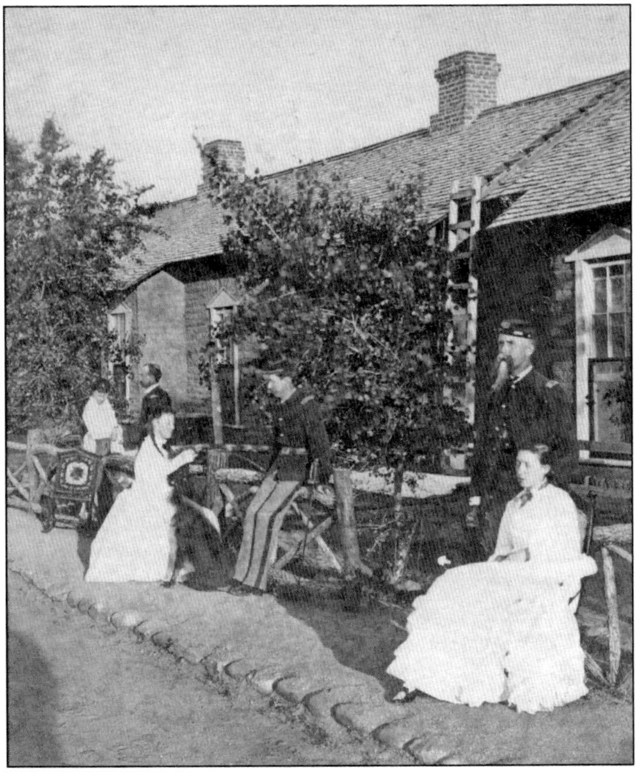

Officers stationed at Fort McDowell and family in front of the officers quarters including (from right to left) Capt. and Mrs. Kendall, Capt. and Mrs. Corliss, and a Mr. Cunningham and a Miss Taylor. (Stereograph by George Rothrock, c. 1877. Collection of the author © vintagephoto.com.)

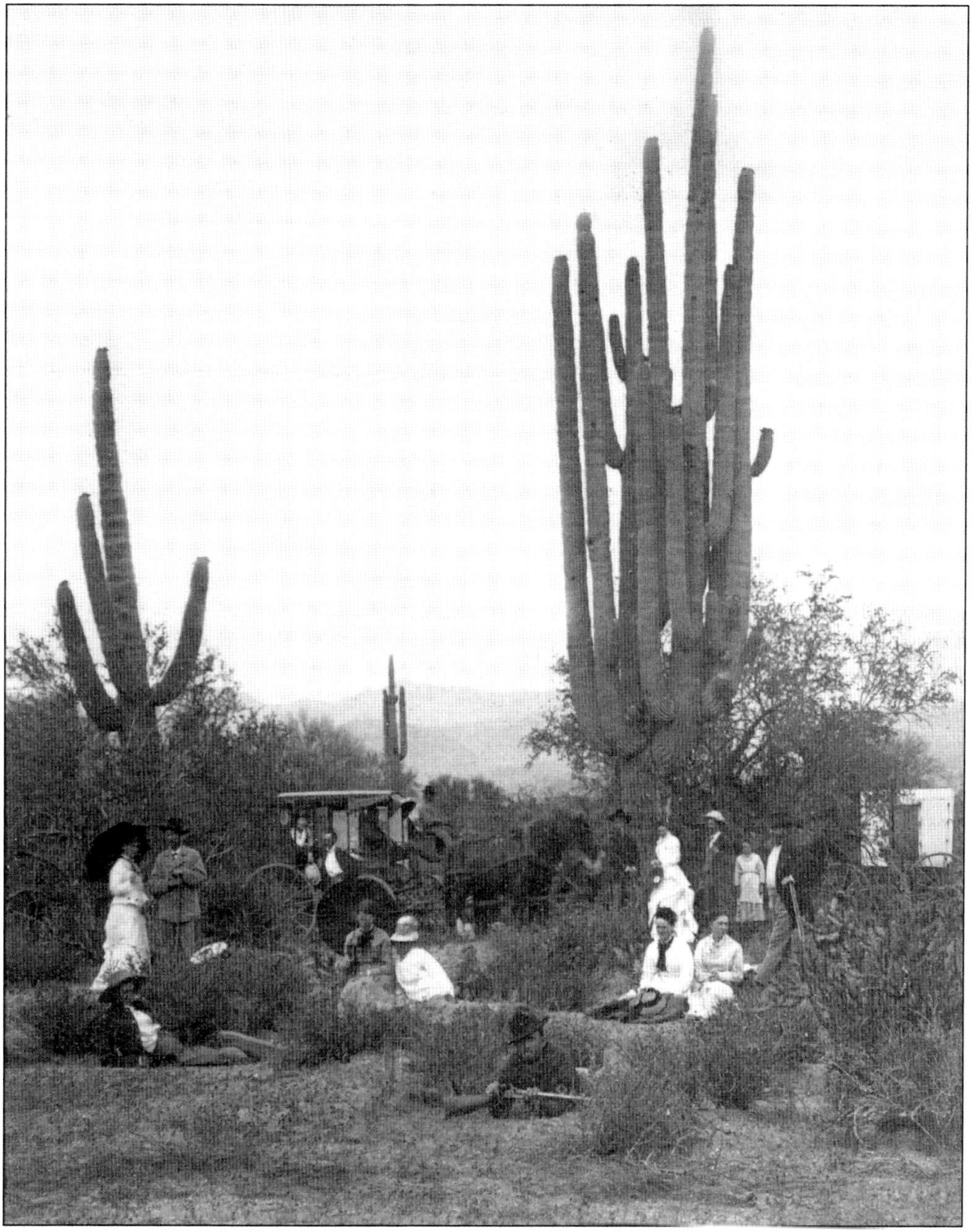

Between campaigns, officers and their wives camped in the hills near the fort. This view shows a Mayday picnic with armed scouts standing guard, and the photographer's white wagon visible at the right rear. (Stereographs by George Rothrock c. 1877. Collection of the author © vintagephoto.com.)

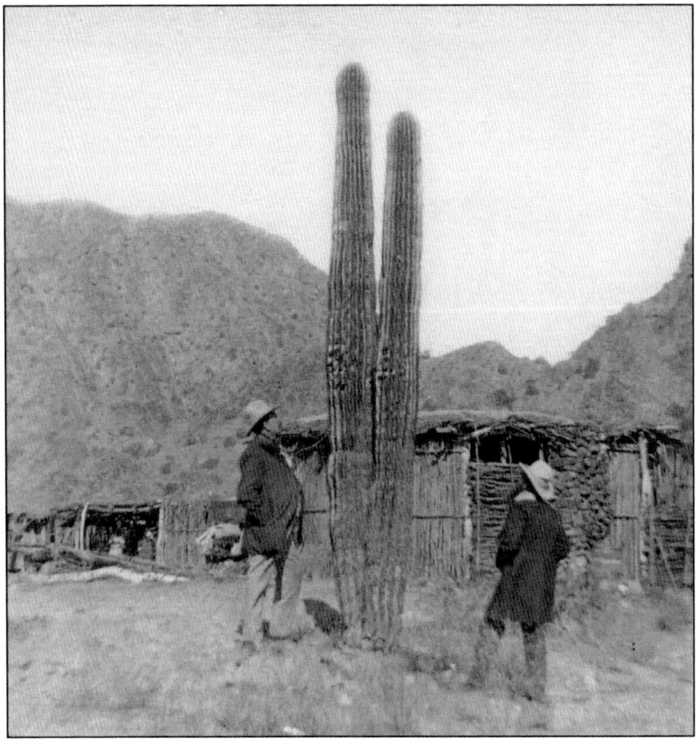

Pima Villages was a settlement along the banks of the Gila River. It lay on the route across central Arizona and was visited by the William Bartlett border survey in 1852 and later became a stagecoach stop in southeastern Maricopa County. (Stereograph, Enoch Conklin photographer, *c.* 1878. Collection of the author © vintagephoto.com.)

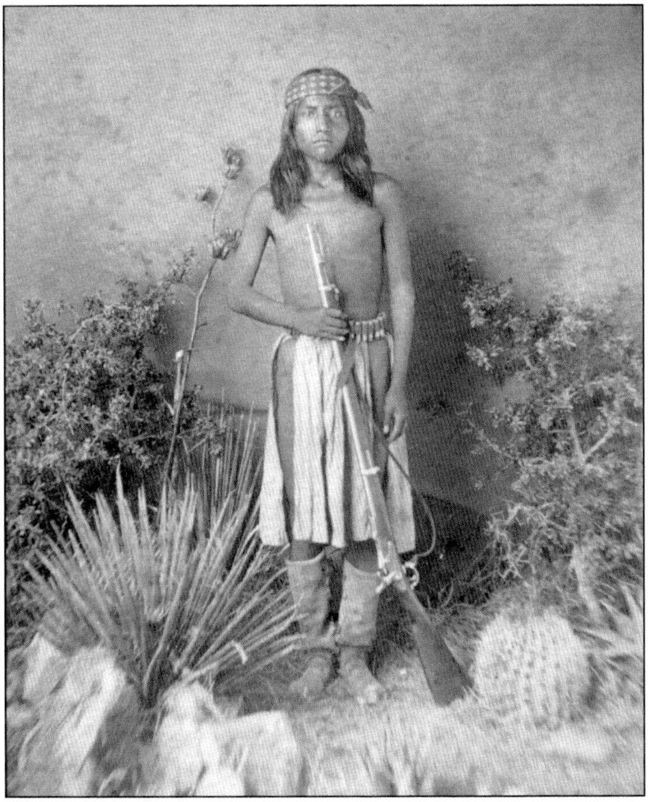

George Rothrock traveled throughout the Territory during the height of the Apache Wars. He photographed many of the chiefs and scouts in his studio. This portrait of Es-ku-lu-jeha shows the Apache Scout posed with his rifle and Rothrock's cactus props. (Stereograph, George Rothrock photographer, *c.* 1877. Collection of the author © vintagephoto.com.)

Two

1881–1888

On February 25, 1881, eight months before the infamous gunfight at the O.K. Corral in Tombstone, Governor Fremont signed documents that established Phoenix as an incorporated city. That year, Phoenix had its first election, began its first daily stagecoach schedule, and established its first cemetery.

New towns soon joined Wickenburg, Tempe, and Phoenix in Maricopa County. Lehi, a small Mormon settlement, was established east of Tempe on the south bank of the Salt River in 1877. Just south of the river, Zenos, which later became Mesa City and eventually Mesa, incorporated in 1883. Goldfield was founded in 1887 by the Superstition Mountains near the new copper and gold mine. In western Maricopa County, the settlement Sydney changed its name to Buckeye about 1889. The wealthy Vulture mine generated dramatic growth. Vulture City now boasted a post office, boarding houses, offices, shops, saloons, and its own school.

The year 1885 saw allocation of three major Territorial resources: the university, the normal school (teacher's college) and insane asylum. Maricopa County won two of the three—the normal school went to Tempe and Phoenix took the insane asylum, seen as a significant revenue source.

By 1886, the irrigation canals had expanded to over 240 miles through construction and clearing of the old Hohokam canals. The system provided irrigation to over 300,000 acres of farmland and was key to continuing development of Maricopa County.

The railroad reached the town of Maricopa then continued through to Tempe in 1887. The bridge across the Salt River at Tempe was completed in June, and the railroad finally reached Phoenix on July 4, 1887. Soon passenger travel between Phoenix and Tempe that had previously taken several hours by horse and wagon was reduced to about 40 minutes.

That same year in Tempe, the local newspaper, the *Salt River Valley News* was renamed the *Tempe News*. The original newspaper office was located in an adobe building near Tempe Butte, above a blacksmith and carpentry shop. A few years later, the office moved to its own building on Fifth Street near Mill Avenue. Curt Miller began his career as publisher of the Tempe paper in 1887 and continued the weekly for the next 55 years.

The railroad expanded throughout Maricopa County and spurred development. Peoria was incorporated northwest of Phoenix along the Atchison, Topeka and Santa Fe rail line in August 1888. Other towns grew dramatically when the railroad reached their communities.

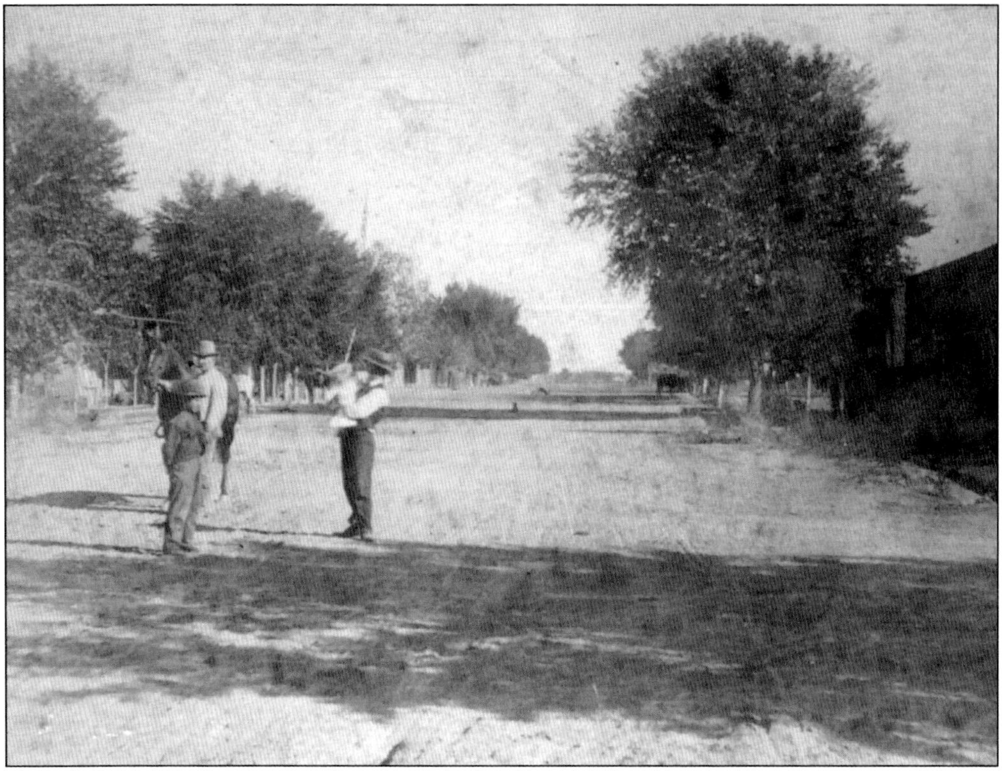

This view looking east down Monroe Street shows unpaved roads and the rural environment of early Phoenix. (Stereograph, George Rothrock photographer, *c.* 1880. Collection of the author © vintagephoto.com.)

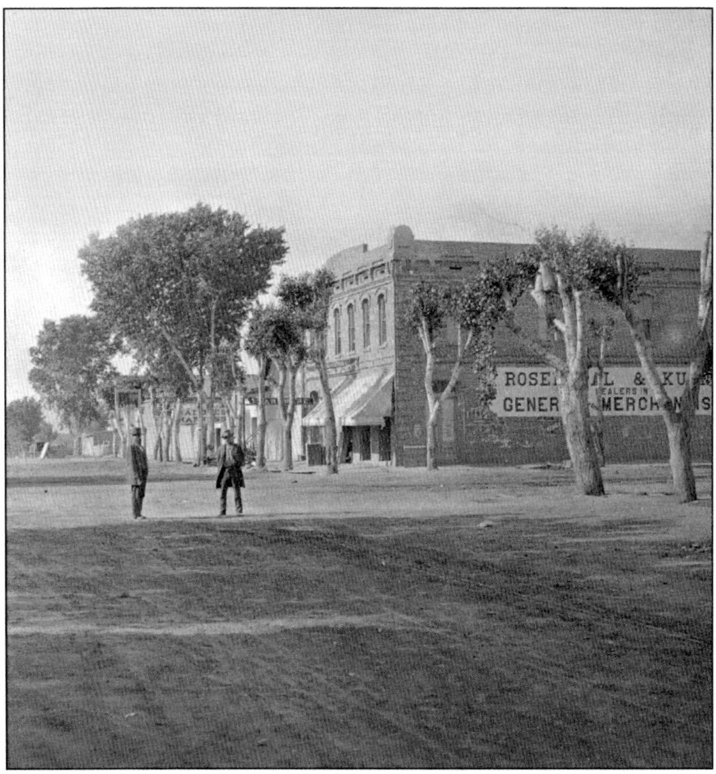

This early view of the downtown Phoenix businesses district was photographed about the time the city was incorporated. (Stereograph, George Rothrock photographer, *c.* 1881. Collection of the author © vintagephoto.com.)

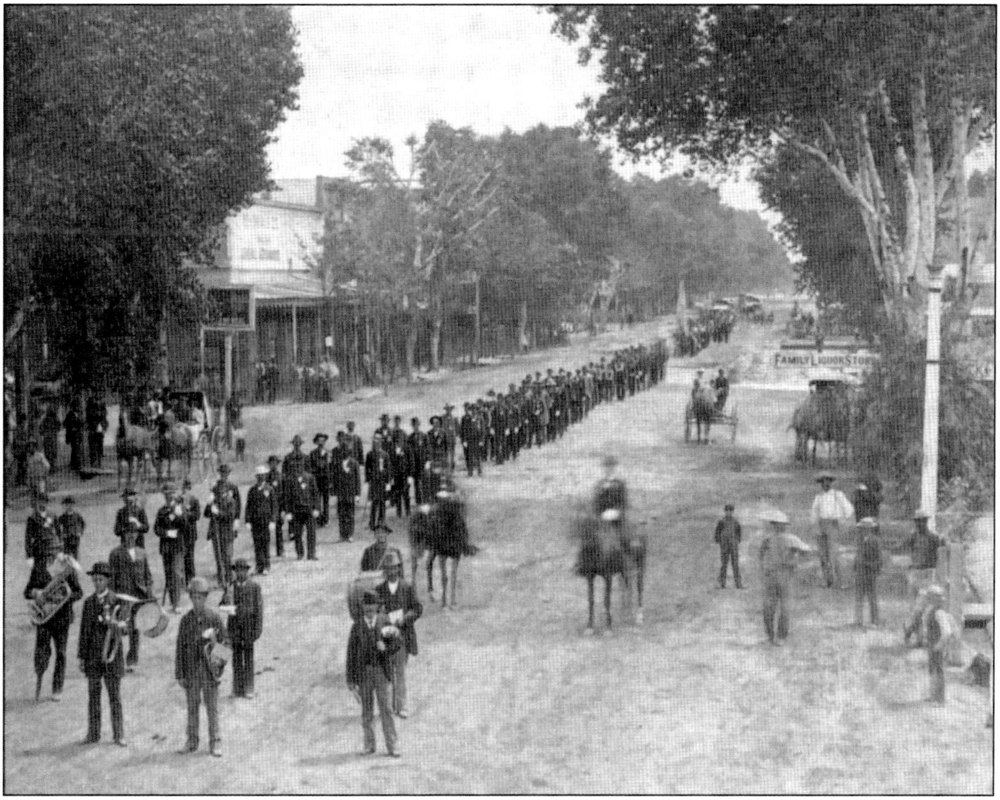

Washington Street in Phoenix was the setting for many parades and local events. Brass bands were popular entertainment, and Phoenix established its own 12-piece band in 1880. Here the International Order of Odd Fellows (IOOF) band leading the parade stops to pose for the photographer. A peg-legged horn player is at the right. (Stereograph, George Rothrock photographer, c. 1880. Collection of the author © vintagephoto.com.)

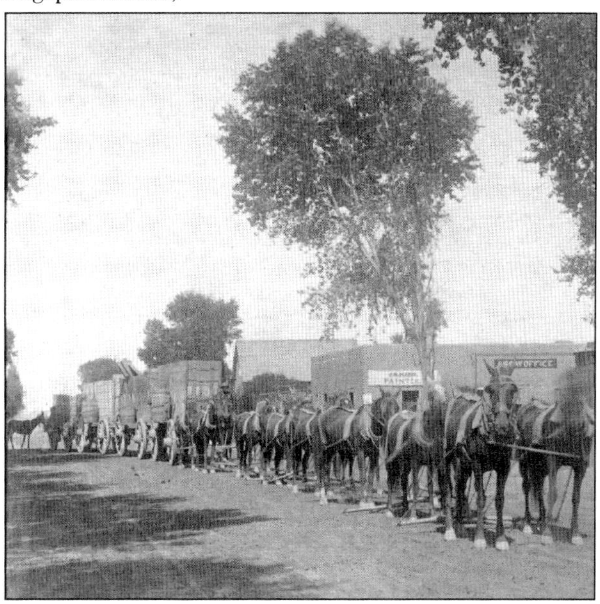

Until the arrival of the railroad, and for many locations not served by rail for decades after, freight teams were the lifeblood of the mines and camps that peppered central Arizona. This 16-horse freight train is preparing to leave from Phoenix. (Stereograph, George Rothrock photographer, c. 1880. Collection of the author © vintagephoto.com.)

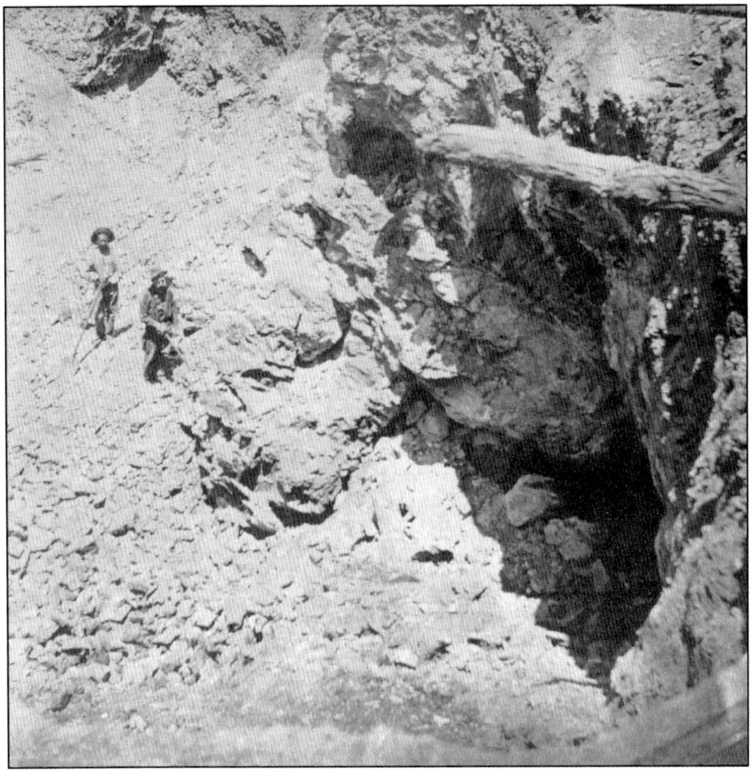

This is an early view of the Vulture Mine, which was discovered by Henry Wickenburg in 1863. The mine was located about 12 miles southwest of Wickenburg. Vulture City, the nearby settlement grew from about 200 in 1870 to over 5,000. (Stereograph, George Rothrock photographer, c. 1880. Collection of the author © vintagephoto.com.)

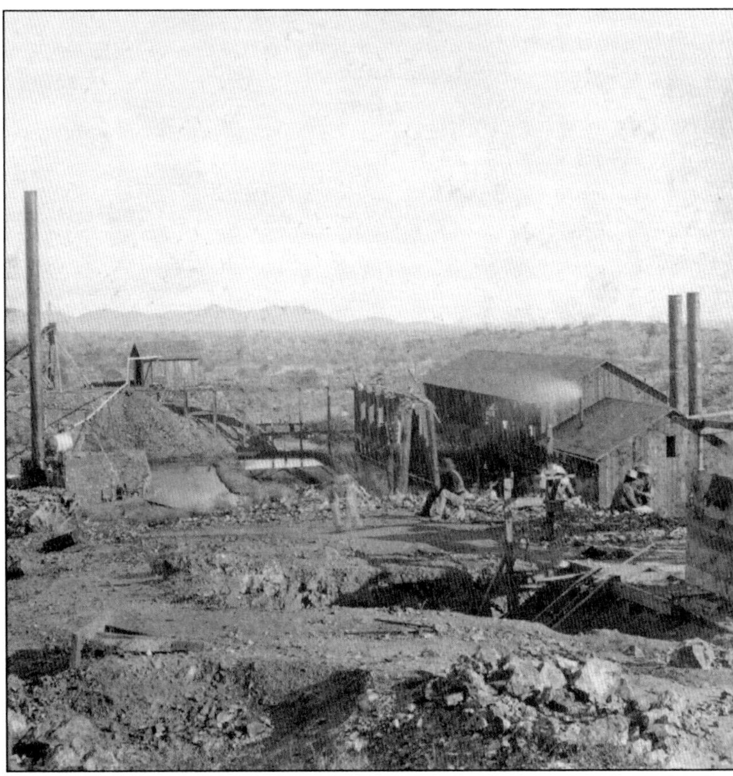

At the height of its operation, an 80-stamp mill operated on the site. During its life, the Vulture mine was one of the richest in Arizona and produced over $2 million worth of gold before it closed in 1942. (Stereograph, George Rothrock photographer, c. 1885. Collection of the author © vintagephoto.com.)

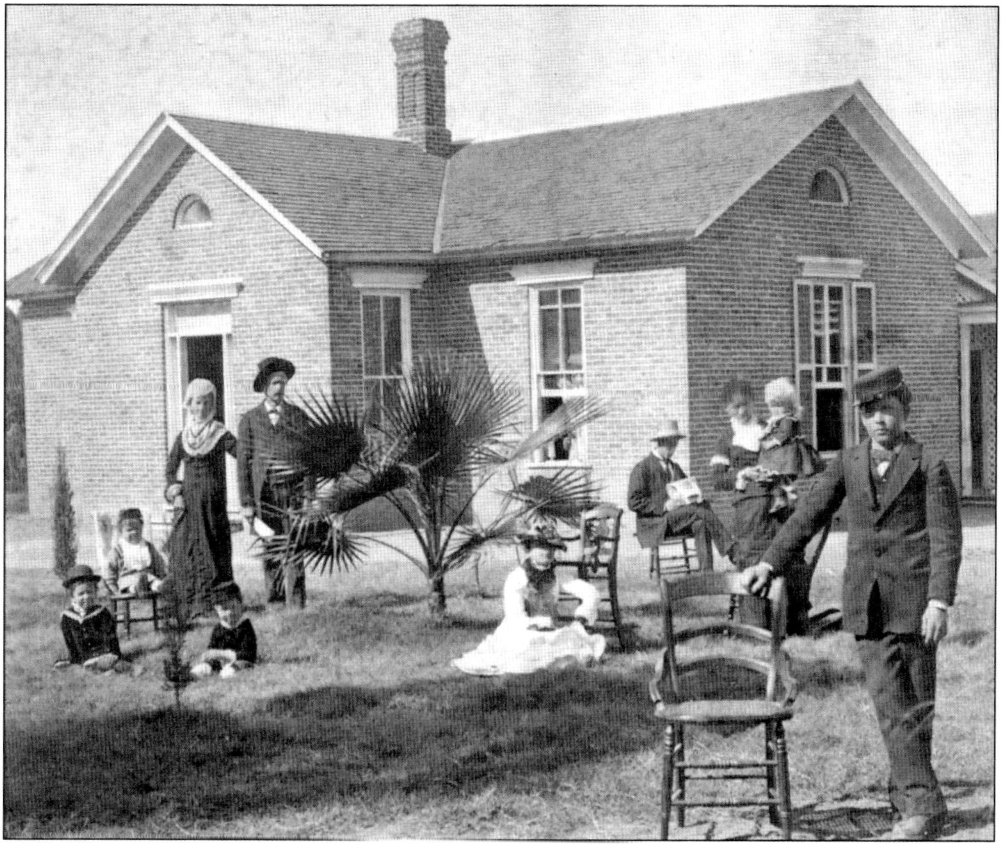

The family of judge and Maricopa County district attorney A. D. Lemon (standing at left), pose in the yard in front of their new brick house in Phoenix. Standing at the right is young Lawrence Lemon, who at the time was known to be "good natured and indolent." Sadly, Lawrence Lemon was arrested for the murder of an acquaintance, Thomas Sheehan, about 10 years later in September 1895. (Stereograph, George Rothrock photographer, c. 1885. Collection of the author © vintagephoto.com.)

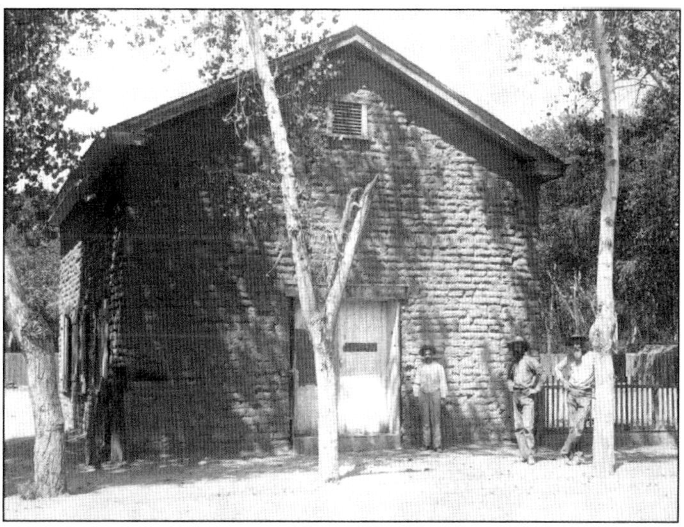

The old schoolhouse on Center Street opened in October 1872 with 21 students. It was the first school building in Phoenix and is a classic example of adobe construction. The first teacher hired was Miss Nellie Shaver who came from Wisconsin for a salary of $100 per month. (Albumen cabinet card, George H. Rothrock photographer, c. 1885. Collection of the author © vintagephoto.com.)

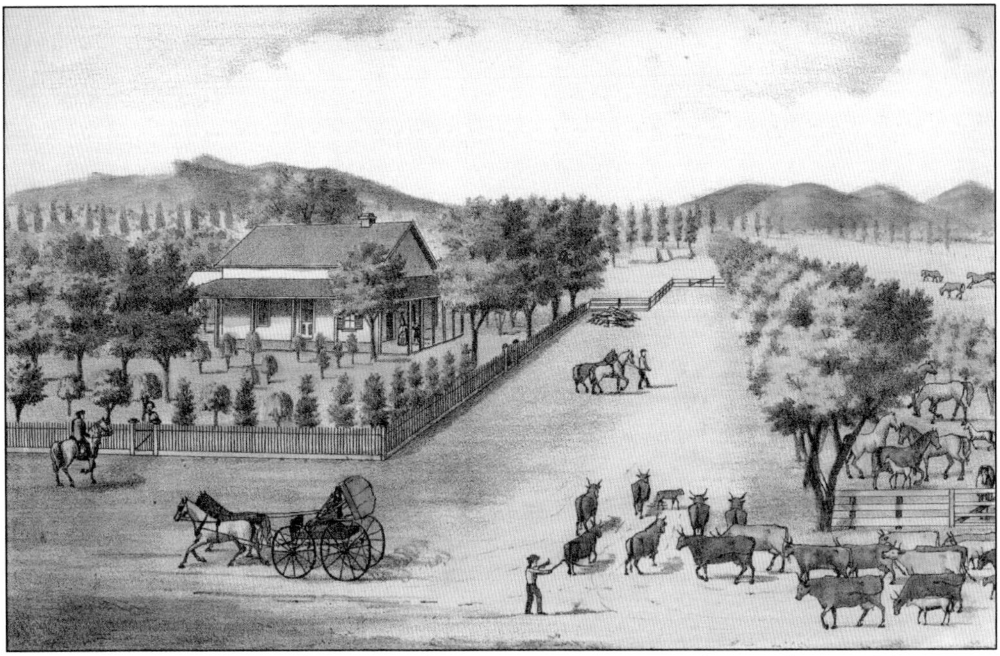

This lithograph shows the farm of William Isaac's Grange, 4 miles northwest of downtown Phoenix. (W. W. Elliott & Co. Lithographers, San Francisco, *c.* 1885. Collection of the author © vintagephoto.com.)

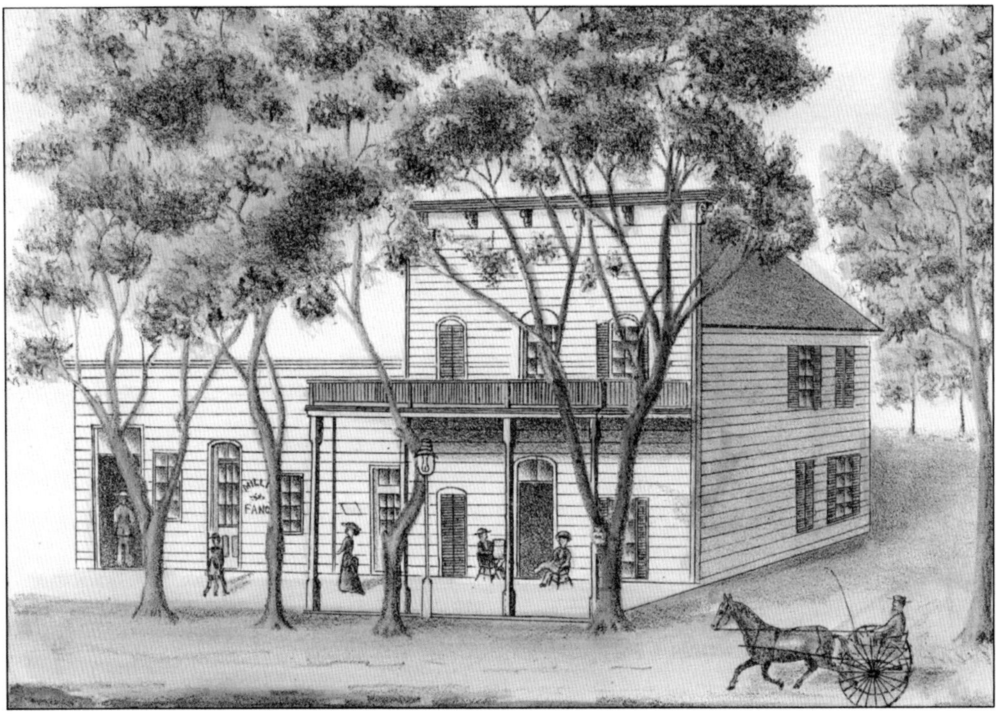

James Morgan Gregory operated a real estate and loan company in addition to the Gregory House hotel located on Washington between Pima and Maricopa Streets in Phoenix. (W. W. Elliott & Co. Lithographers, San Francisco, *c.* 1885. Collection of the author © vintagephoto.com.)

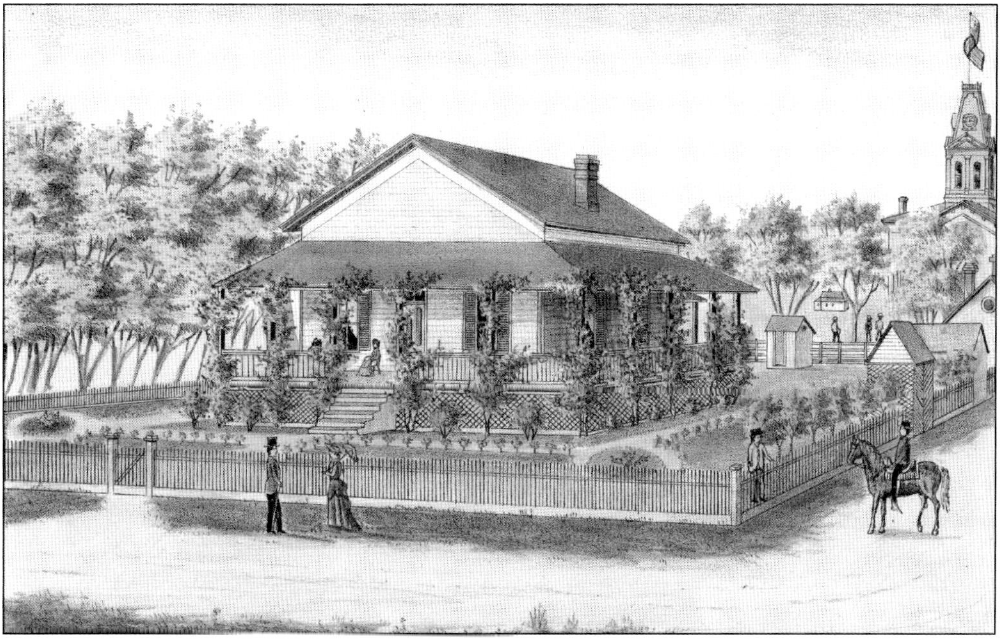

This lithograph shows the residence of Phoenix Lawyer H. N. Alexander on the corner of Adams and Mohave. W. W. Elliott & Co. Lithographers, San Francisco, *c.* 1885. Collection of the author © vintagephoto.com.

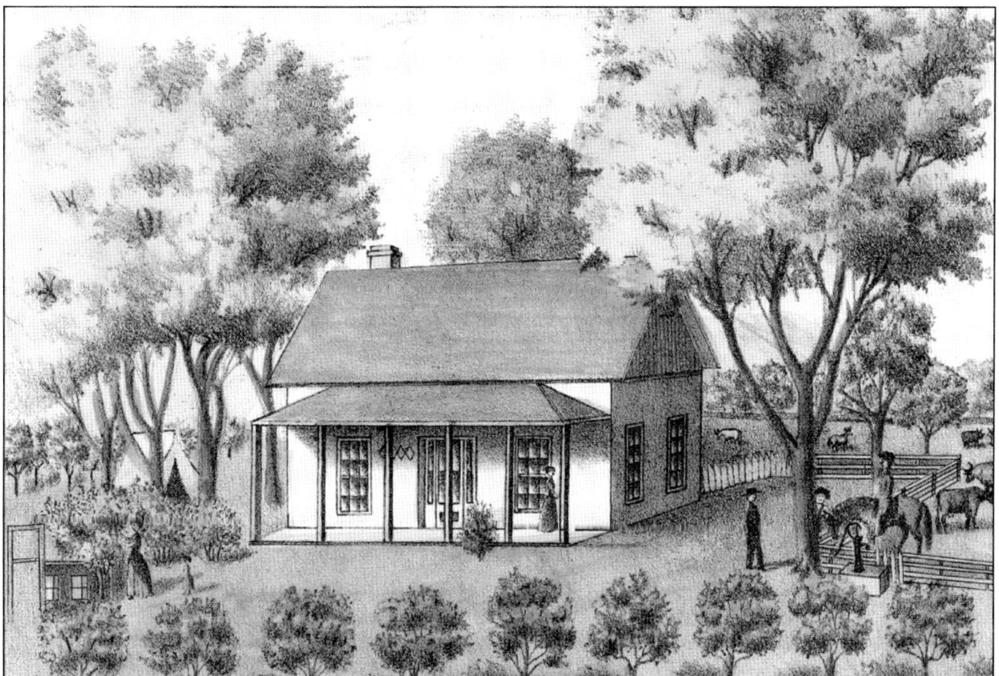

The residence of Maricopa County sheriff John B. Montgomery was located on Cortez Street in the Montgomery addition of Phoenix. (W. W. Elliott & Co. Lithographers, San Francisco, *c.* 1885. Collection of the author © vintagephoto.com.)

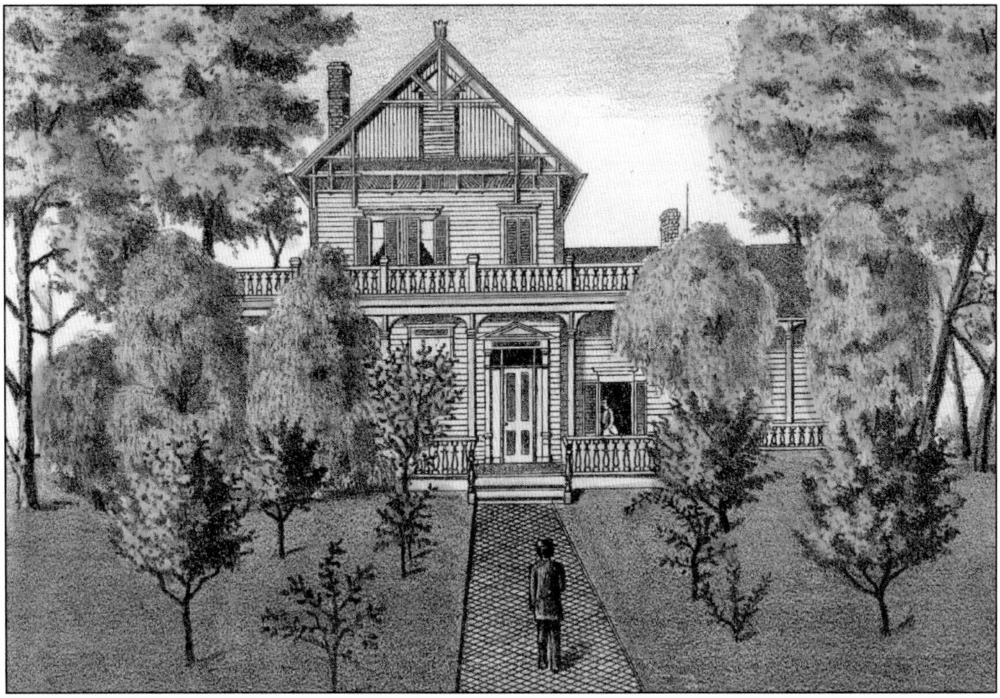

This lithograph shows the residence of M. W. Kales, president of the National Bank of Arizona in Phoenix. (W. W. Elliott & Co. Lithographers, San Francisco, *c.* 1885. Collection of the author © vintagephoto.com.)

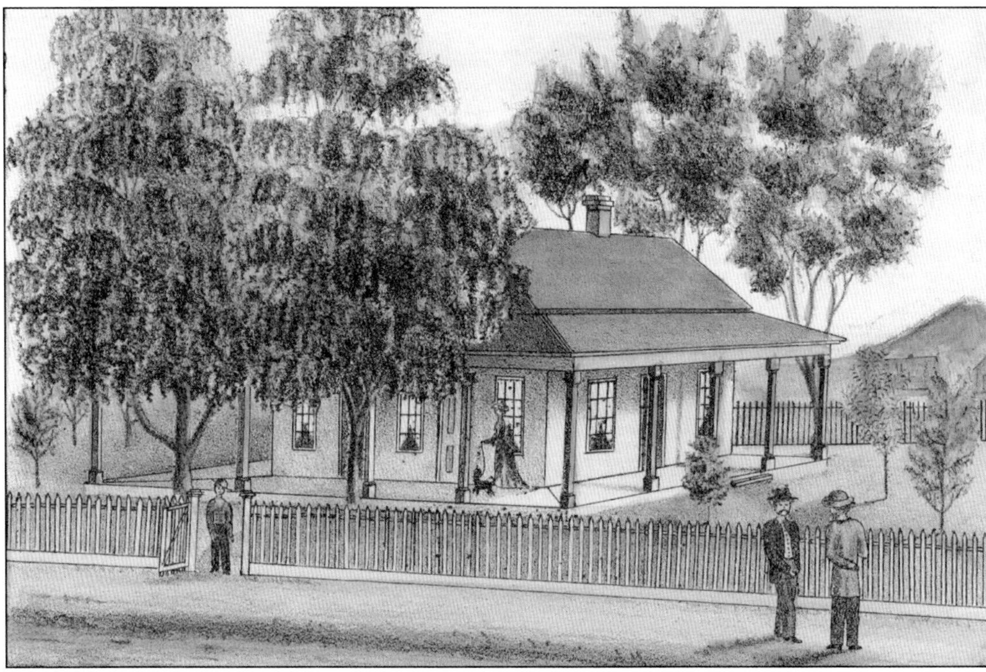

The residence of N. Herrick was located on the corner of Cortez and Jefferson in Phoenix. (W. W. Elliott & Co. Lithographers, San Francisco, *c.* 1885. Collection of the author © vintagephoto.com.)

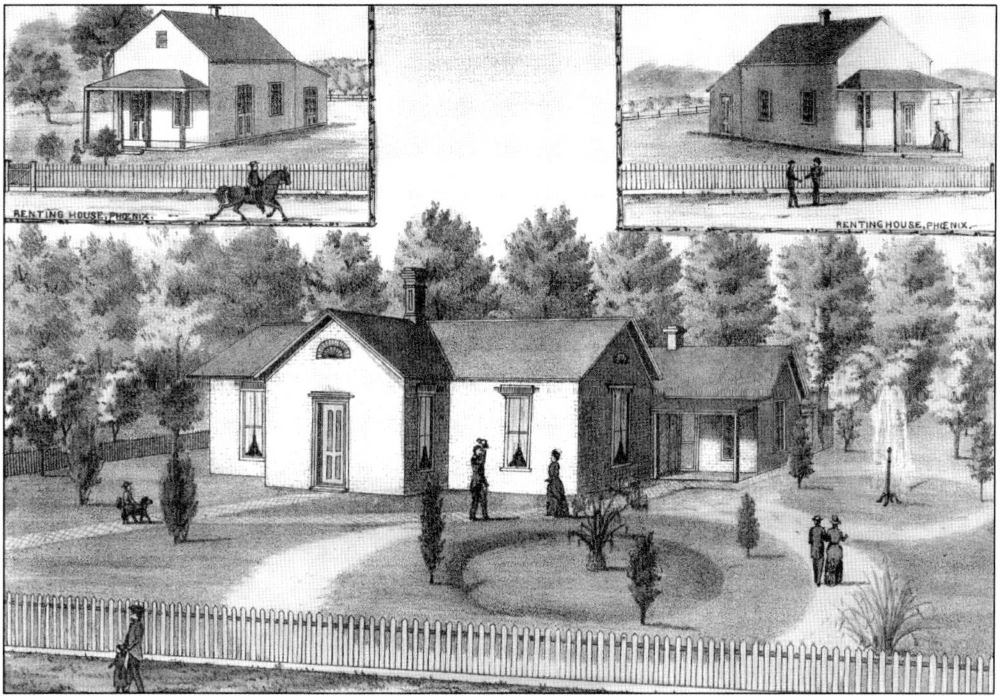

This lithograph shows the residence of Phoenix butcher Ira Stroud on Jefferson between Apache and Arizona Avenues. (W. W. Elliott & Co. Lithographers, San Francisco, c. 1885. Collection of the author © vintagephoto.com.)

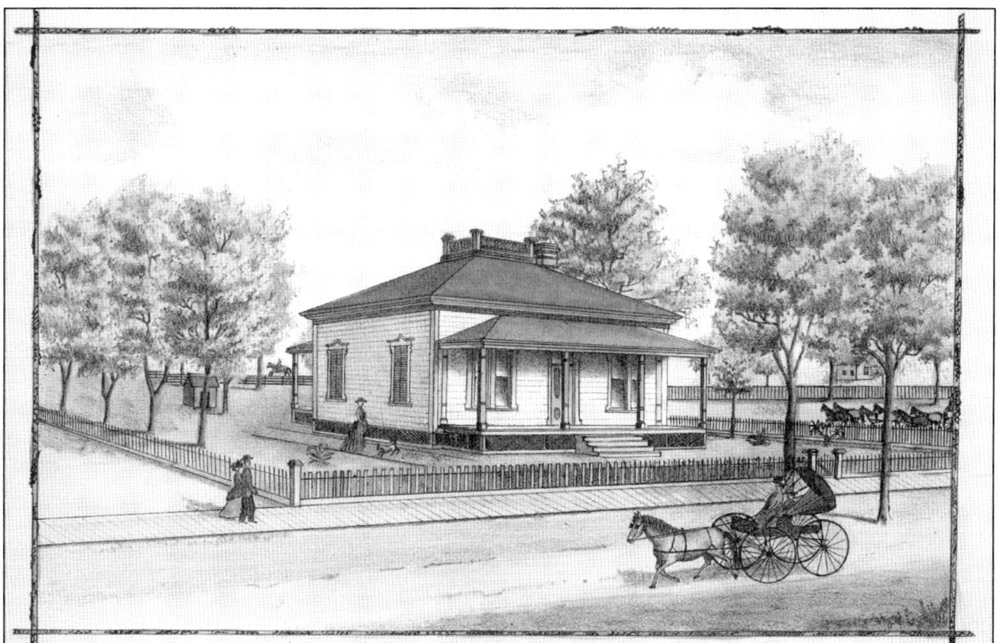

The residence of A. C. Baker, partner in the law firm of Baker and Campbell, was located on Mohave between Adams and Monroe, in Phoenix. (W. W. Elliott & Co. Lithographers, San Francisco, c. 1885. Collection of the author © vintagephoto.com.)

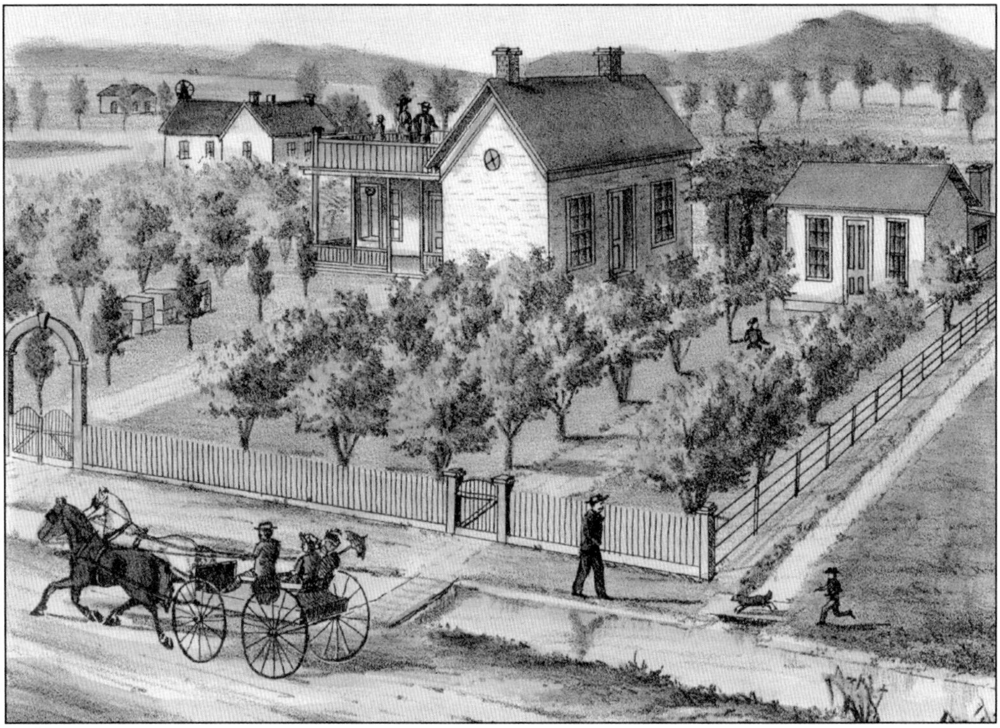

This lithograph shows the residence of Mesa farmer Daniel Bagley on South First Street between Center and Macdonald. (W. W. Elliott & Co. Lithographers, San Francisco, *c.* 1885. Collection of the author © vintagephoto.com.)

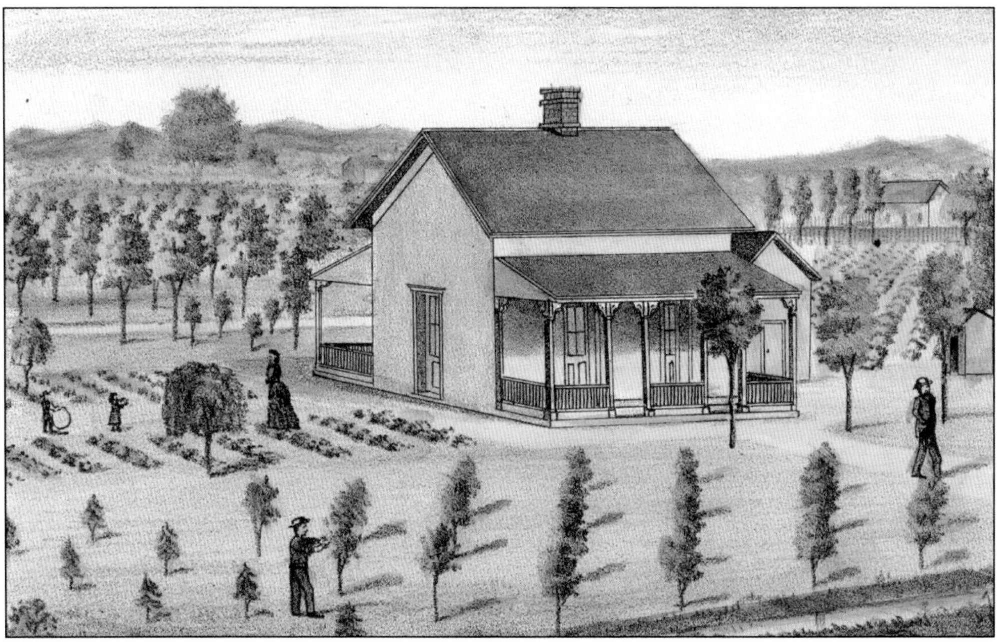

The residence of Mesa farmer John H. Pomeroy was located on the corner of Center and Main. (W. W. Elliott & Co. Lithographers, San Francisco, *c.* 1885. Collection of the author © vintagephoto.com.)

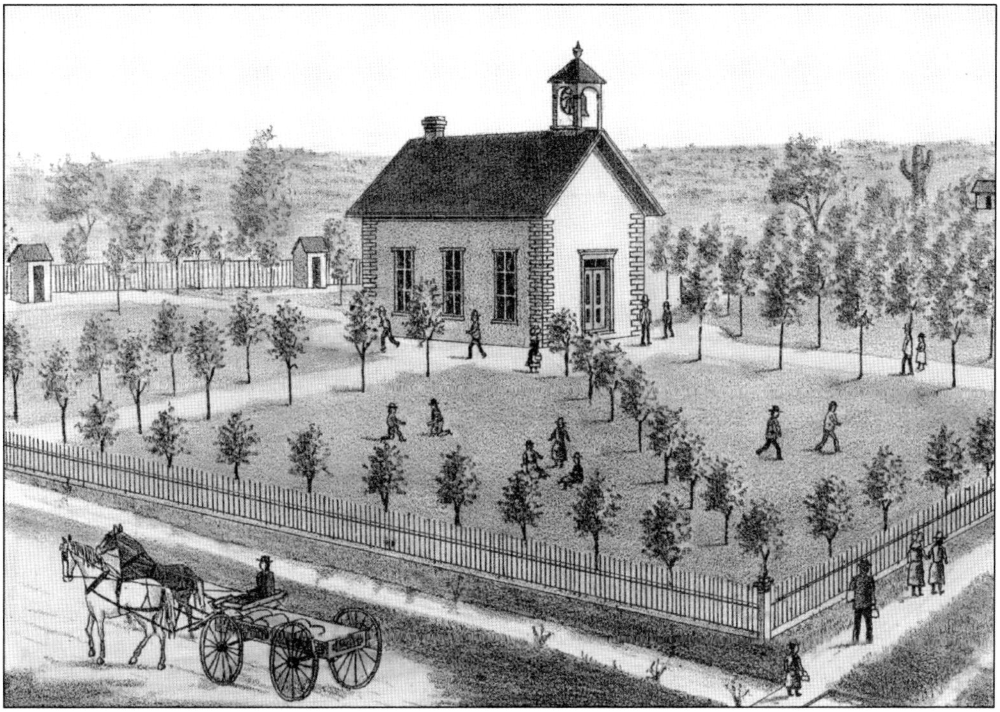

This lithograph shows the Lehi Public School, northwest of Mesa City. (W. W. Elliott & Co. Lithographers, San Francisco, *c.* 1885. Collection of the author © vintagephoto.com.)

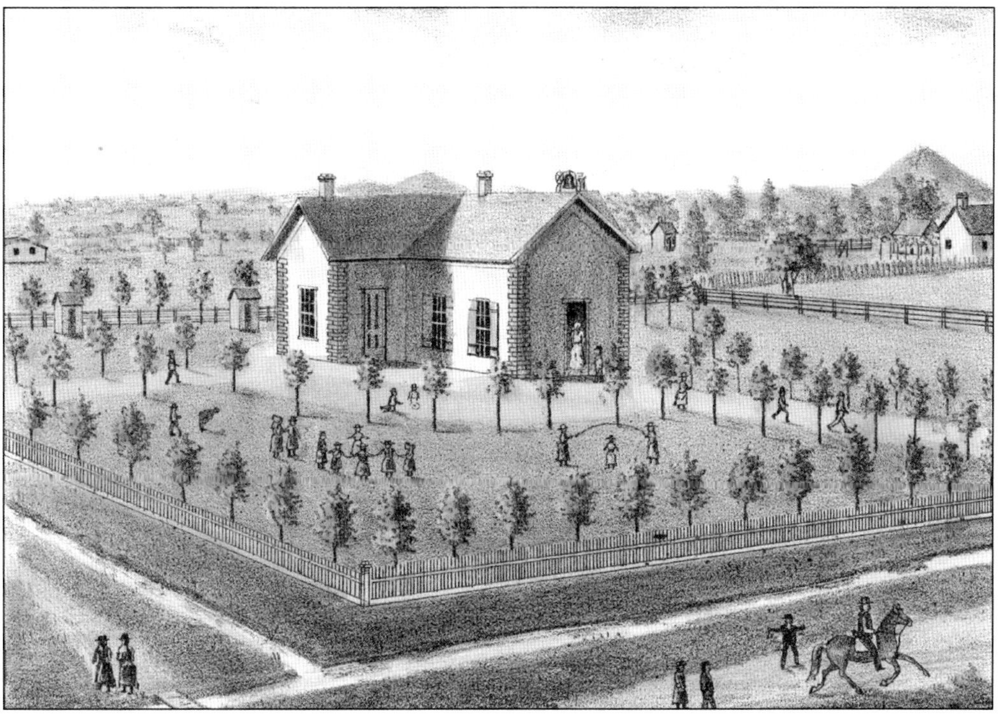

The Mesa City Public School, *c.* 1885. (W. W. Elliott & Co. Lithographers, San Francisco. Collection of the author © vintagephoto.com.)

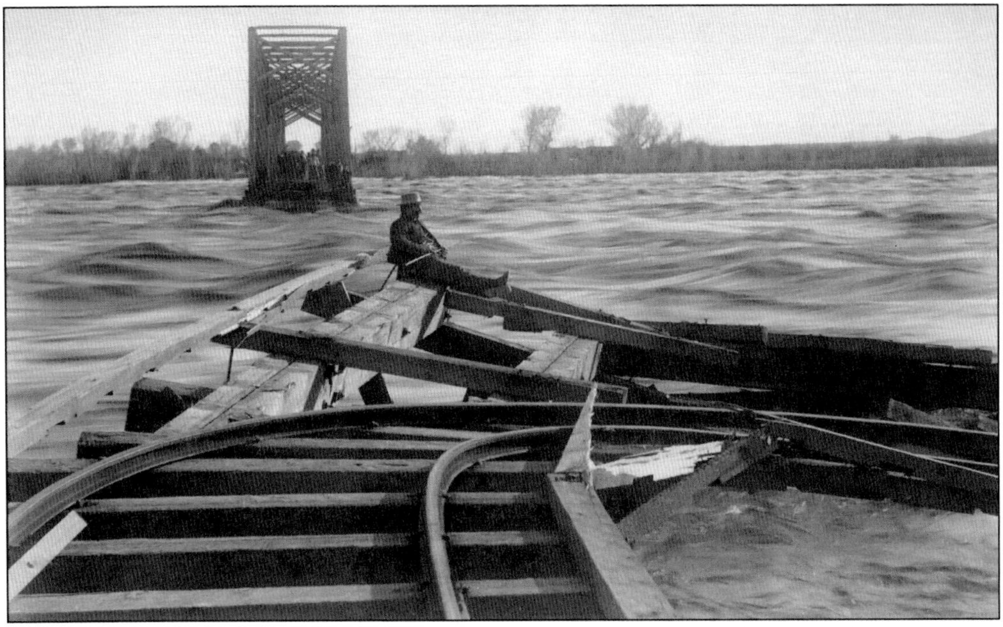

February 1891 saw the highest flow of the Salt River through Tempe and Phoenix. Water flowing at over 300,000 cubic feet per second washed out buildings along the river and the railroad bridge at Tempe. (Boudoir cabinet card, George Rothrock photographer. Collection of the author © vintagephoto.com.)

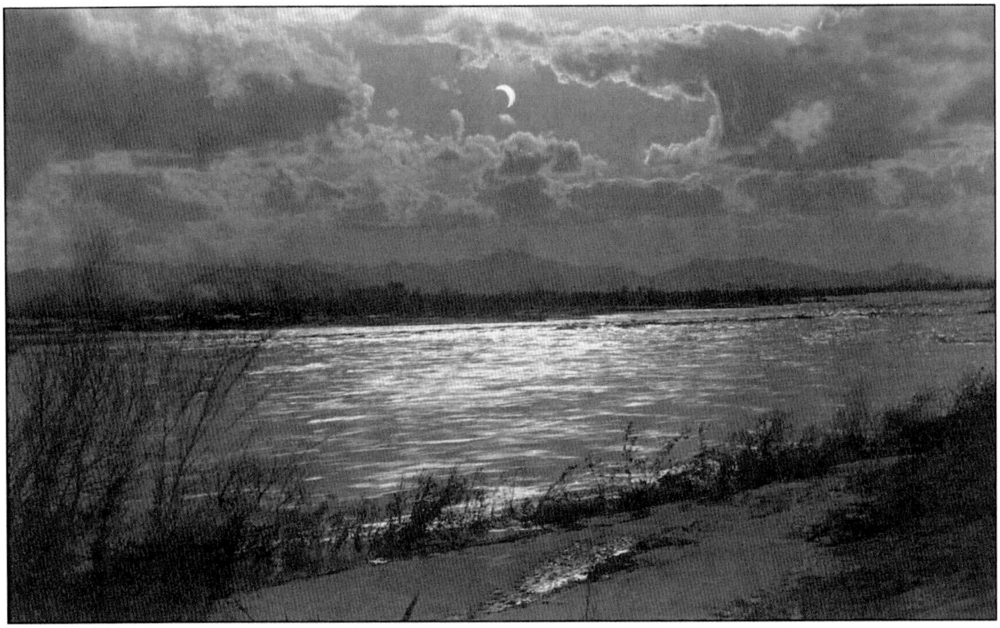

The Salt River had been respected and appreciated ever since humans settled in the Salt River Valley. Photographer George Rothrock created a dramatic composite of images made in daylight, printed to emulate night photography, which was extremely difficult at the time. Titled "Moonlight on Salt River" and taken near Phoenix, the image includes a paper punch artificial moon as a final touch. (Boudoir cabinet card, George Rothrock photographer, c. 1890. Collection of the author © vintagephoto.com.)

Three

1889–1892

The contentious move of the territorial capital from Tucson to Phoenix in 1889 provided an additional incentive for development. By this time he population of Maricopa County had grown to about 10,000 with county assets of $7 million Phoenix had grown from a population of 50 in 1868 to over 3,000 though it remained relatively primitive according to a description from that period: "Phoenix had 2 blocks of boardwalks, water was precarious, and barley, wheat and alfalfa were the primary crops. The volunteer pioneer hose company provided fire service."

Phoenix also had one three-story building, three men who delivered milk, and rail fare at 10¢ per passenger mile and 15¢ freight fare for the single train a day that connected Phoenix to the rest of the country. Freight teams linked Phoenix with the mines and cattle camps. There were two hotels and the "Chinese monopolized the restaurant business."

During the 1890s, Phoenix began the transition from small town to urban city as its population doubled. Phoenix had its own Chinatown, home to about 200 Chinese, including merchants, restaurateurs, and their families in an area roughly bounded by First and Second Streets between Madison and Jefferson.

In addition to carrying passengers and freight, the railroads brought mail that connected Maricopa County to the world. Rural Farm Delivery was established in 1891 and would provide regular mail delivery that connected the ranches and farms throughout Maricopa County with the world outside of Arizona.

Construction of an Indian School complex north of Phoenix was funded in 1891and the first building was completed the following year. 1891 also saw a major flood of the Salt River. At its peak in February 1891, water flowed at over 300,000 cubic feet per second and did substantial damage. It took over 3 months for crews to replace the Tempe Bridge and reconnect the railroad through to Phoenix.

In the valley northwest of Phoenix, the New England Land Company established the city of Glendale, originally on a 360 acres plot, on February 27, 1892. The principal early residents were members of the Church of the Brethren from Illinois. The town originally began as homesteads near the Grand Avenue crosscut canal, but soon the Santa Fe Railroad passed through Glendale, dramatically spurring both growth of the town and development of agriculture in the region.

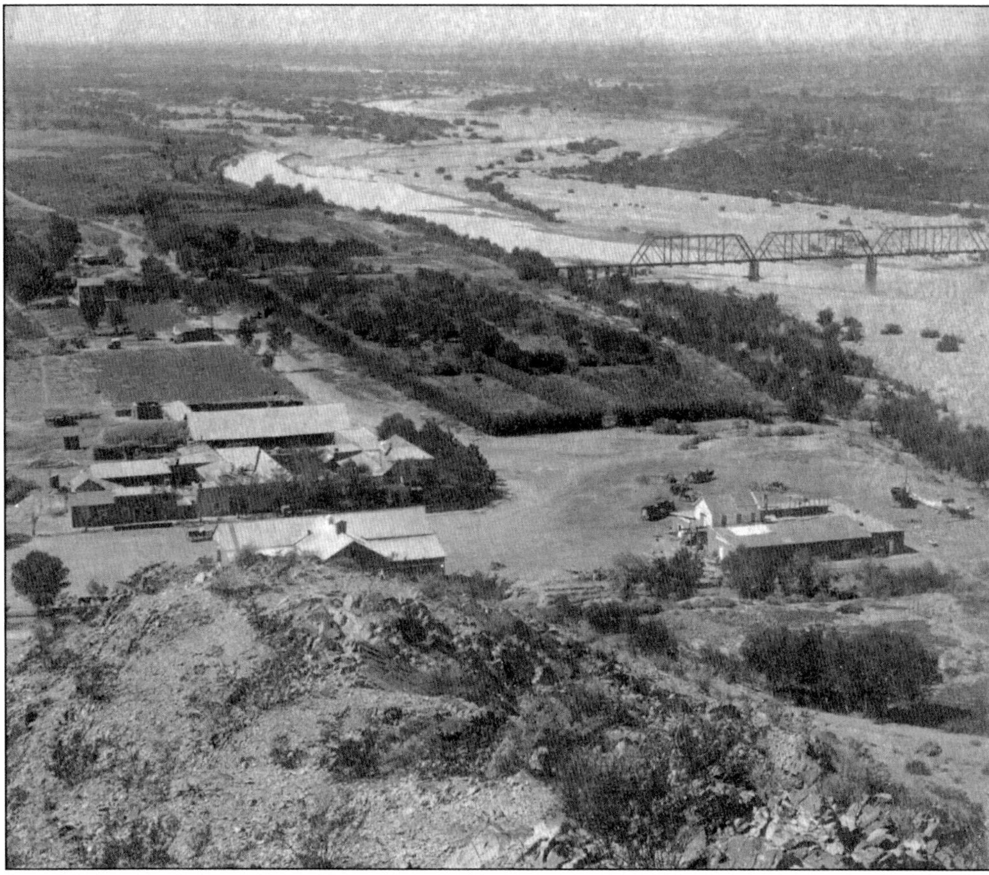

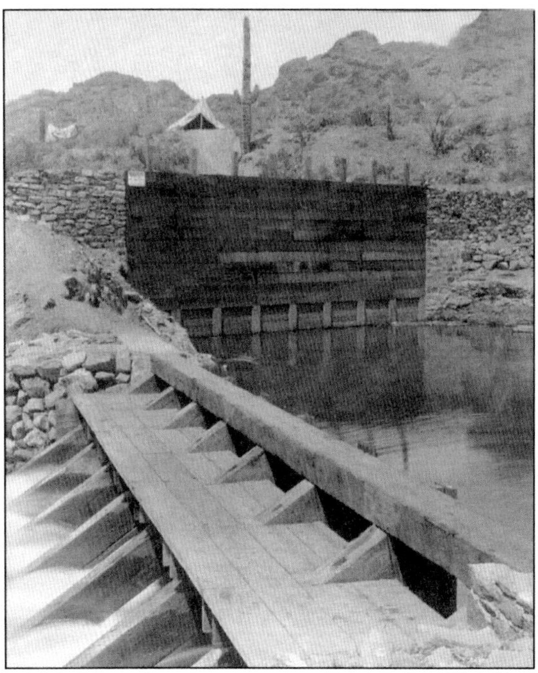

This view from Tempe Butte shows the Hayden Flour mill in the foreground and the new railroad bridge spanning the Salt River in this classic view looking west toward Phoenix. (Stereograph, George Rothrock photographer, c. 1889. Collection of the author © vintagephoto.com.)

The spring flood in 1886 destroyed the original dam and head gate of the Arizona Canal on the Salt River, east of Phoenix. Construction of the new diversion dam and head gate required 32 freight cars of lumber. (Stereograph, George Rothrock photographer, c. 1889. Collection of the author © vintagephoto.com.)

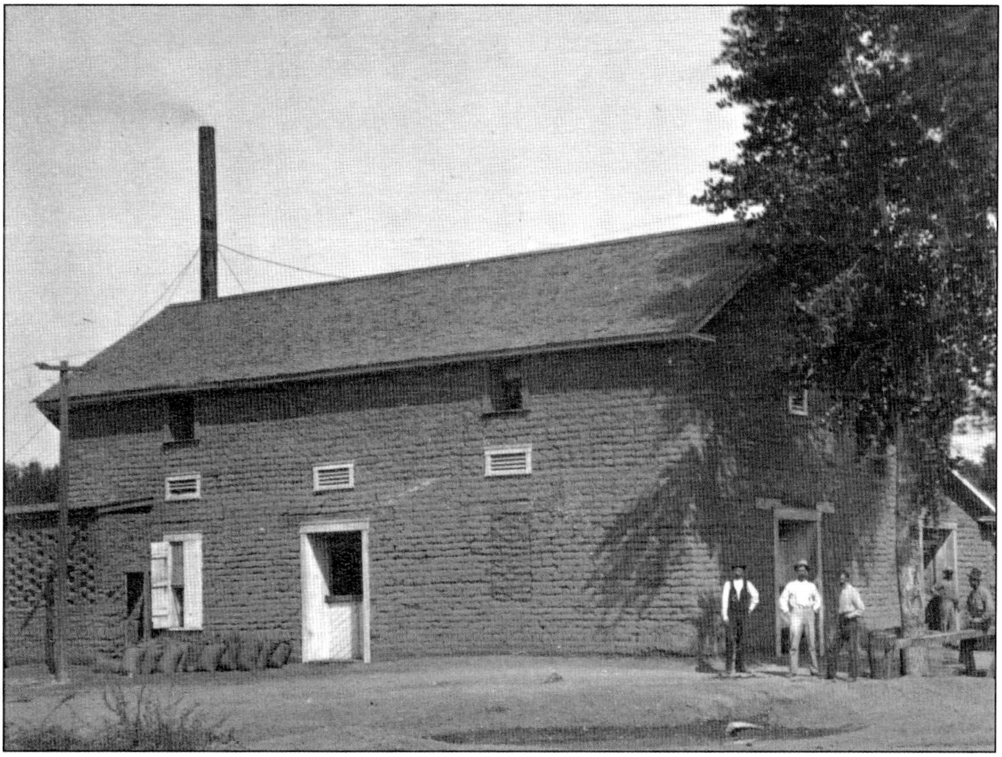

Pictured is Smiths Mill near Seymour on the Hassayampa River near the northern edge of Maricopa County. (Stereograph, Daniel Mitchell photographer, c. 1885. Collection of the author © vintagephoto.com.)

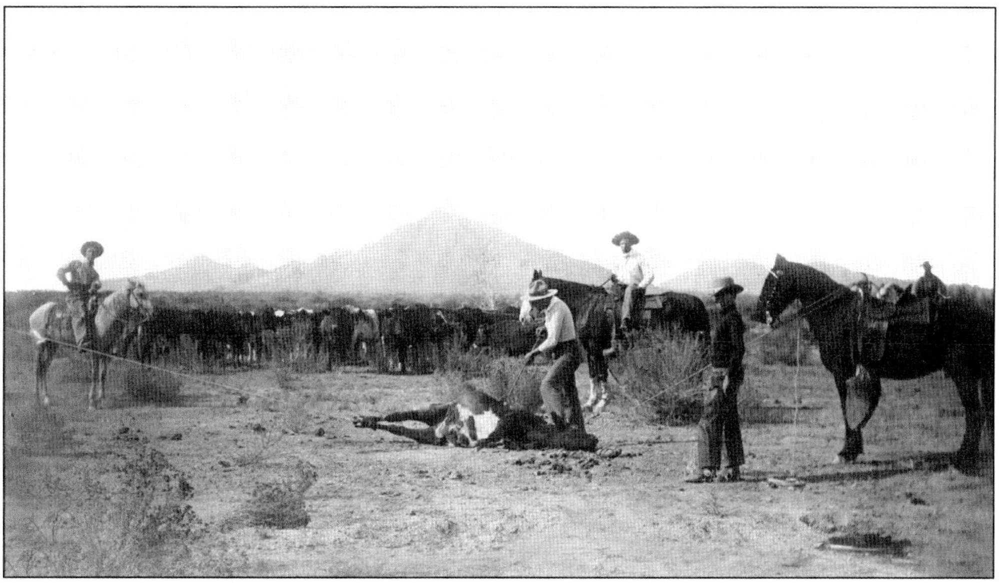

Cattle ranching grew as economical hay and forage became available locally. By 1891, Tempe ranches shipped over 11,000 head of cattle to California. This unidentified branding scene is in central Maricopa County near Phoenix. (Albumen cabinet card, George H. Rothrock photographer, c. 1890. Collection of the author © vintagephoto.com.)

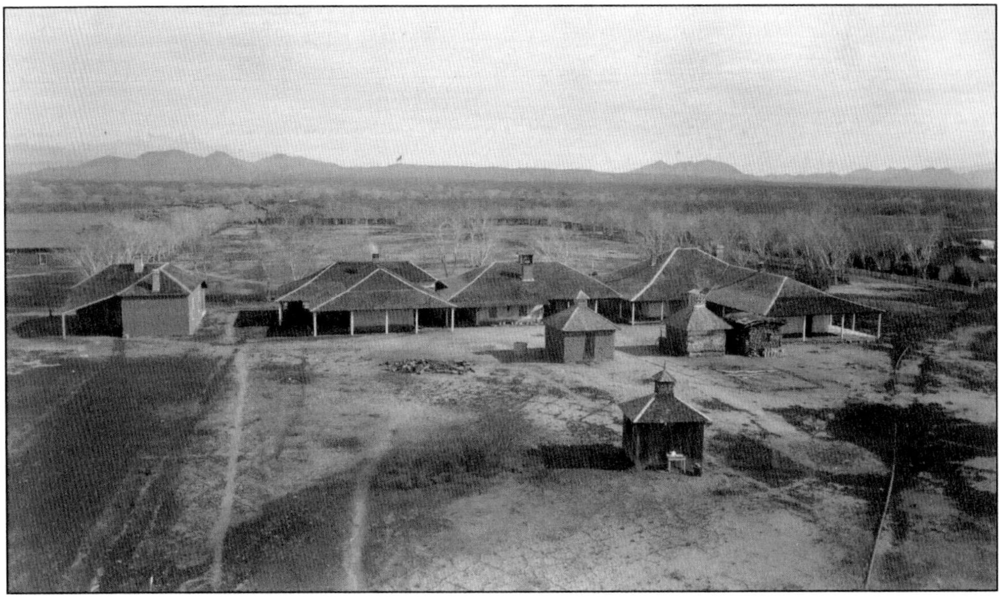

An early military base was established at the end of the Civil War in 1865 by the California Volunteers along the Verde River to help protect settlers along the Salt and Gila Rivers in Central Arizona. By the 1870s, nine detachments of soldiers at Camp McDowell worked to control the Apache raiding the emerging mines and settlements. After the end of the Apache era, the facility became part of the Fort McDowell Indian Reservation on April 10, 1890. (Boudoir cabinet card, George Rothrock photographer, *c.* 1892. Collection of the author © vintagephoto.com.)

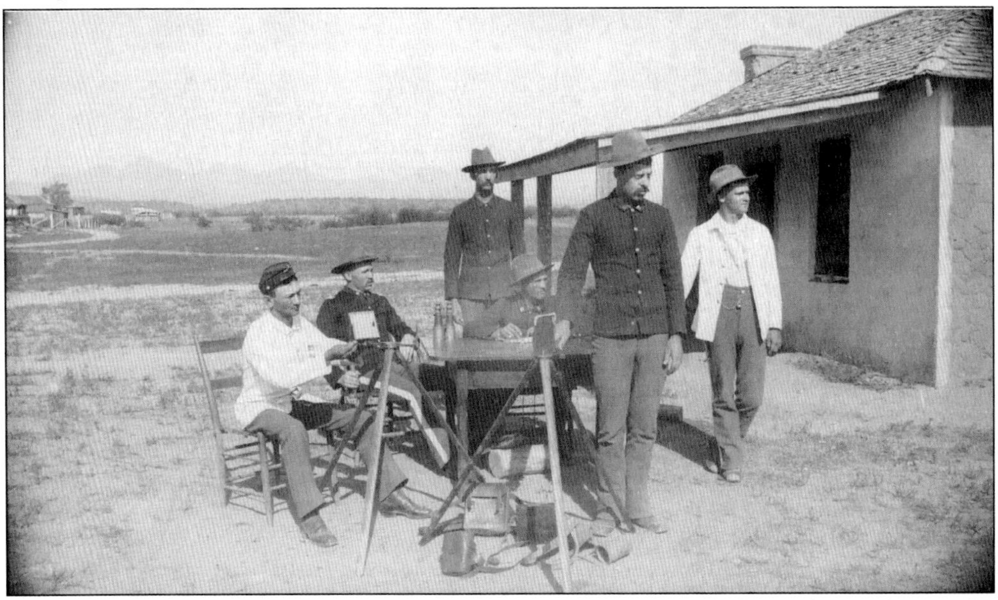

Effective communication between soldiers and forts was a continual challenge during the Apache War. Telegraph wires were easy targets for disruption. The heliograph was a wireless communication technique that used shutters to control reflections from mirrors to send Morse code. Heliographs could communicate for up to 30 miles under ideal circumstances, required little equipment, and were highly portable as seen in this image taken at Fort McDowell. (Boudoir cabinet card, photographer unknown, *c.* 1890. Collection of the author © vintagephoto.com.)

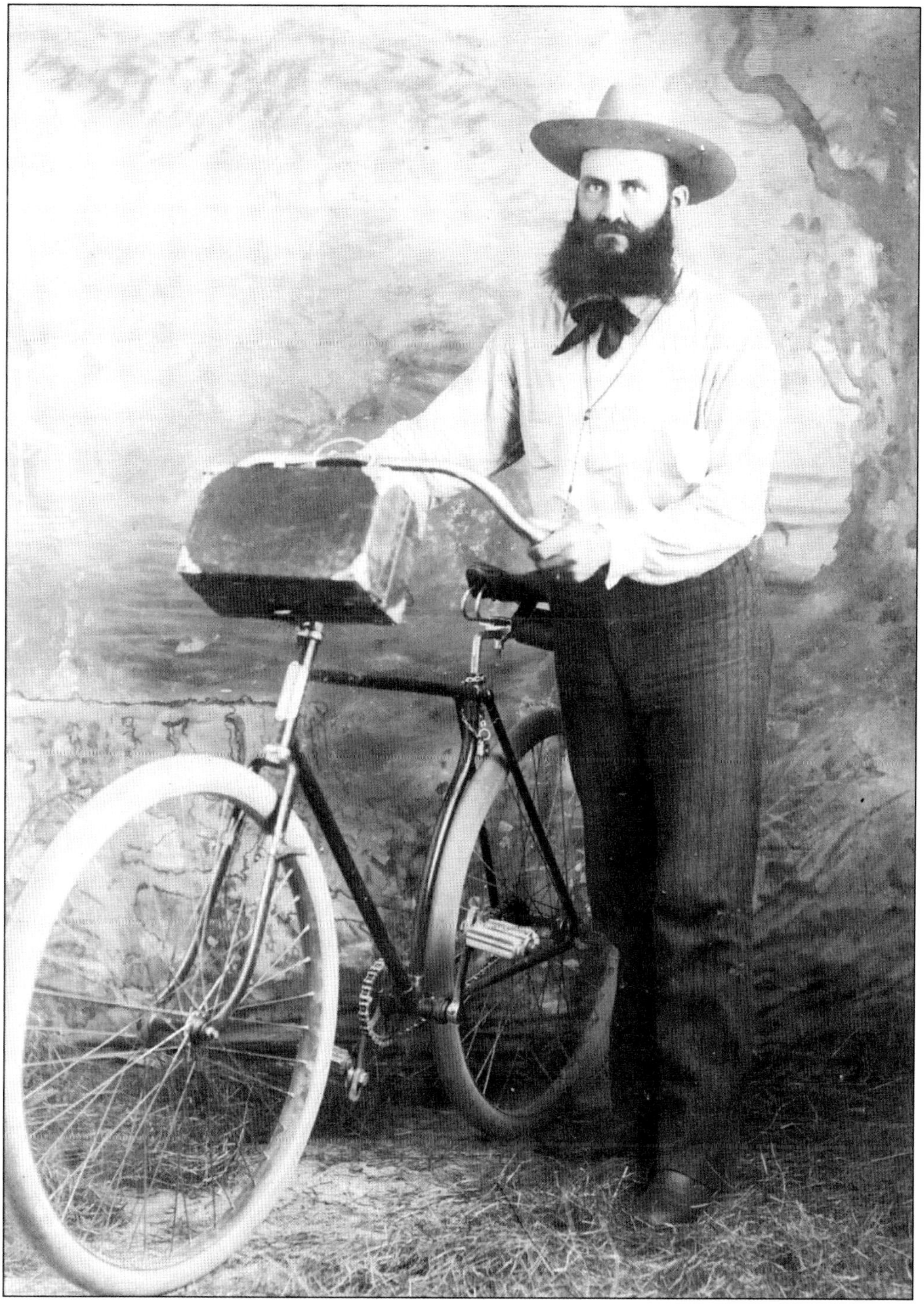

Handheld cameras became popular for both amateurs and professionals seeking to work outside of the studio in the 1890s. This self-portrait of George Rothrock in his Tempe studio shows him posed with his bicycle and camera case mounted below the handlebars. (Cabinet card, George Rothrock photographer, *c.* 1892. Collection of the author © vintagephoto.com.)

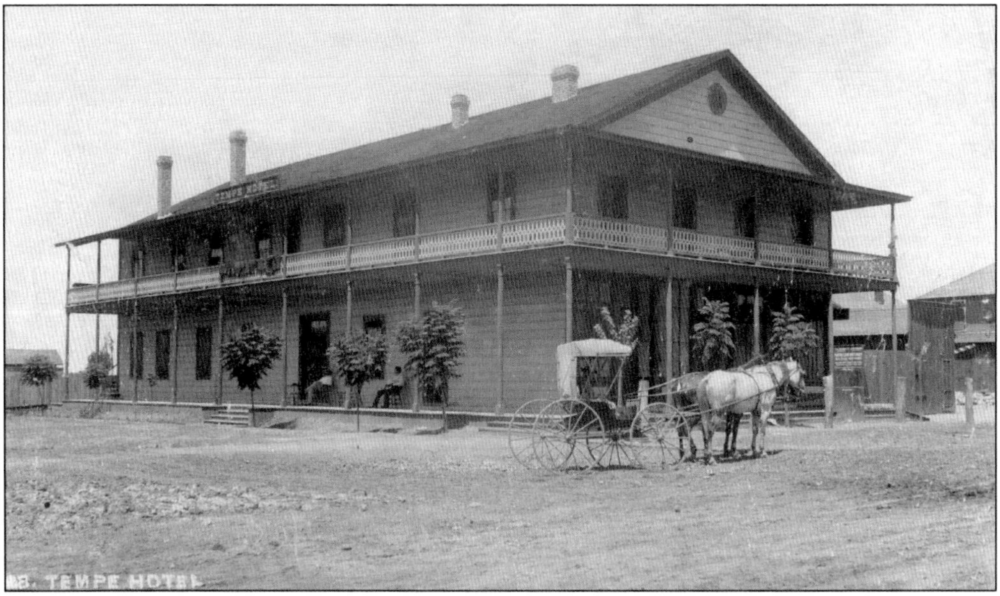

The Tempe Hotel was located on the northwest corner of Fourth Street and Mill Avenue. The original building burned in May 1894 and was replaced by the Casa Loma Hotel. (Albumen print, photographer unknown, c. 1893. Collection of the author © vintagephoto.com.)

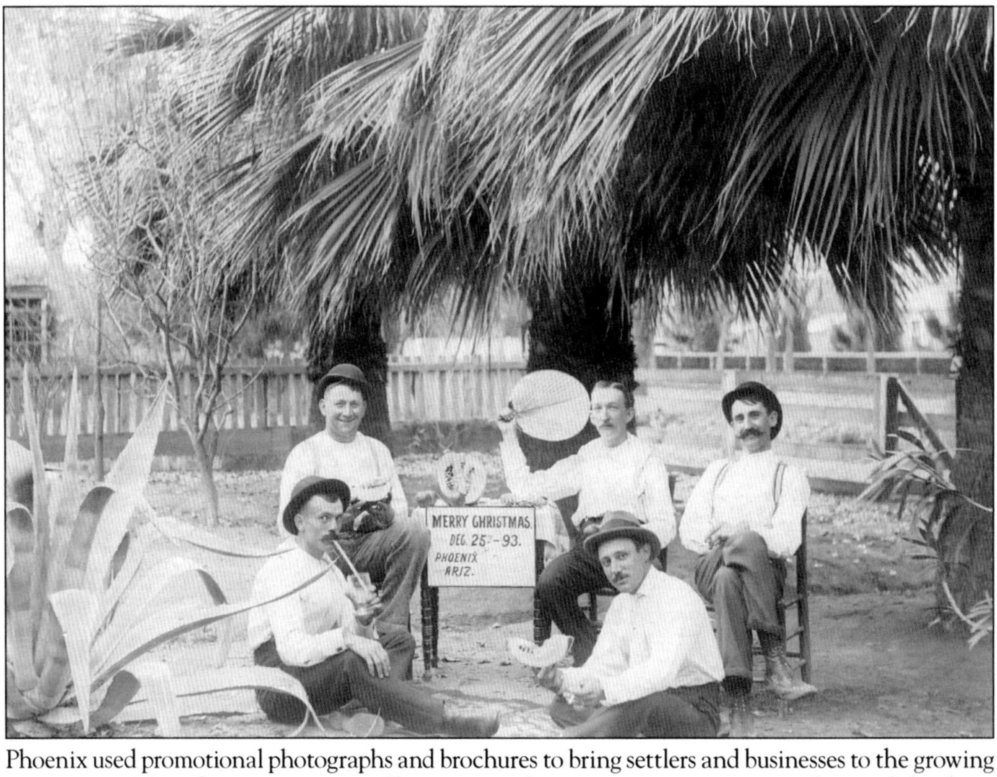

Phoenix used promotional photographs and brochures to bring settlers and businesses to the growing community. Here five men pose at Christmas without coats, eating watermelon and drinking lemonade amid palm trees and cactus to promote the mild Arizona winters. (Boudoir cabinet card, Frank Hartwell photographer, 1893. Collection of the author © vintagephoto.com.)

Four

1893–1897

The horse-drawn Phoenix street railway went electric in 1893. Washington Street in Phoenix was now 3 miles long, and "lined on either side for blocks with handsome businesses." Every major city needed a quality hotel to draw travelers and entertain traveling businessmen. The upscale Adams Hotel, completed on the Center Street north of Washington Street in December 1896 met that criterion.

The railroad and normal school fostered growth in Tempe. The Tempe Hotel was built on the corner of Fourth Street and Mill Avenue. In May 1894, the hotel burned down, but the Casa Loma Hotel replaced it at the same location. Tempe shipped over 1,100 head of cattle to California in 1891. A few years later, the human population of Tempe had almost kept up, growing to about 1,000 by 1895.

Dr. E. W. Wilbur and C. F. Crouse founded the Mesa City Bank at Main and McDonald streets in 1893. A two-story brick building, the Alhambra Hotel, was constructed just north of downtown Mesa, at 43 McDonald Street in November 1894 at a cost of $4,000. The first railroad arrived in Mesa in 1895, linking the town with Tempe and Phoenix, which was now only about 45 minutes away by rail.

The railroad in Maricopa County soon extended from Phoenix to Wickenburg, where the depot was dedicated on July 29, 1895. By the mid-1890s the population of Maricopa County had grown by another 20 percent, to about 12,000. Around 250 miles of canals, mostly in the Salt River Valley, provided water for the burgeoning agricultural industries.

Maricopa County continued to add new towns, including Scottsdale established in 1896 around a farm homesteaded by Maj. Gen. Winfield Scott in the Salt River Valley. Like other Maricopa County towns looking to grow, Scottsdale also promoted its climate and lifestyle to health seekers.

But forces were at work that sought to divide Maricopa County in two. In 1897, James C. Goodwin introduced a bill to create a new county out of eastern Maricopa County with Tempe as the county seat called Butte County. Despite the link by railroad, proponents of the new county stated that travel to Phoenix by horse and buggy was arduous enough to justify a new county seat. One can only imagine how Wickenburg, Gila Bend, and other communities that were located even farther away from Phoenix reacted to the proposal.

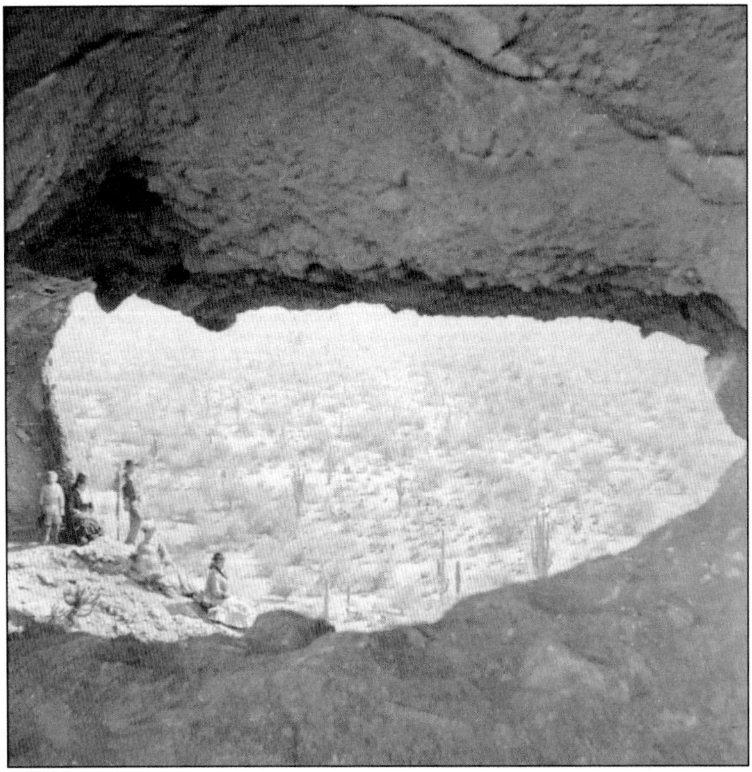

Papago Park was designated part of the Maricopa and Papago reservation in 1879 and was a popular carriage destination for picnickers and sightseers east of Phoenix near Tempe. A popular feature of the park was a natural tunnel in a sandstone hill at the center of the park. "Hole-in-the-Rock" framed the desert and provided for Victorian visitors a view of Phoenix in the distance. (Stereograph, J. C. Burge photographer, c. 1895. Collection of the author © vintagephoto.com.)

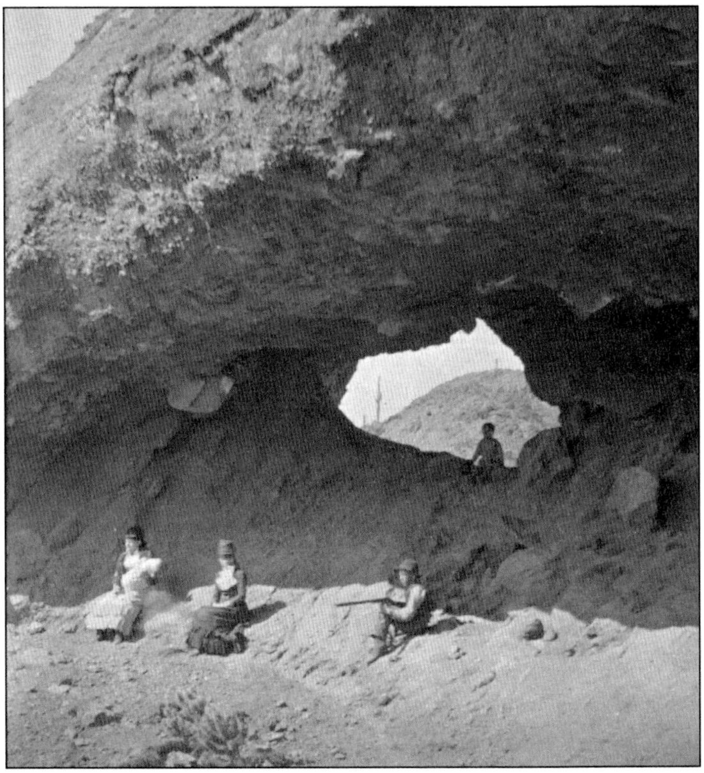

Both amateur and professional photographers were drawn to "Hole-in-the-Rock" at Papago Park. George Rothrock added a large graffiti advertisement for his photographic studio in Phoenix on the roof of the opening. His advertisement was cropped out of this image by a rival photographer. A similar Rothrock studio ad is still visible in a cave at Montezuma's Well, north of the Verde Valley. Note the same individuals appear in the view above. (Stereograph, J. C. Burge photographer, c. 1895. Collection of the author © vintagephoto.com.)

After the end of the Apache wars, the mystique of the West began to coalesce into myth. Photographers were quick to build on interest and create salable images of Arizona and the West. The same individuals appear once again in this tableau of an armed settler protecting two women from an Indian posed at lower right. This image was actually made on the southeast of the large butte at Papago Park. (Stereograph, J. C. Burge photographer, c. 1895. Collection of the author © vintagephoto.com.)

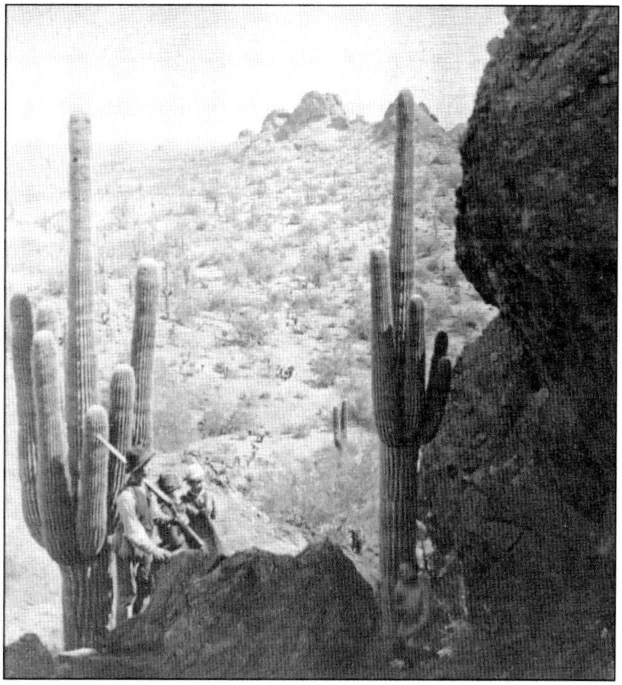

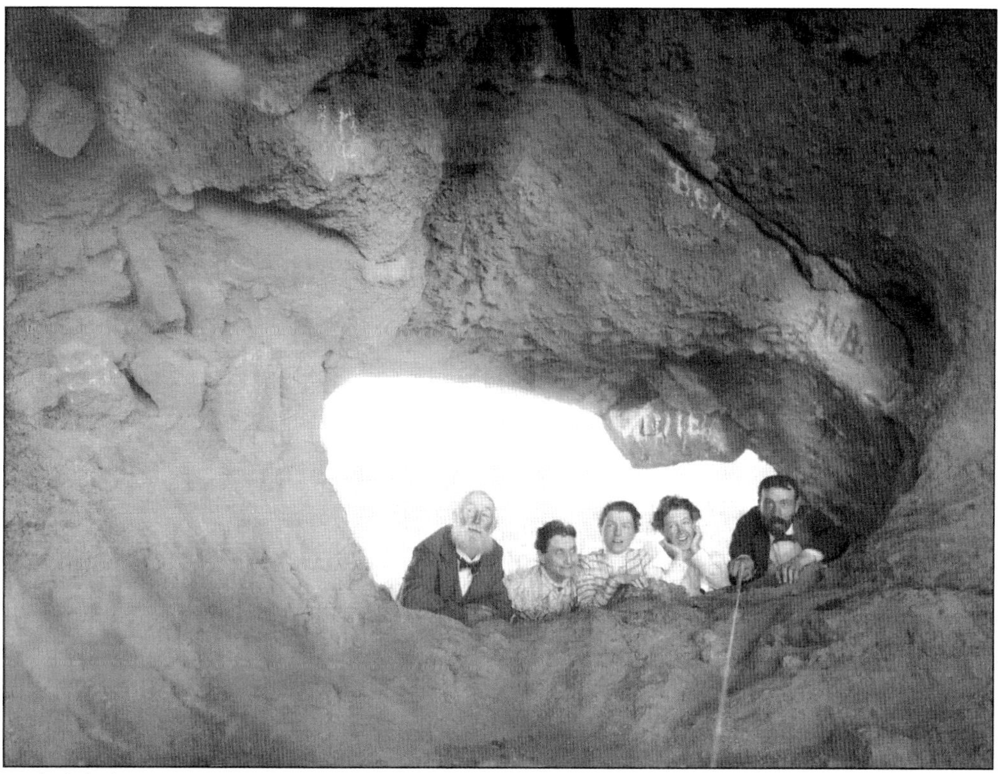

A slightly later image of visitors to Hole-in-the-Rock at Papago Park shows the group posing for the camera. The gentleman on the right is pulling a string to trip the shutter and take the picture. (Silver print, photographer unknown, c. 1900. Collection of the author © vintagephoto.com.)

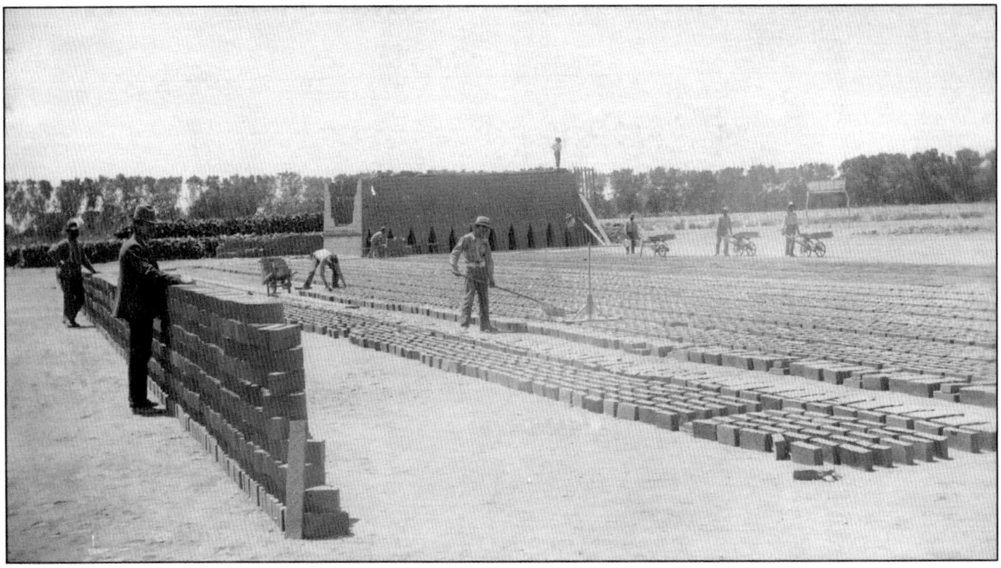

As Phoenix grew, adobe was still a popular and economical building material. This scene shows adobe brick production near Phoenix. A work crew is drying the formed adobe bricks, and a test wall is inspected at the left of the image. (Boudoir cabinet card, George Rothrock photographer, c. 1890. Collection of the author © vintagephoto.com.)

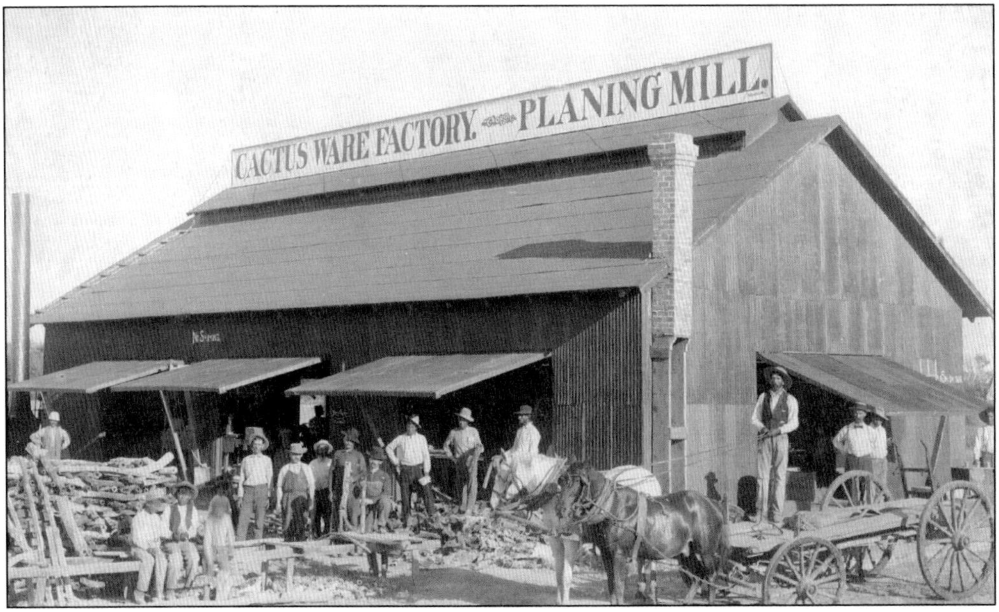

The unique natural materials of the Southwest were soon incorporated into products for the burgeoning tourist trade. The Cactus Ware Factory and Planning Mill in Phoenix was an early adopter, using cholla cactus skeletons to make unique decorator items. (Albumen boudoir cabinet card, Frank A. Hartwell photographer, c. 1895. Collection of the author © vintagephoto.com.)

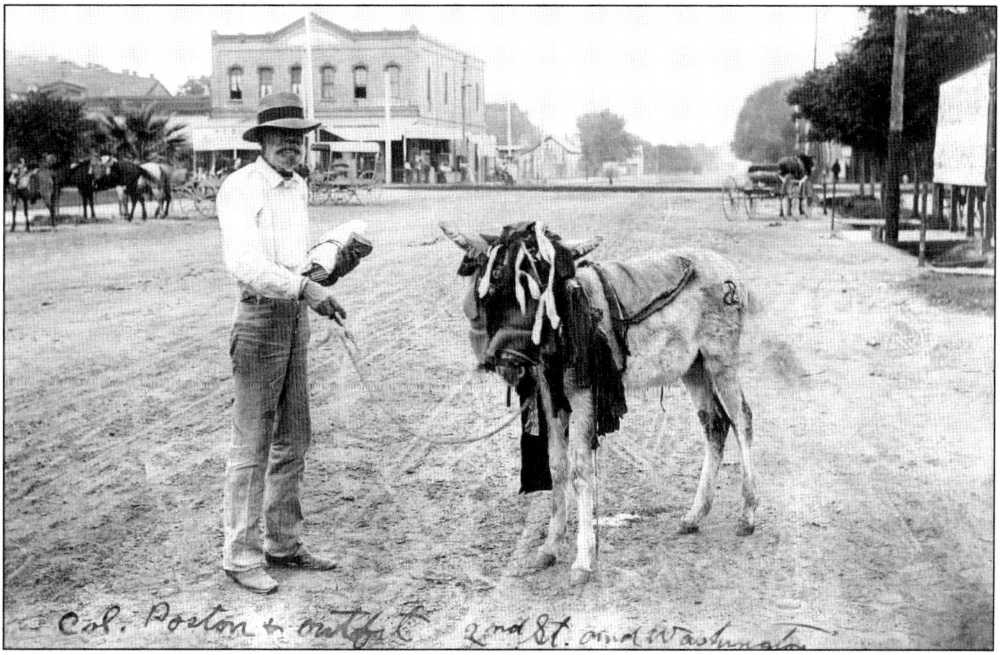

Col. Charles Debrille Poston, an Arizona pioneer, was an explorer, miner, and first delegate to the House of Representatives in Washington, D.C. Colonel Poston is often referred to as the "Father of Arizona." Unfortunately his notoriety did little to help him late in life when he lived on the streets of Phoenix with his mules. Though finally recognized and given a small pension in 1897, Col. Poston died a pauper on June 24, 1902. (Albumen boudoir cabinet card, Frank A. Hartwell photographer, c. 1895. Collection of the author © vintagephoto.com.)

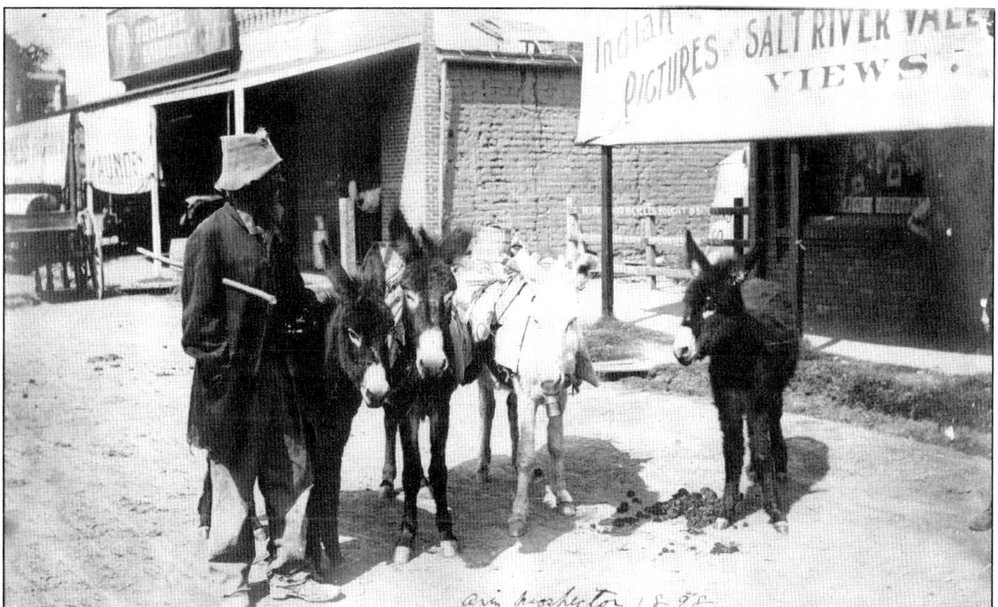

Poston poses with his mules in front of an unidentified Phoenix photographic studio. (Albumen boudoir cabinet card, Frank A. Hartwell photographer, c. 1895. Collection of the author © vintagephoto.com.)

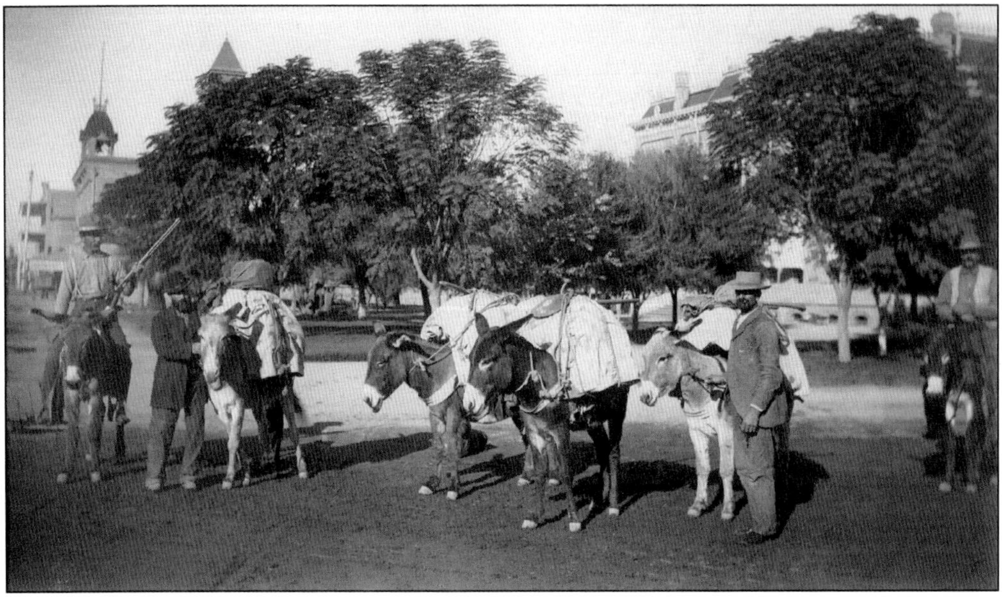

Though Phoenix was not known for its mining wealth, prospectors still provisioned there and before setting out to strike it rich. Jacob Waltz, also known as the "Lost Dutchman," died in Phoenix soon after the 1891 flood. His legend drew scores of dreamers to the hunt for this lost mine in the nearby Superstition Mountains. (Boudoir cabinet card, Frank Hartwell photographer, c. 1895. Collection of the author © vintagephoto.com.)

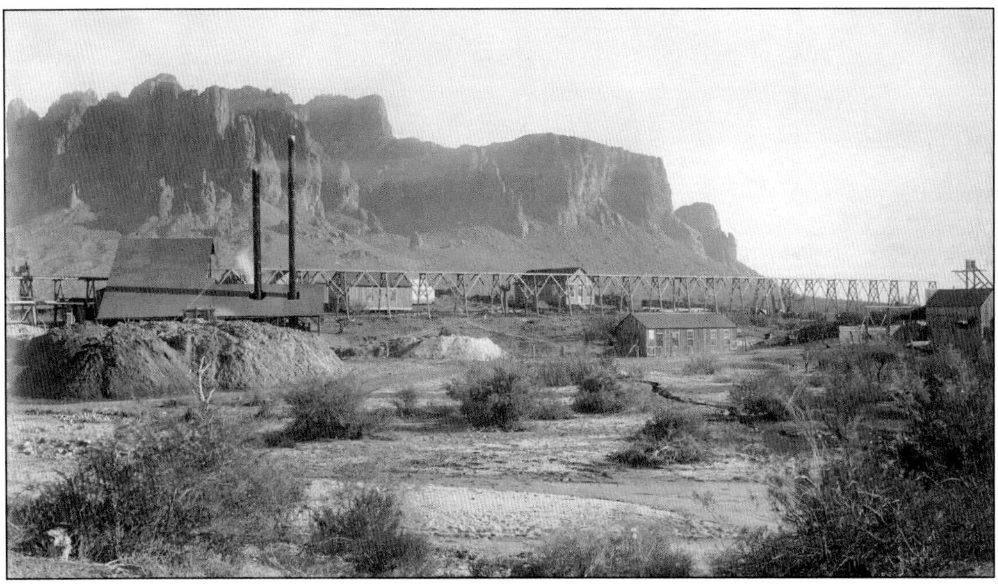

Goldfield, at the base of the Superstition Mountains (near Apache Junction today), was founded in 1887 as a copper and gold mine. By the time the mill was built in 1893, about 150 people lived in the area. (Boudoir cabinet card, photographer unknown, c. 1895. Collection of the author © vintagephoto.com.)

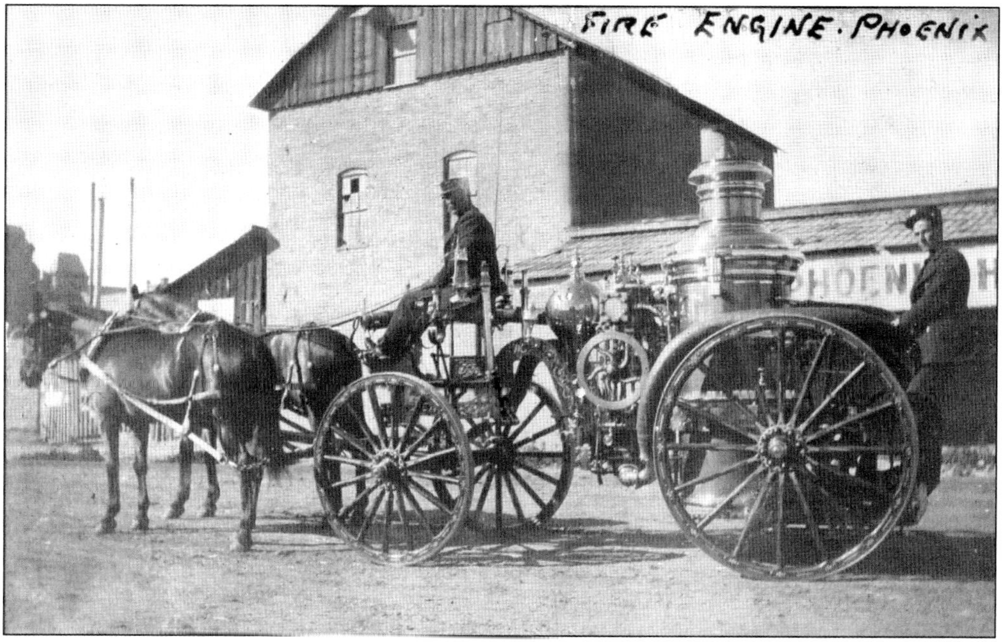

Major fires in 1885 and 1886 led to formation of a volunteer fire department composed of the Pioneer Hose Company and Hispanic Yucatec Hose Company No. 2. This horse-drawn fire pump augmented the precarious water supply to help contain fires and protect the growing city center. The first fire station in Phoenix was completed in 1894 at the corner of First Street and Jefferson. Phoenix was ahead of other Valley cities; Tempe would not organize a volunteer fire department until 1902. (Albumen print. photographer unknown, c. 1895. Collection of the author © vintagephoto.com.)

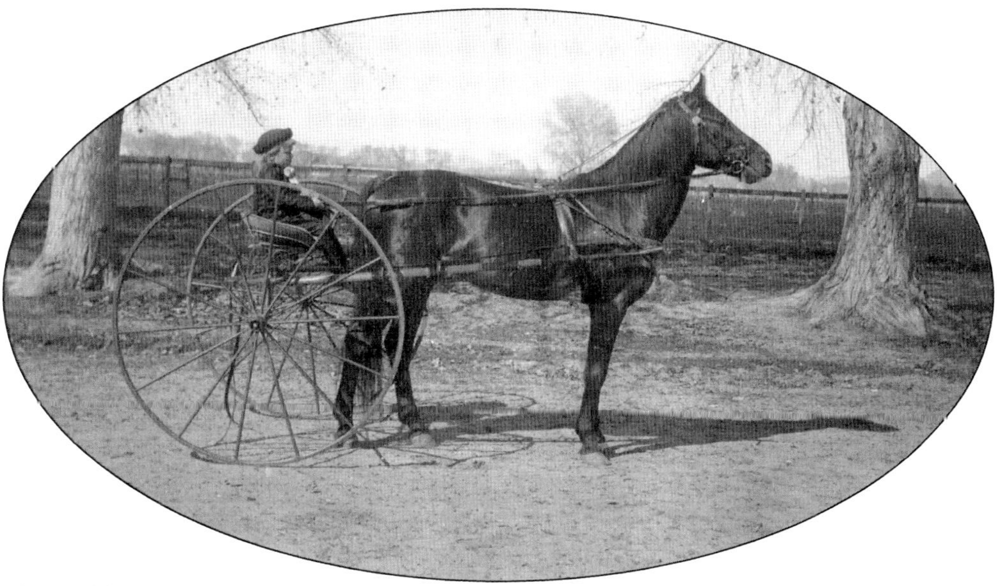

Thoroughbred horses have always been popular demonstrations of wealth. Born in 1888, Outward was a record winning trotter bred by George Loring and E. B. Kirkland of Phoenix. Outward poses with his sulky and an unidentified young boy at a farm in Mesa. (Boudoir cabinet card, Barnett photographer, c. 1895. Collection of the author © vintagephoto.com.)

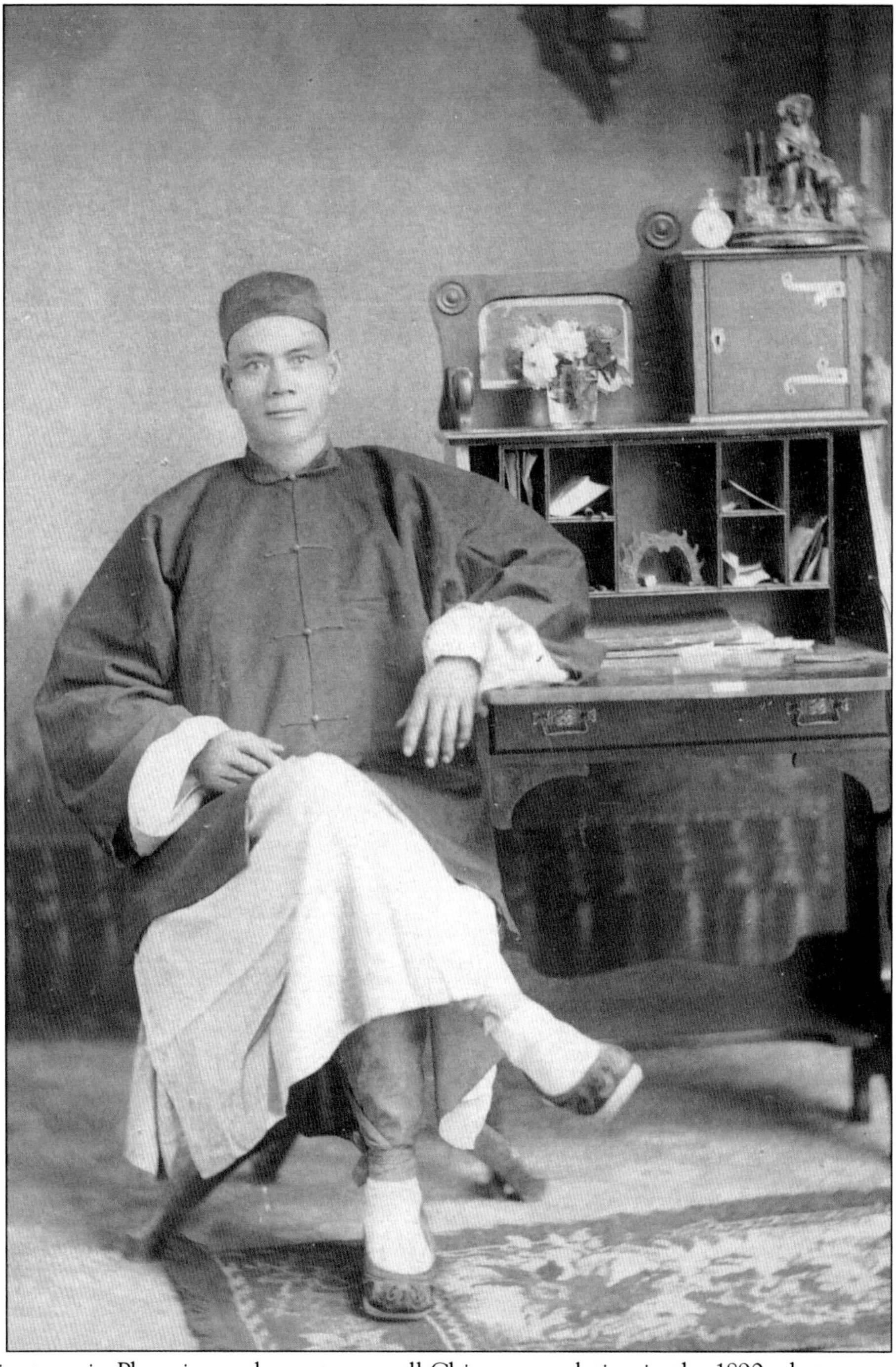

Chinatown in Phoenix was home to a small Chinese population in the 1890s that grew to an area bounded by Jackson, Jefferson between First and Third Streets by 1910. In addition to many of the successful restaurants in Phoenix at the time, Chinatown had saloons, opium dens, and other less savory businesses. This Chinese businessman brought his desk as a prop for his formal studio portrait. (Cabinet card, F. A. Hartwell photographer, c. 1898. Collection of the author © vintagephoto.com.)

Five

1898–1901

Maricopa County saw a period of unusual growth in photographic activity as several prolific photographers created exceptional bodies of work between 1898 and 1901, including Frank Hartwell, A. F. Messinger and partner William Altenburgh, J. P. Rhodes and a score of talented amateurs. They documented parades and public events, new schools and buildings, and emerging recreational activities that included day trips to Papago Park, camping and swimming in the canals and Salt River. Historic images were regularly reprinted or copied from old photographs. The market for photographs of Arizona's Native American population remained strong, and photographers happily provided images for regional and national markets.

The population of Maricopa County continued to grow even more rapidly in the second half of the 1890s, fully doubling between 1890 and 1900, to 20,457. Phoenix now accounted for 25 percent of the population of the County, with the rest reflecting the growth of Tempe, Mesa, and the smaller towns, mines, and ranches.

As the irrigation canals continued to extend throughout the Salt River Valley, so did the farms and ranches. The mild winter climate helped Arizona farmers respond to national demand for winter fruits and produce. Maricopa County farms produced crops including corn, wheat, oats, barley, pink beans, Irish potatoes, watermelons, cantaloupe, peaches, apricots, plums, pears, blackberries, strawberries, grapes, raisins, dates, tomatoes, and cabbage. Livestock, including cattle, sheep, and ostrich, were also important Arizona exports.

Phoenix needed a capitol building. In 1889, the same year the Capital moved to Phoenix, M. H. Sherman and Marcellus E. Collins donated land at the west end of Washington Street for a building to house the capitol and legislature. The following year, 1890, George Houton Smith was engaged to create a major garden on the capitol grounds. Contractor Tom Lovell was hired to oversee building construction in 1900, after the legislature appropriated $100,000 in bonds to fund the project. The completed Arizona capital was dedicated by Gov. Nathan O. Murphy on February 25, 1901.

Also in May 1901, local developer Frank Murphy who had built the Santa Fe, Prescott and Phoenix railway and was principal owner of the Congress Gold Mining Company persuaded Pres. William McKinley and his entourage to stop in Maricopa County while traveling by rail from New Orleans to Portland, Oregon. McKinley paraded from the Phoenix railroad depot to the capitol building for a speech before leaving for the Congress mine, arriving on May 7, 1901.

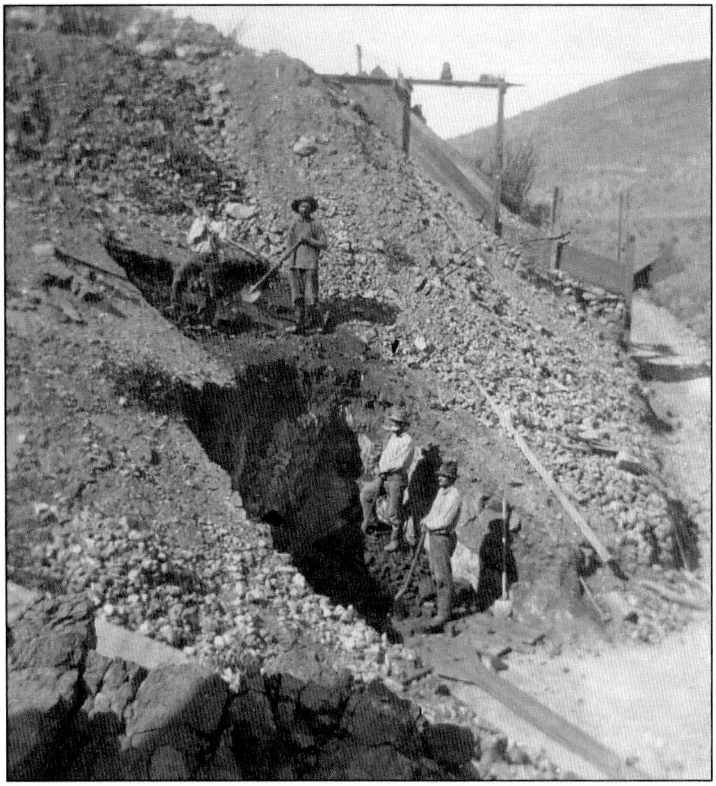

Small individual mining claims were sprinkled throughout Maricopa County. This image shows a shoot for loading ore into wagons for transport at the right. The unidentified small works is attributed to being near the Vulture Mine near Wickenburg. (Silver print, photographer unknown, *c.* 1898. Collection of the author © vintagephoto.com.)

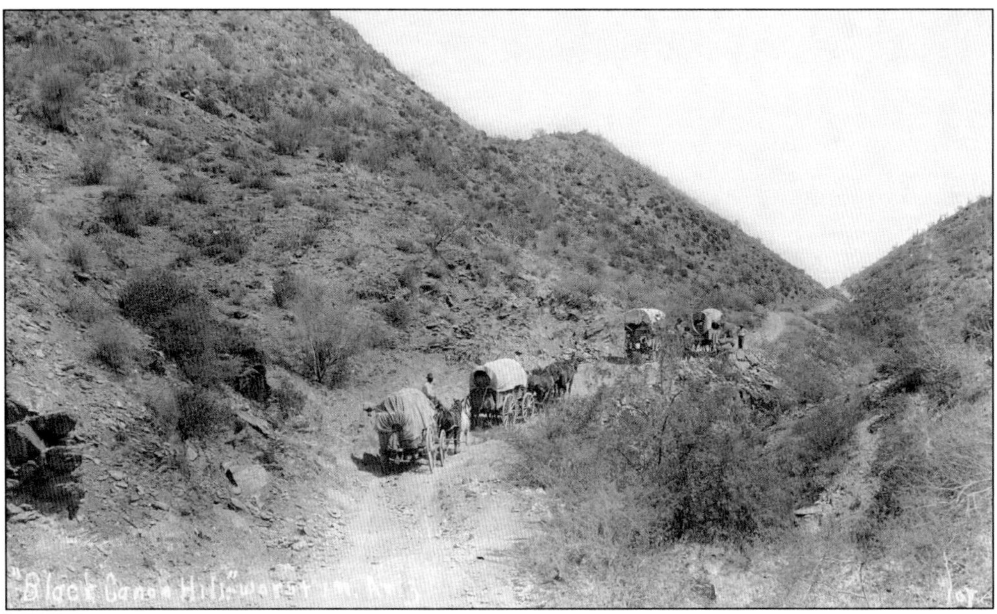

A freight wagon train is shown starting up the incline at Black Canyon on the trail from Phoenix to Prescott. (Silver print, A. F. Messinger photographer, *c.* 1898. Collection of the author © vintagephoto.com.)

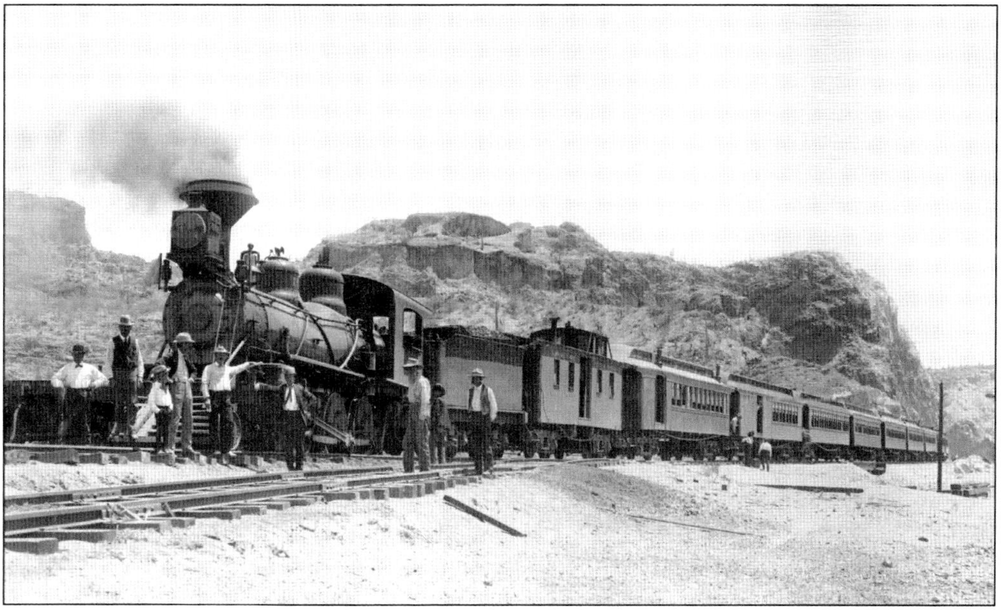

The Santa Fe Prescott and Phoenix Railway was incorporated in 1891 and linked Phoenix and Prescott on February 28, 1895. The line provided passenger and freight service between the cities and access to the Atchison, Topeka and Santa Fe via Ash Fork. (Silver print, Frank A. Hartwell photographer, *c.* 1898. Collection of the author © vintagephoto.com.)

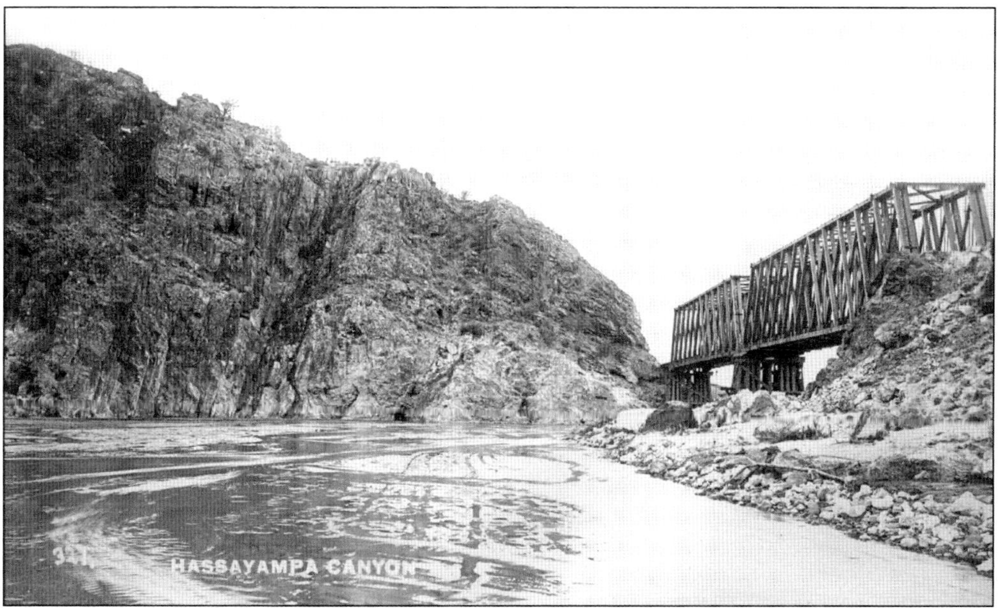

Pictured is the Phoenix and Prescott Railroad Bridge across the Hassayampa River, south of Wickenburg. (Silver print, A. F. Messinger photographer, *c.* 1898. Collection of the author © vintagephoto.com.

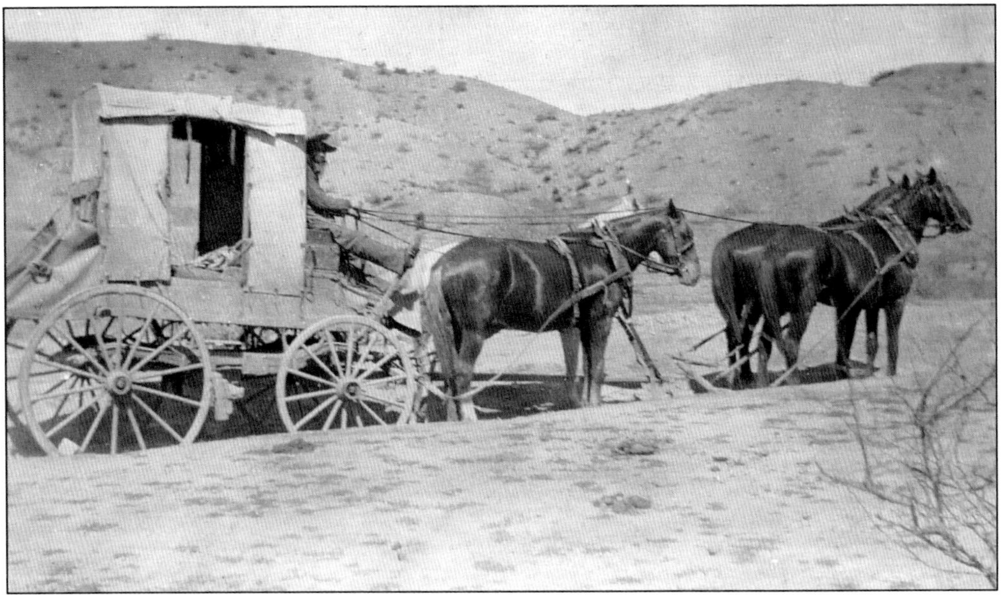

Travel between railroad depots in Maricopa County consisted of stagecoaches for passengers and freight wagons to carry goods and supplies. This coach illustrates the deep ruts that heavy traffic wore into the hard desert soil. (Silver print, photographer unknown, c. 1897. Collection of the author © vintagephoto.com.)

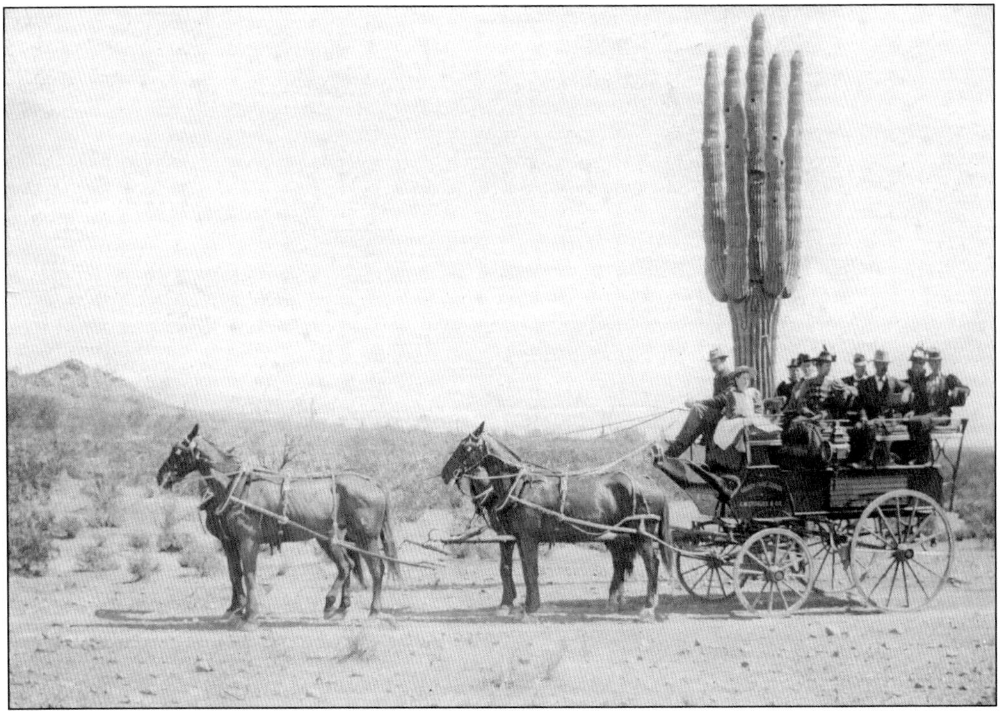

The north side of Camelback Mountain was still mostly untouched desert. A well-dressed excursion party travels in a much more upscale 19th-century stagecoach as they visit Paradise Valley for a picnic. (Silver print, photographer unknown, c. 1898. Collection of the author © vintagephoto.com.)

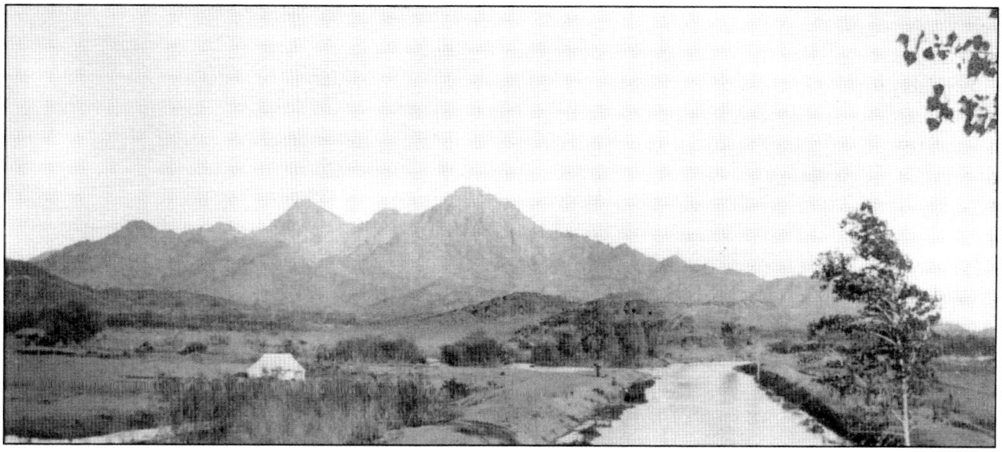

This example of a tent dwelling in this *c.* 1897 silver print is far outside of Phoenix, north of the Arizona Canal near the base of Squaw (now Piestewa) Peak, just north of Glendale, and at about Twelfth Street today. (Silver print, photographer unknown. Collection of the author © vintagephoto.com.)

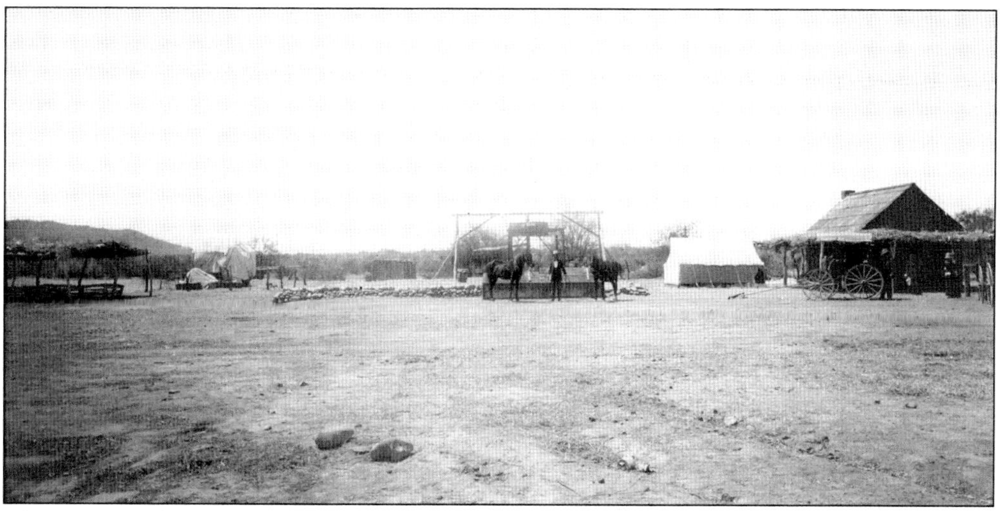

The stagecoach stop owned by Phoenix Pioneer Darrel Duppa, called Duppa Station, was abandoned in 1875. A post office was established at the site in 1898 as New River. (Silver print, photographer unknown, *c.* 1900. Collection of the author © vintagephoto.com.)

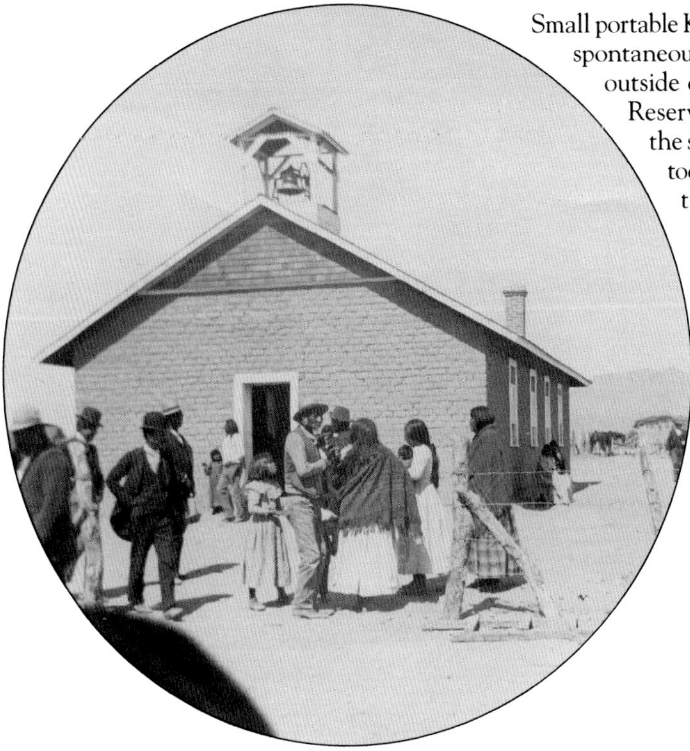

Small portable Kodak cameras permitted more spontaneous photography, like this group outside of the church on the Papago Reservation. The earliest cameras, the string set and ordinary models, took circular images and required the cameras to be sent back to the Kodak factory for processing. (Silver print, photographer unknown, c. 1897. Collection of the author © vintagephoto.com.)

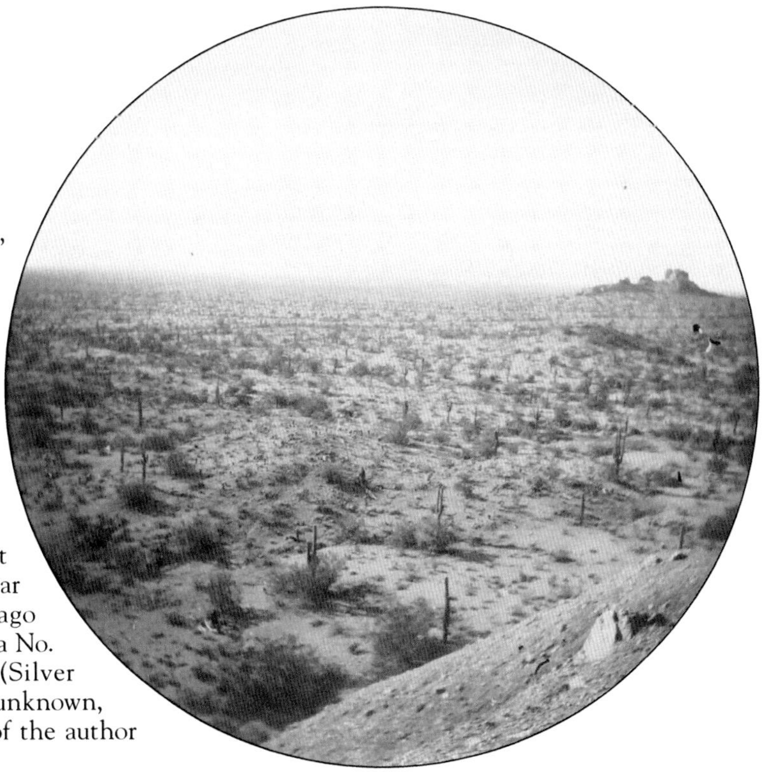

Availability of simple, handheld Kodak cameras fueled the rise of amateur photography that coincided with increased leisure time and the rise of the middle class in the 1890s. This view of the desert below Hole-in-the-Rock at Papago Park, the popular destination in Papago Park, was made with a No. 1 string set Kodak.(Silver print, photographer unknown, c. 1897. Collection of the author © vintagephoto.com.)

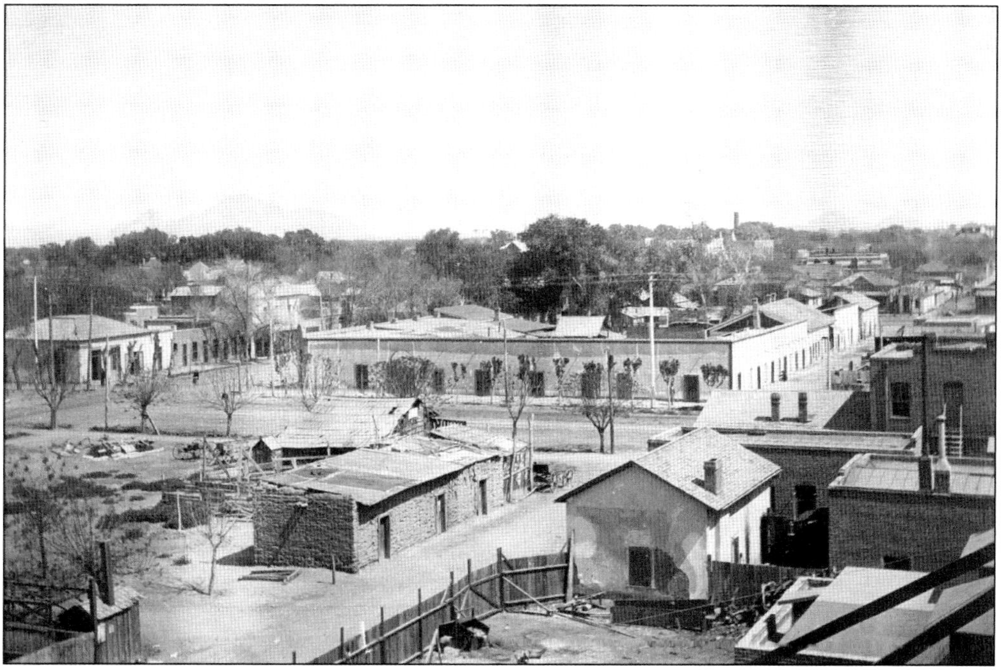

The Adams Hotel quickly became a local landmark and provided one of the highest vantage points to look out over Phoenix. A photographer made these two images from the balcony, looking north (above) and looking across Adams Street to Washington (below). (Silver prints, photographer unknown, *c.* 1897. Collection of the author © vintagephoto.com.)

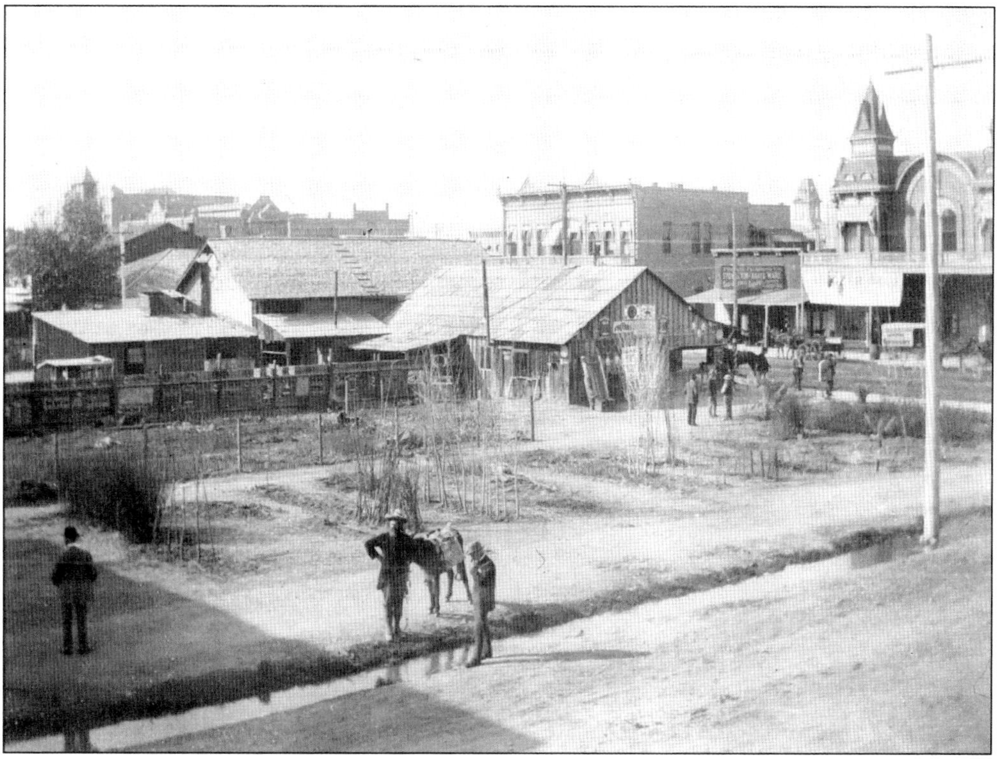

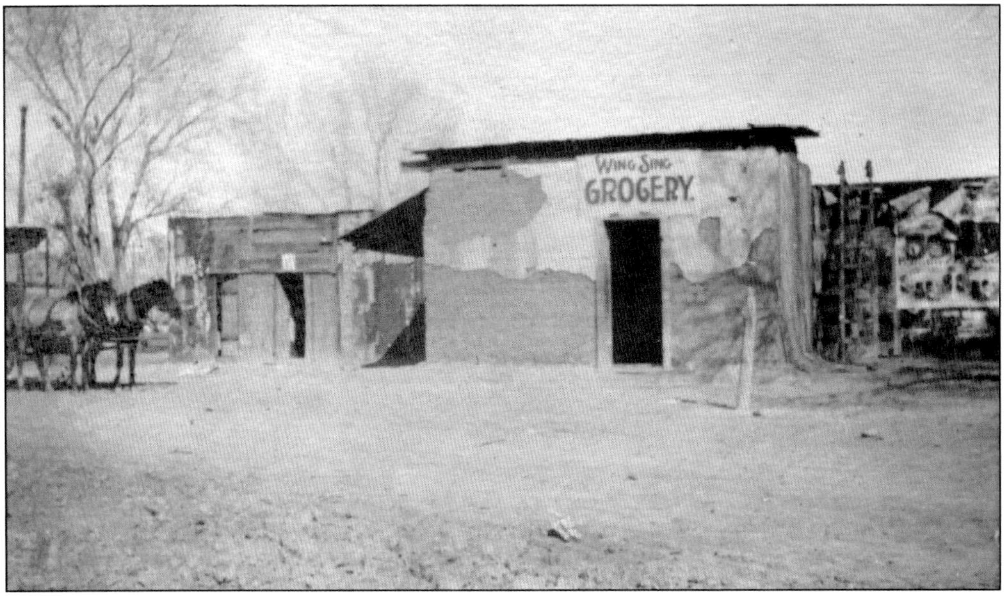

Though business buildings on Washington and in the downtown Phoenix core were modern, many businesses, like Wing Sing's grocery at 612 East Jackson, continued to occupy primitive adobe structures well into the 20th century. (Silver print, photographer unknown, c. 1898. Collection of the author © vintagephoto.com.)

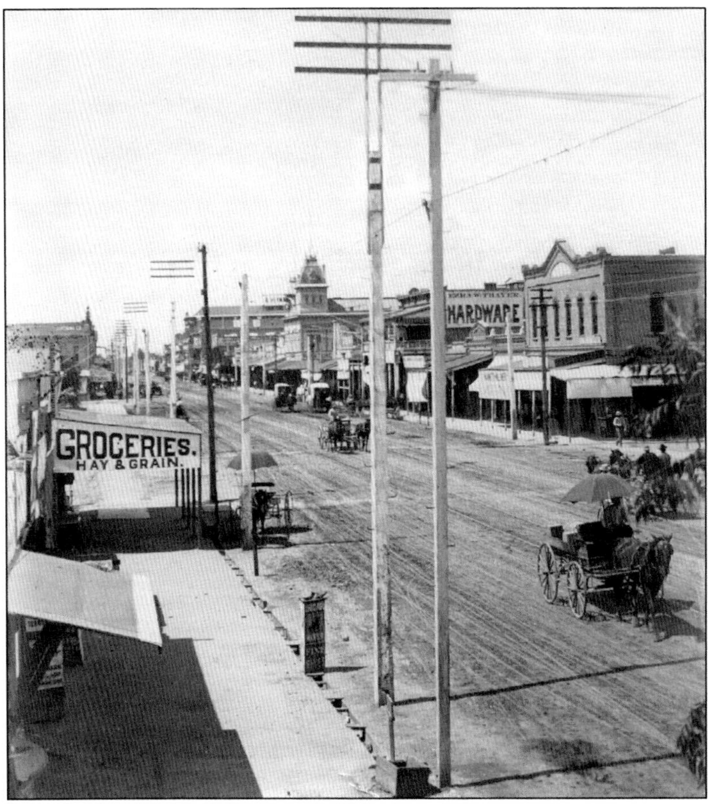

Amateur photographers sought high points to make photographs of the young city. This view down the boardwalk along Washington from Second Street was composed to show the modern electric poles as well as the carriage traffic. (Silver print, photographer unknown, c. 1898. Collection of the author © vintagephoto.com.)

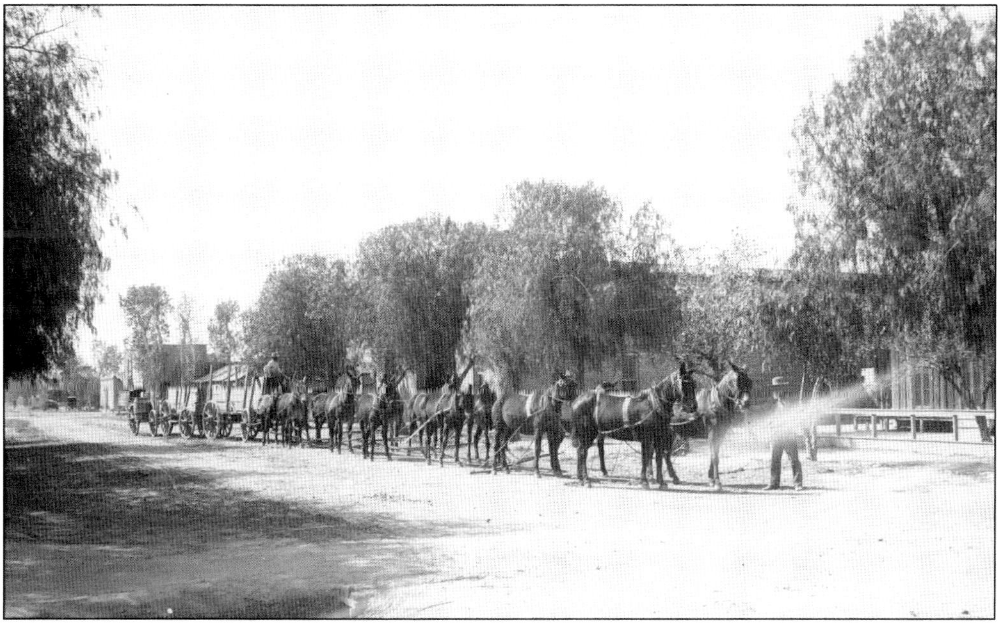

Even after the arrival of the railroad, freight wagons remained important means of transporting goods throughout the County. The freight wagon trains were popular photographic subjects as they traveled through Phoenix. Silver print, photographer unknown, c. 1897. Collection of the author © vintagephoto.com.

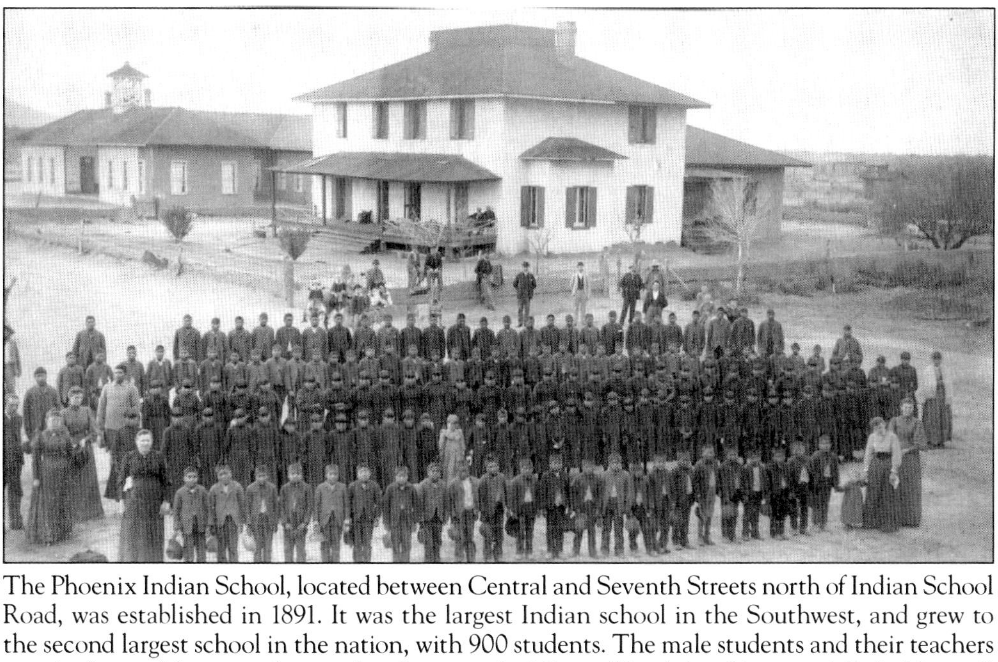

The Phoenix Indian School, located between Central and Seventh Streets north of Indian School Road, was established in 1891. It was the largest Indian school in the Southwest, and grew to the second largest school in the nation, with 900 students. The male students and their teachers pose in front of the recently completed campus buildings. (Boudoir cabinet card, F. A. Hartwell photographer c. 1898. Collection of the author © vintagephoto.com.)

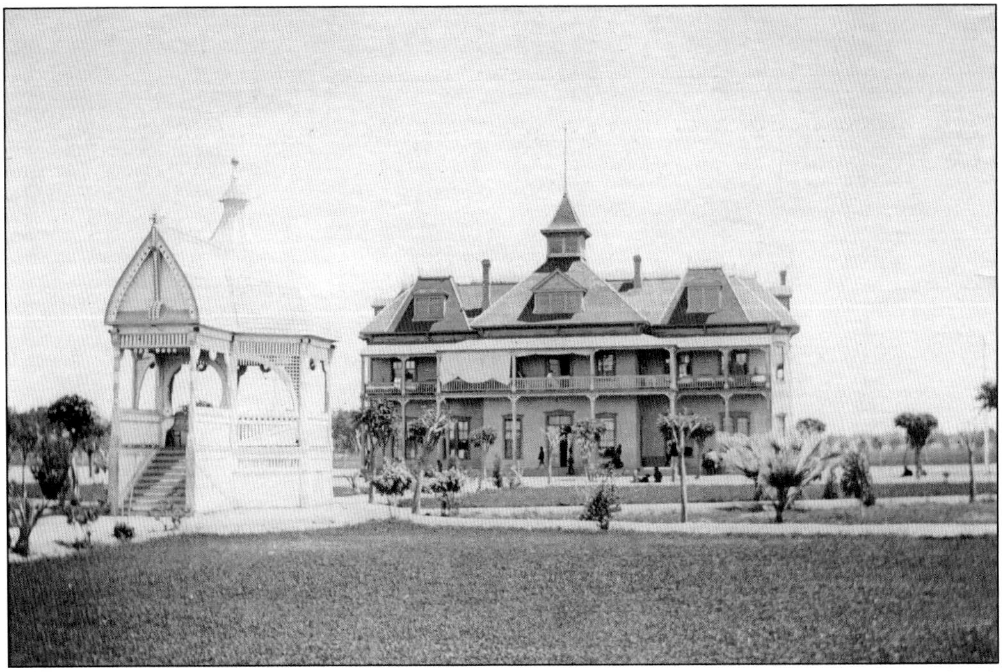

This view of the bandstand and Girls Building shows the newly completed Phoenix Indian School, with freshly planted grounds. (Silver print, photographer unknown, *c.* 1898. Collection of the author © vintagephoto.com.)

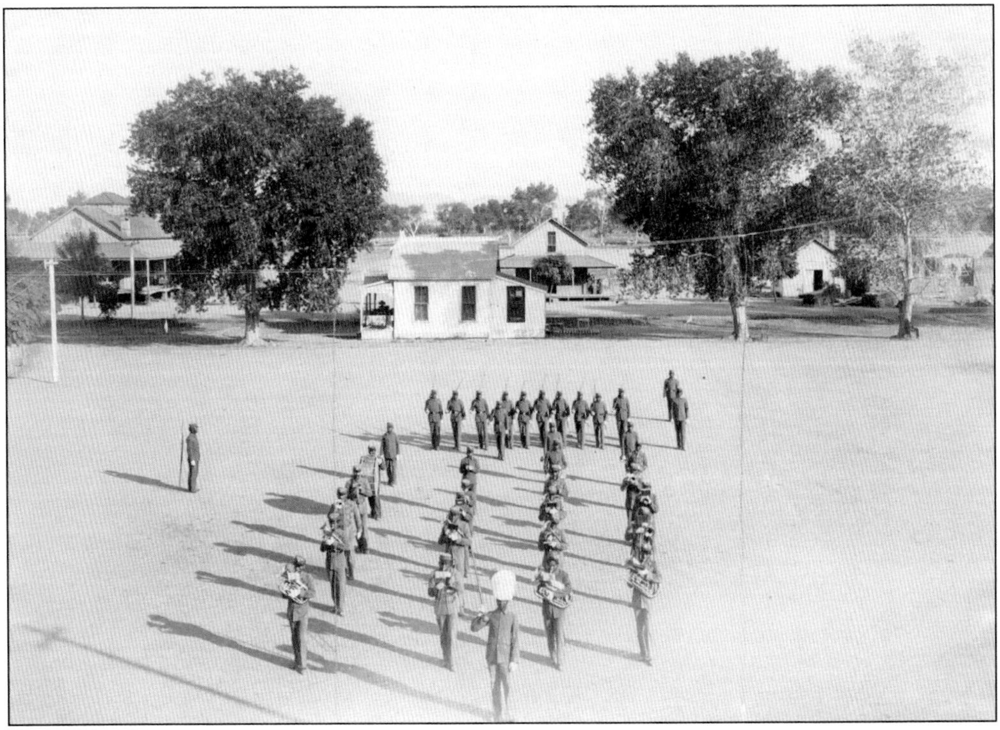

Male cadets are in formation during a drill on the parade ground at the Phoenix Indian School. (Silver print, photographer unknown, *c.* 1898. Collection of the author © vintagephoto.com.)

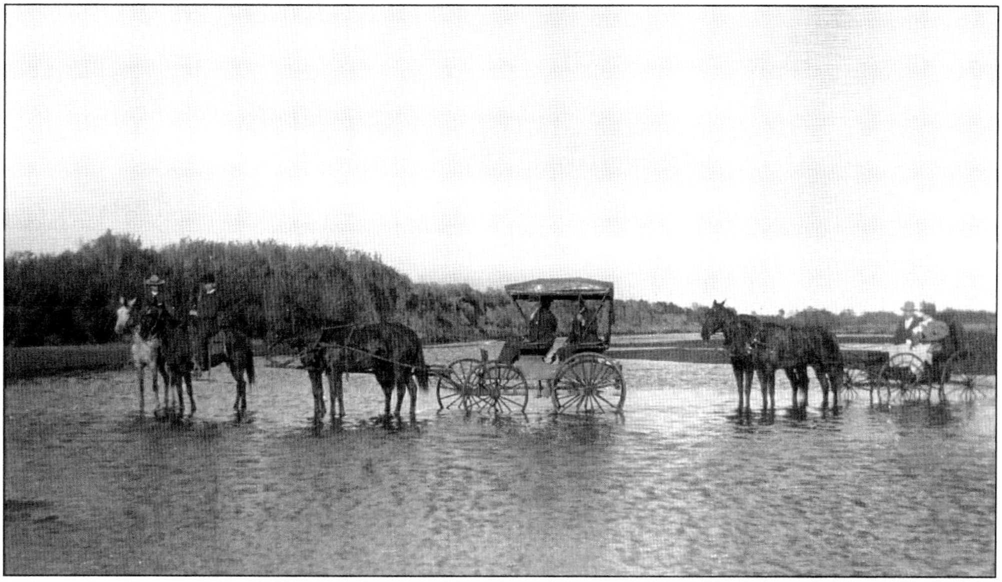

When the flow of the Salt River dropped, it was possible to ford the river by carriage or on horseback near the Tempe Railroad Bridge. The photographer apparently walked downstream to take this photograph of such a river crossing in March 1898. (Silver print, photographer unknown. Collection of the author © vintagephoto.com.)

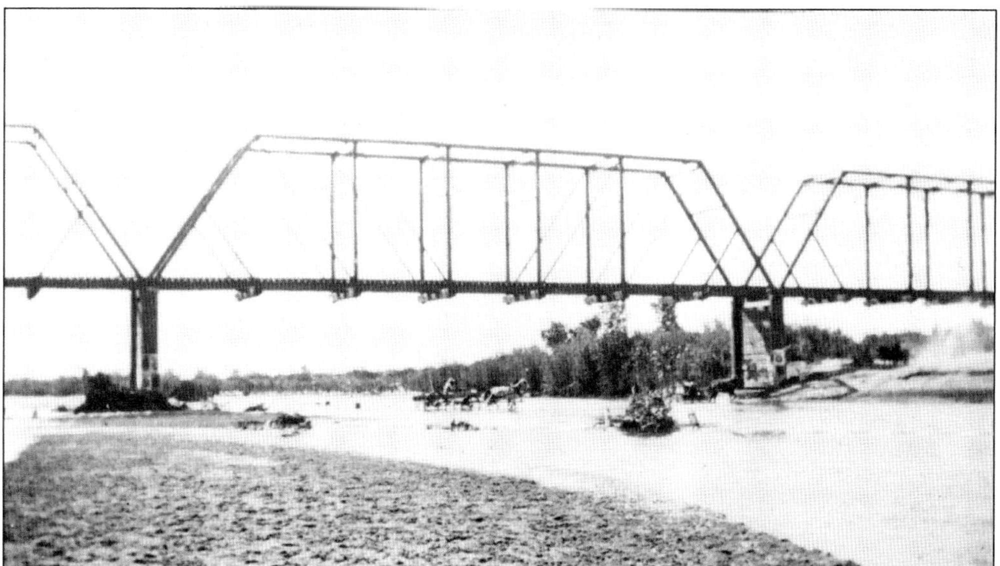

The railroad bridge across the Salt River at Tempe was rebuilt after the 1891 flood but was still susceptible to damage from high water. A new, more robust bridge replaced the simple span structure after the flood of 1905. (Silver print, photographer unknown, c. 1898. Collection of the author © vintagephoto.com.)

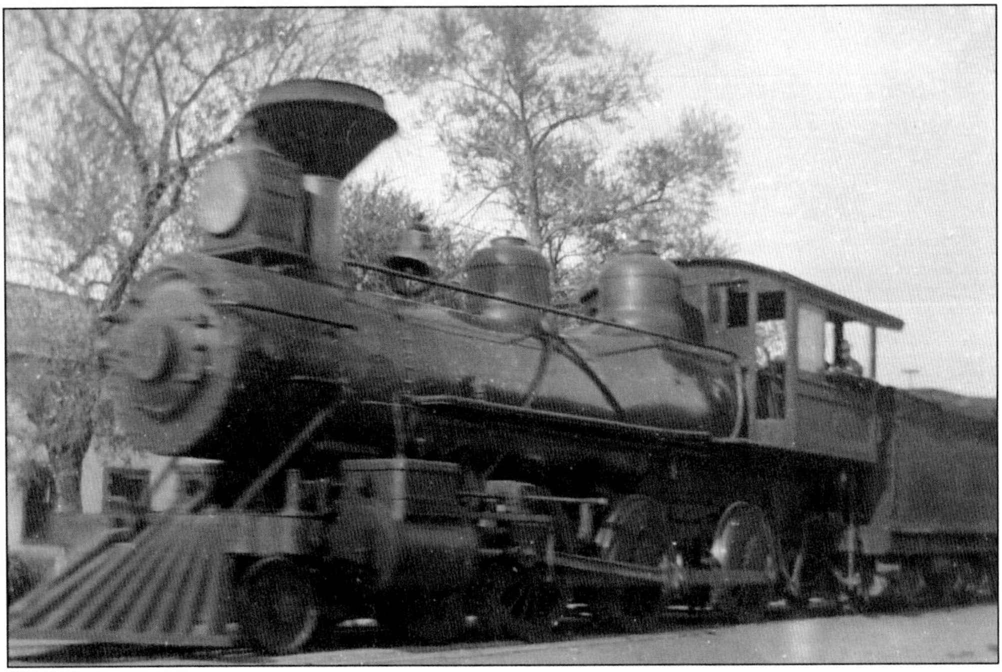

Railroad accidents were common occurrences, and ranged from minor derailment and collisions to collapsed bridges. This Maricopa, Phoenix, and Salt River Railroad engine wrecked between Phoenix and Tempe on April 12, 1898. (Silver print, photographer unknown. Collection of the author © vintagephoto.com.)

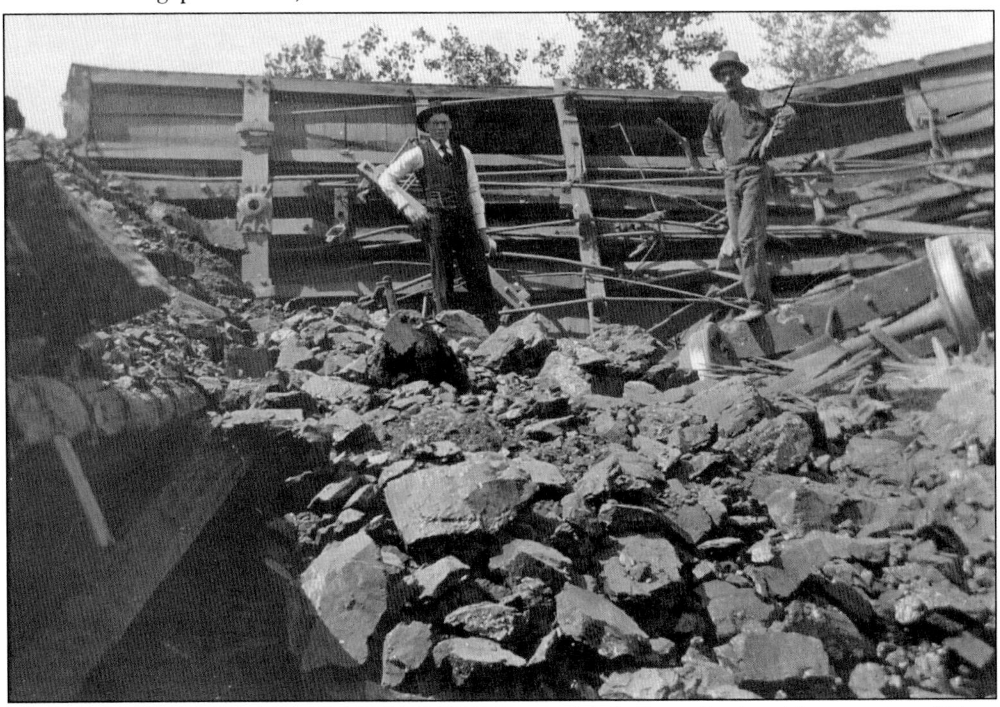

Men explore the wreck of the Maricopa, Phoenix, and Salt River Railroad locomotive. (Silver prints, photographer unknown, April 1898. Collection of the author © vintagephoto.com.)

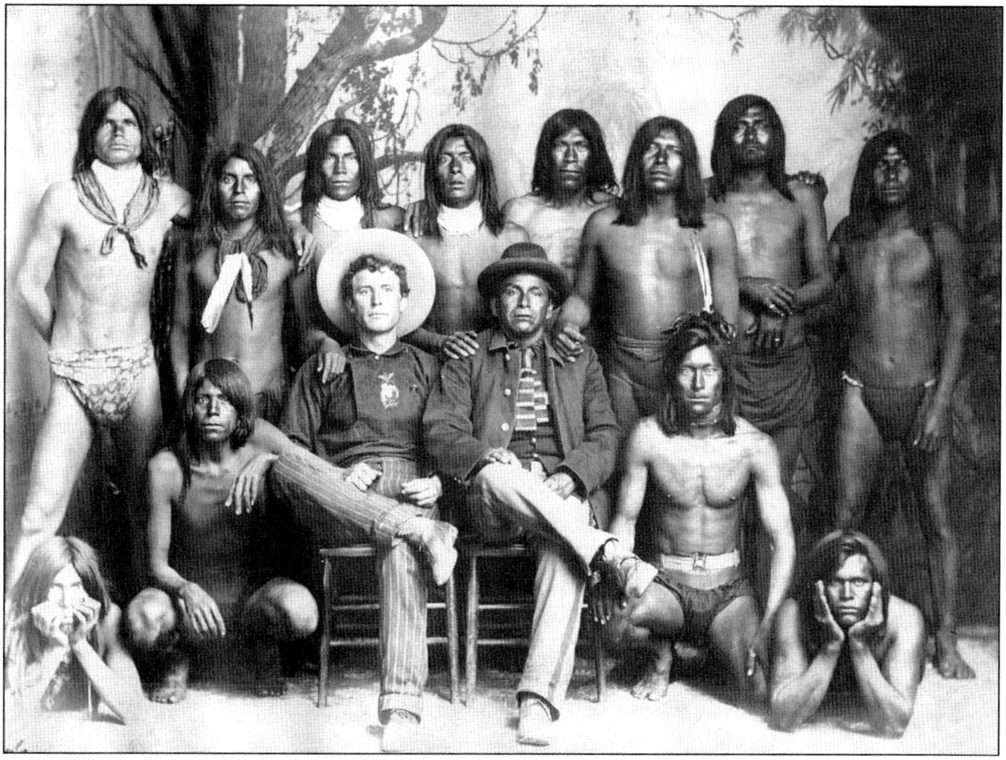

Native American imagery continued to be popular long after the end of the Apache wars in the 1880s. Phoenix hosted a number of Indian parades and fairs to promote business development in Phoenix. Entrepreneurial photographers took advantage of these events to make studio portraits for sale, like this view of an unidentified Anglo cowboy and group of Pima and Papago "warriors." (Boudoir cabinet card, Frank Hartwell photographer, c. 1899. Collection of the author © vintagephoto.com.)

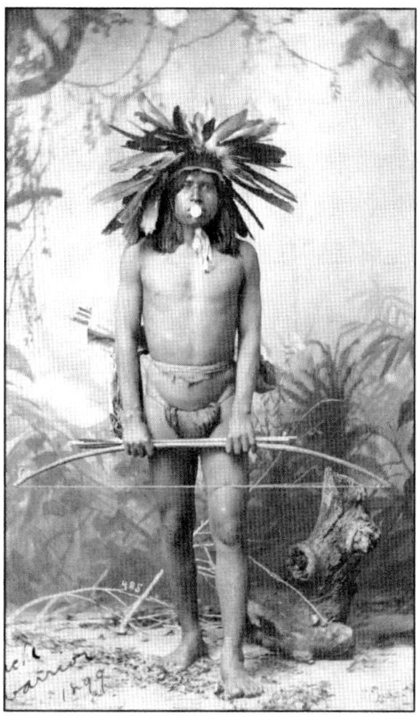

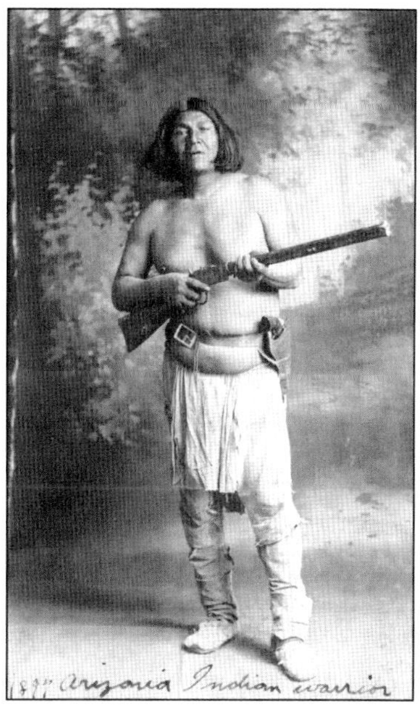

These individual portraits of local Indians are labeled as "Apache" warriors. Boudoir cabinet cards, Frank Hartwell photographer, c. 1899. Collection of the author © vintagephoto.com.

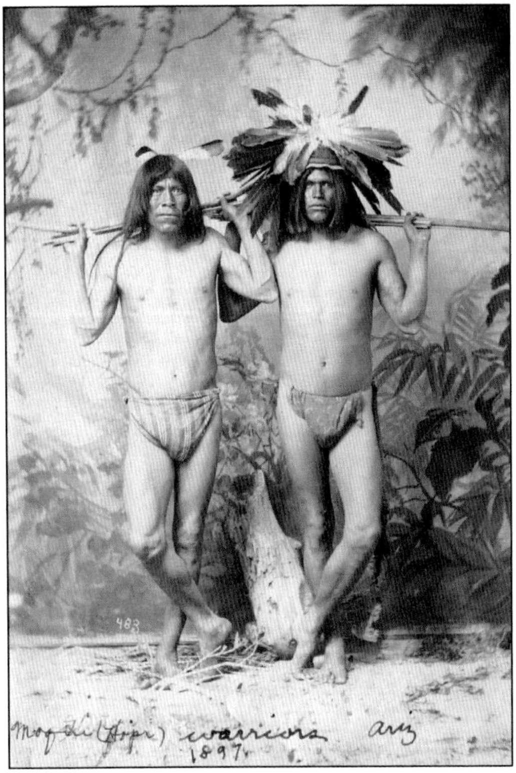

A very unique studio pose for two Maricopa men. (Boudoir cabinet card, Frank Hartwell photographer, *c.* 1899. Collection of the author © vintagephoto.com.)

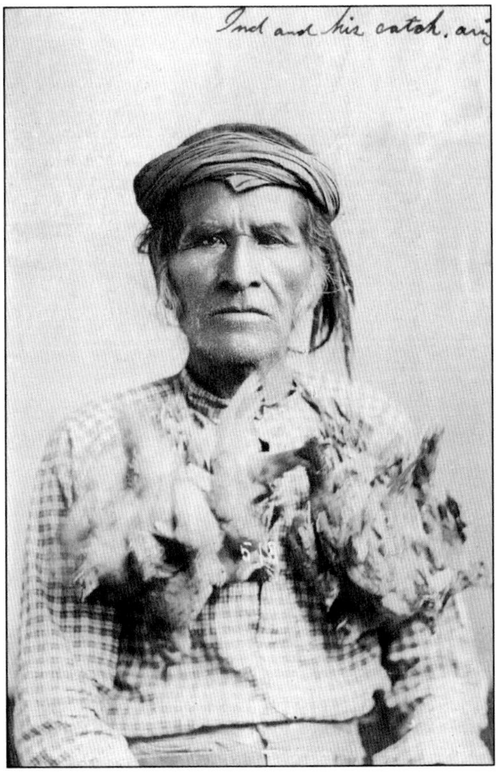

This proudly posed studio portrait of a Pima man shows the results of a successful quail hunt. (Albumen print, F. A. Hartwell photographer, c. 1898. Collection of the author © vintagephoto.com.)

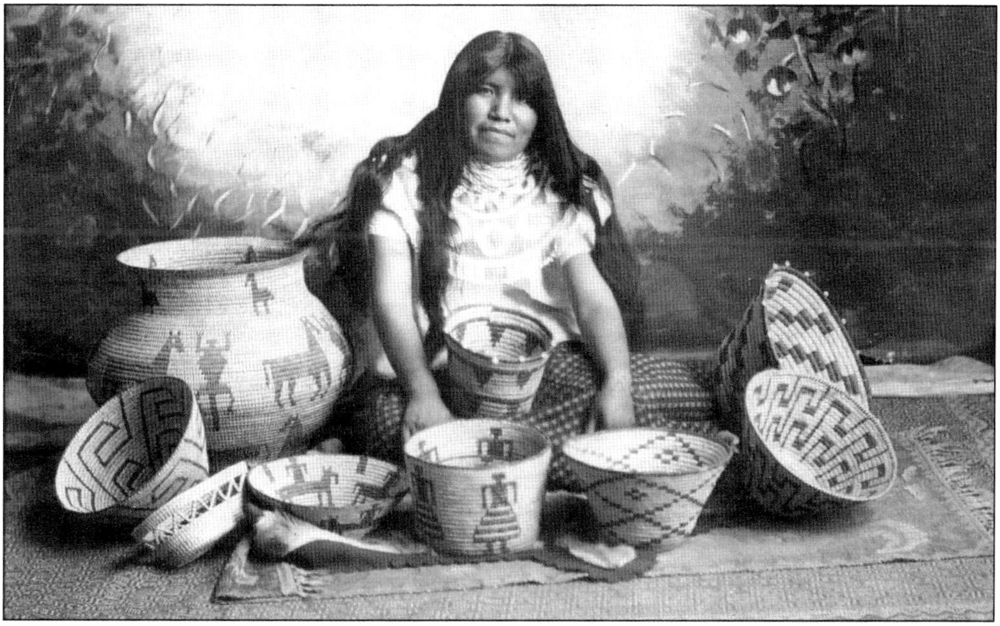

Native American artisans quickly became popular photographic subjects. This Papago basket maker poses in Frank Hartwell's studio with a number of examples of her craft. This image was quite popular and sold well as a postcard, even decades after it was originally made in 1898. (Silver print, Frank A. Hartwell photographer. Collection of the author © vintagephoto.com.)

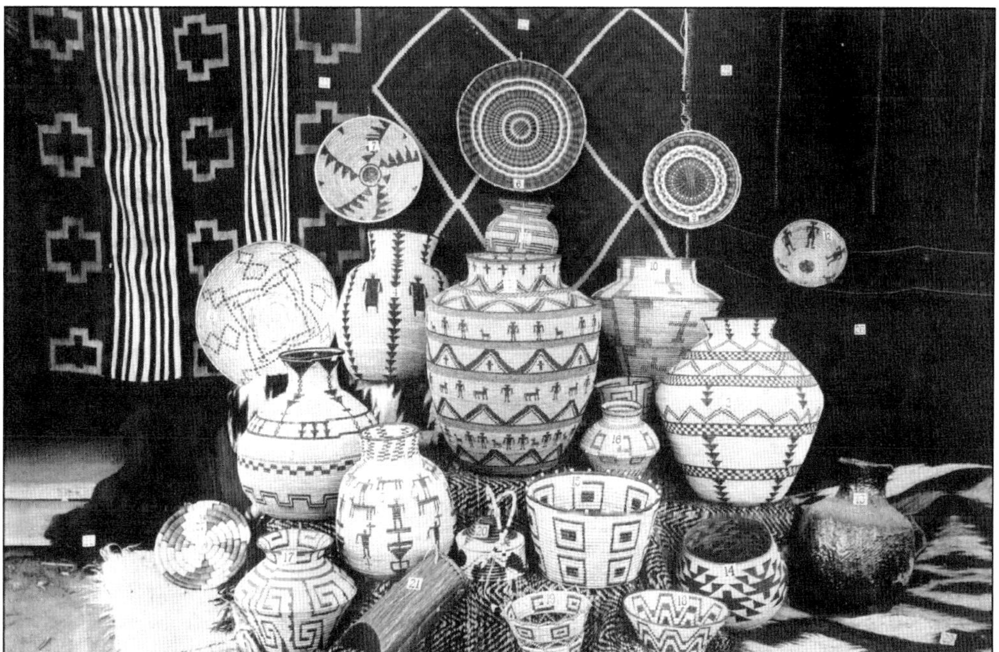

Many new residents of Maricopa County collected and displayed Native American crafts and artifacts. Some were small collections of a few items; others exhibited the Victorian passion for middle class display of new disposable income. (Silver print, photographer unknown, c. 1900. Collection of the author © vintagephoto.com.)

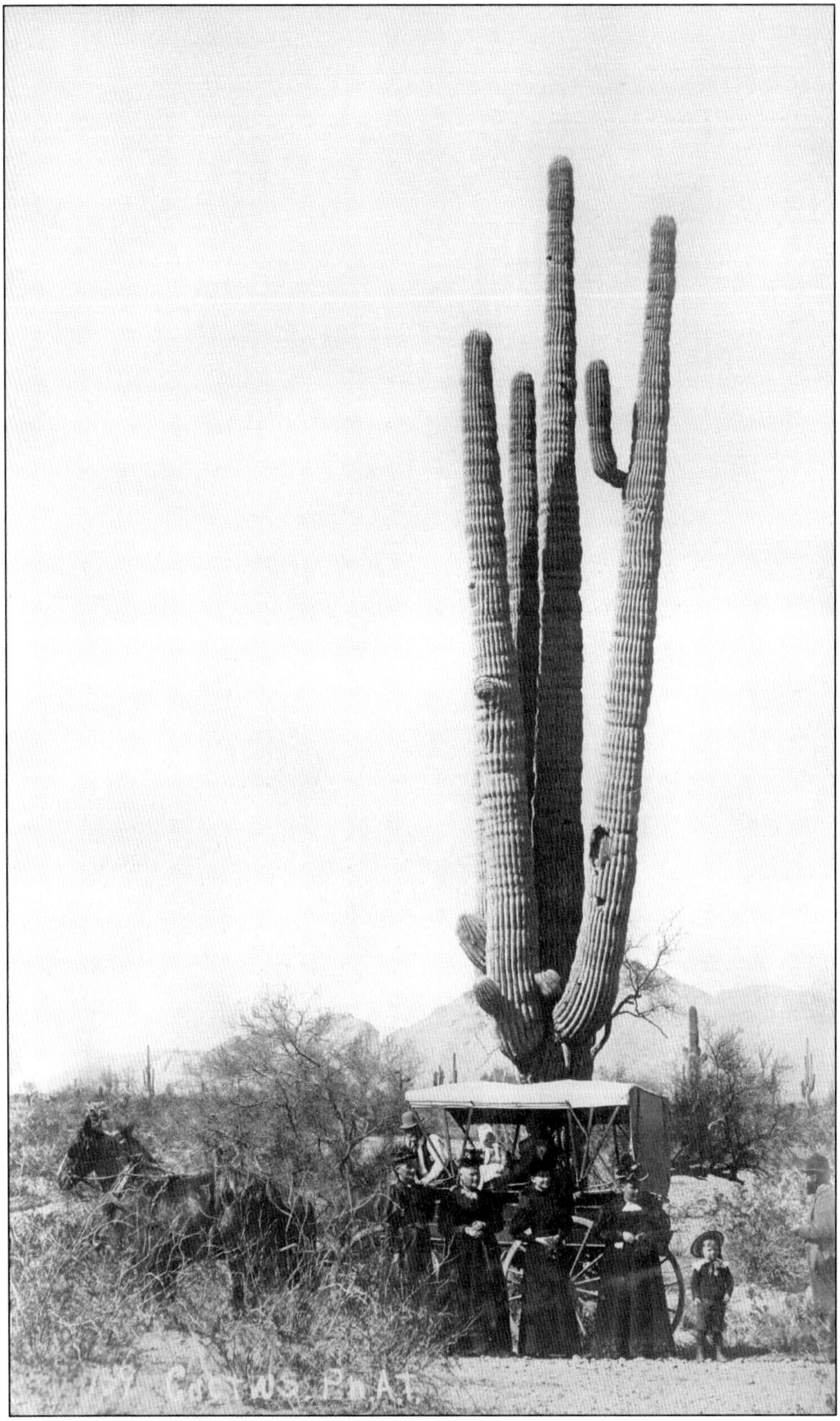

Picnickers and their carriage are pictured near the northwest corner of Papago Park with saguaro cactus and Camelback Mountain in the background. (Silver print, photographer unknown, c. 1898. Collection of the author © vintagephoto.com.)

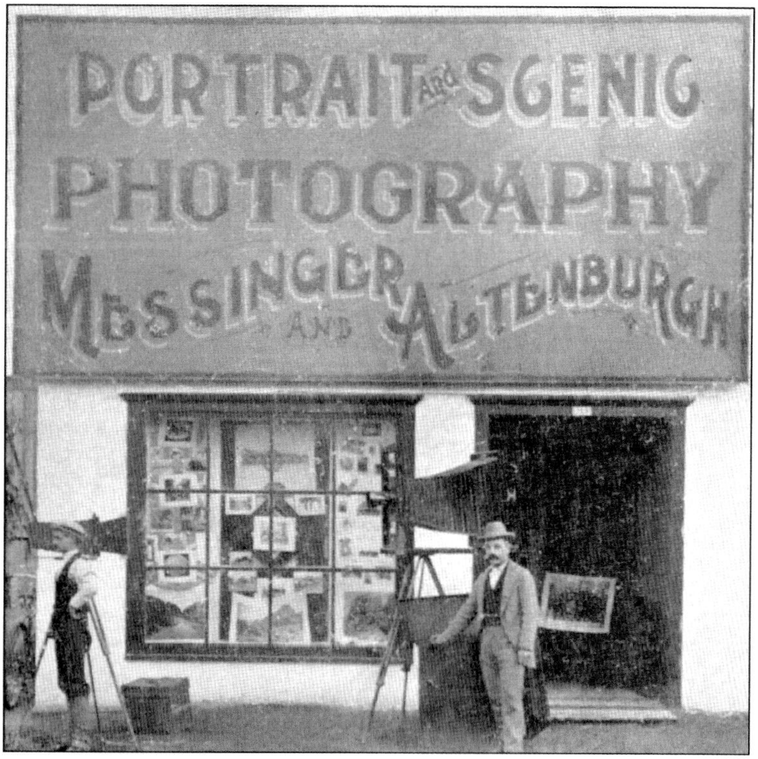

A. F. Messinger was an accountant and part-time photographer who formed a partnership with William Altenburgh from about 1898 to 1901. The partners produced hundreds of images of parades, mining, Native Americans, and life in Central Arizona. This advertisement shows the pair in front of their studio with their cameras. (Boudoir cabinet card imprint. Collection of the author © vintagephoto.com.)

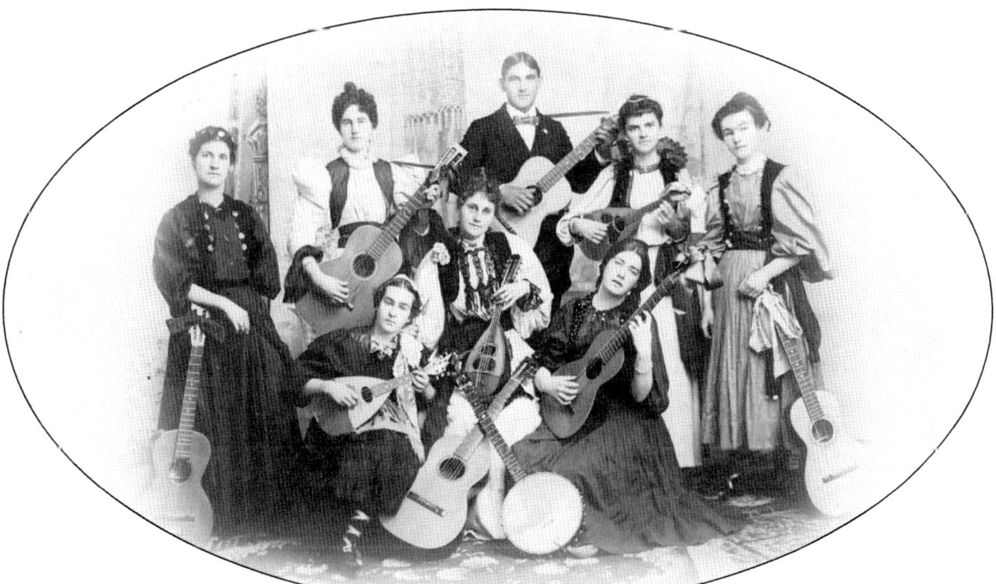

Phoenix worked hard to acquire all the cultural trappings of a big city. Guitar, banjo, and mandolin instruction was offered by F. S. Gerrish in the O'Neill building prior to the establishment of the Phoenix School of Music in 1904. (Boudoir cabinet card, F. A. Hartwell photographer, c. 1897. Collection of the author © vintagephoto.com.)

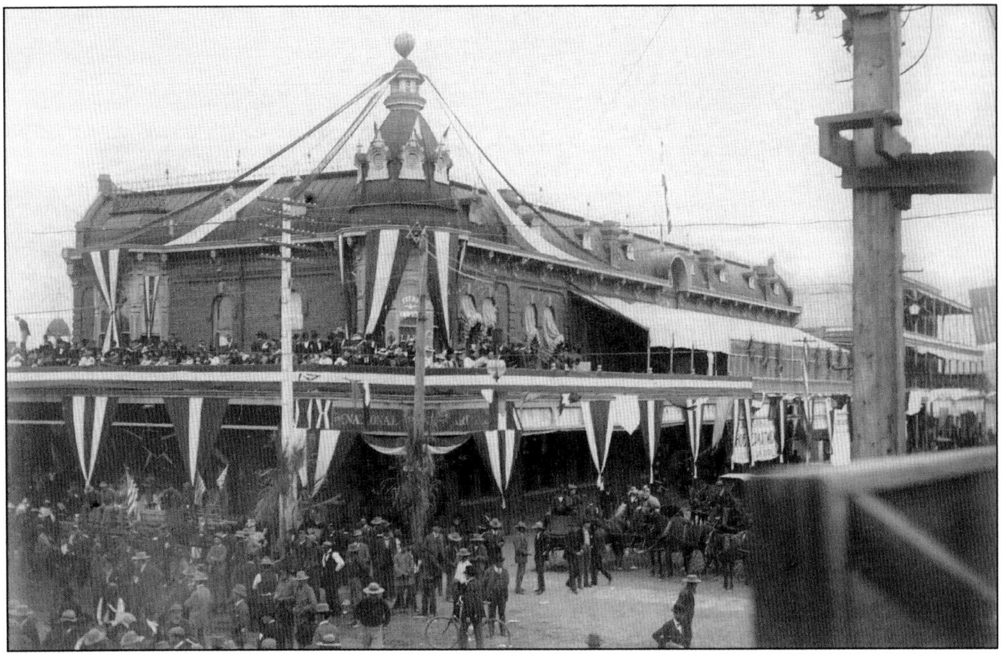

In addition to parades, community celebrations were common events in downtown Phoenix. The National Bank of Arizona in the Cotton Block at the corner of Center and Washington was decked out in style for this unidentified celebration. (Boudoir cabinet card, J. P. Rhodes photographer, c. 1897. Collection of the author © vintagephoto.com.)

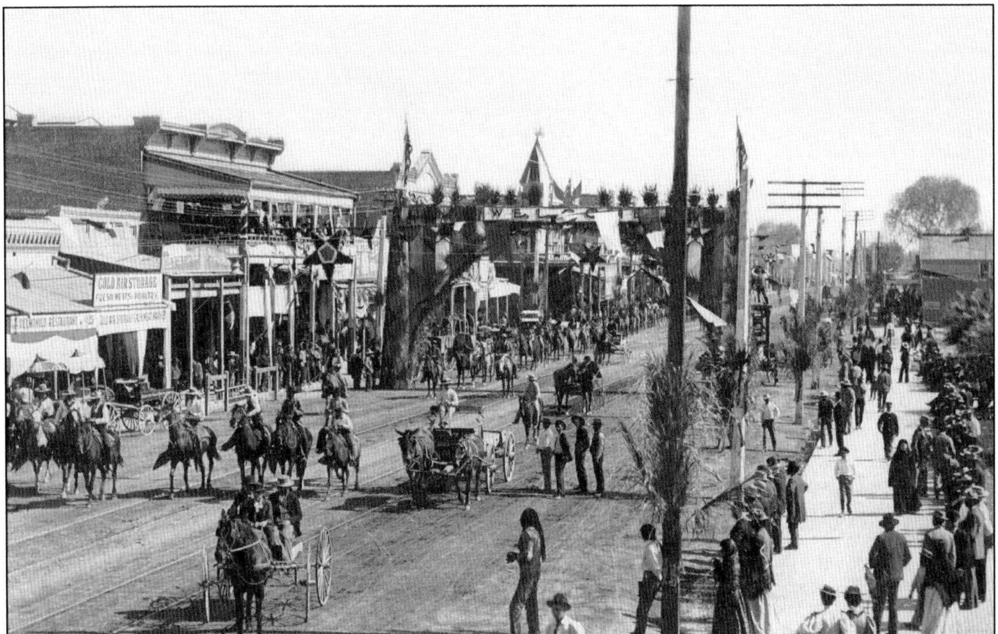

Downtown parades were common public events in early Phoenix. Several photographers, including one on a stand with his large format camera at right center, documented this parade on East Washington Street in Phoenix. (Albumen boudoir cabinet card, Messinger and Altenburgh photographers, c. 1898. Collection of the author © vintagephoto.com.)

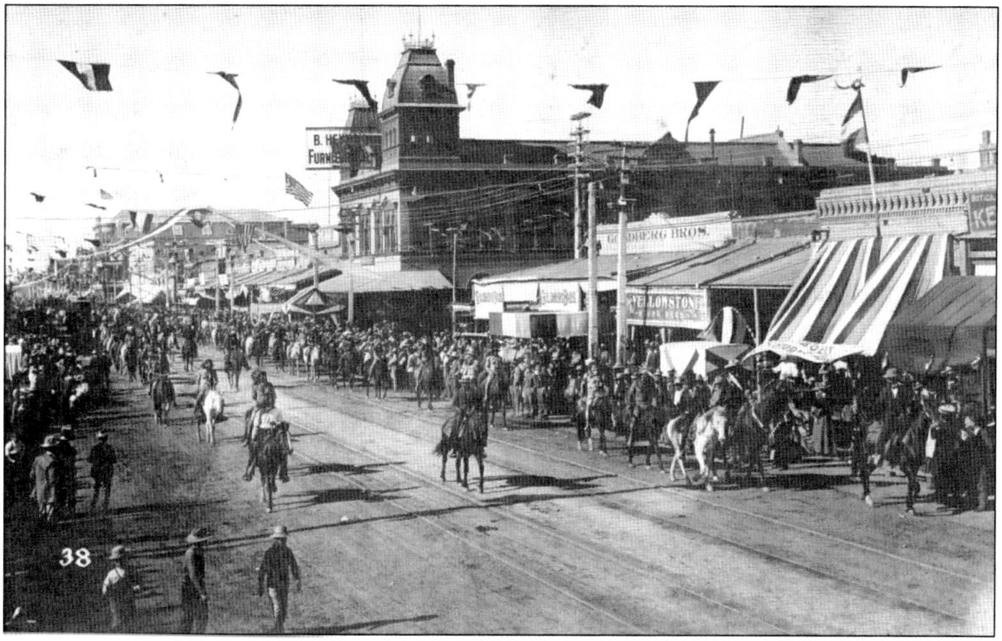

Phoenix took advantage of the increasing interest in the Wild West by hosting Indian Fairs beginning in the late 1890s. This view of the parade looks west down Washington as the parade passed the twin towers of the Anderson Building. The Indian Fairs were accompanied by rodeos and other related activities. (Boudoir cabinet card, Hartwell and Hammaker photographers, c. 1898. Collection of the author © vintagephoto.com.)

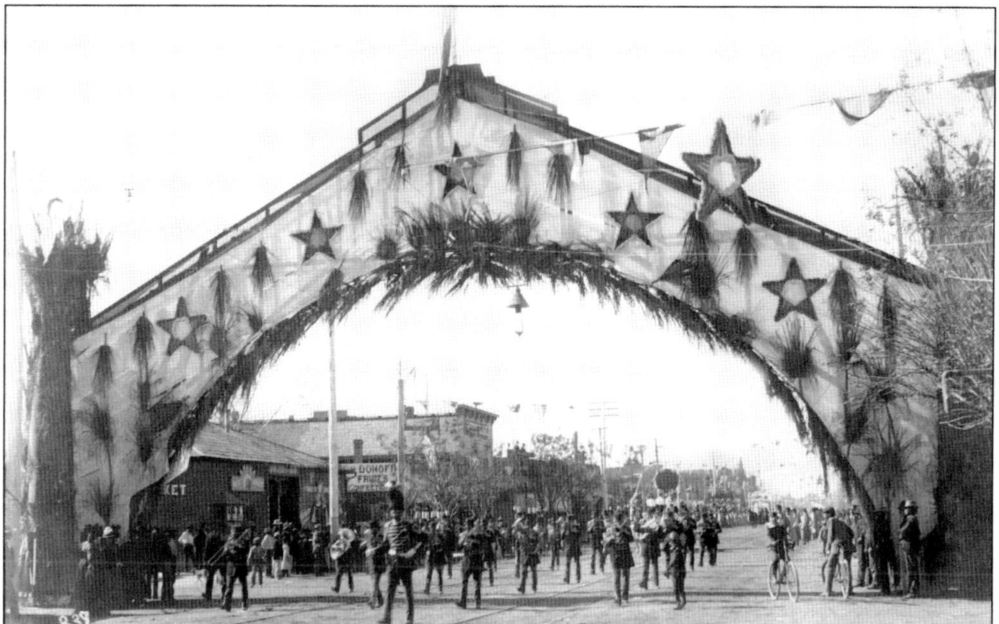

This image looks west down Washington Street at the Phoenix Indian and Cowboy Festival. Sam Donofrio operated the fruit and confectionary store at 231–233 East Washington at left below the arch. (Silver print, A. F. Messinger photographer, c. 1899. Collection of the author © vintagephoto.com.)

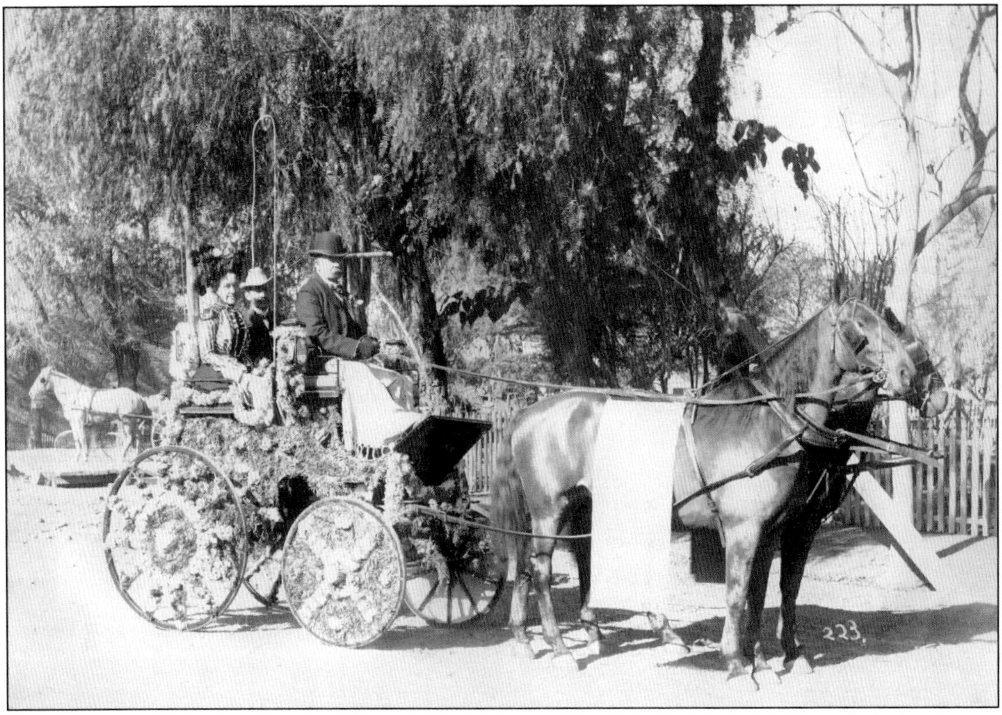

An unidentified parade float is pictured at the Phoenix Indian and Cowboy Festival. (Silver print, A. F. Messinger photographer. Collection of the author © vintagephoto.com.)

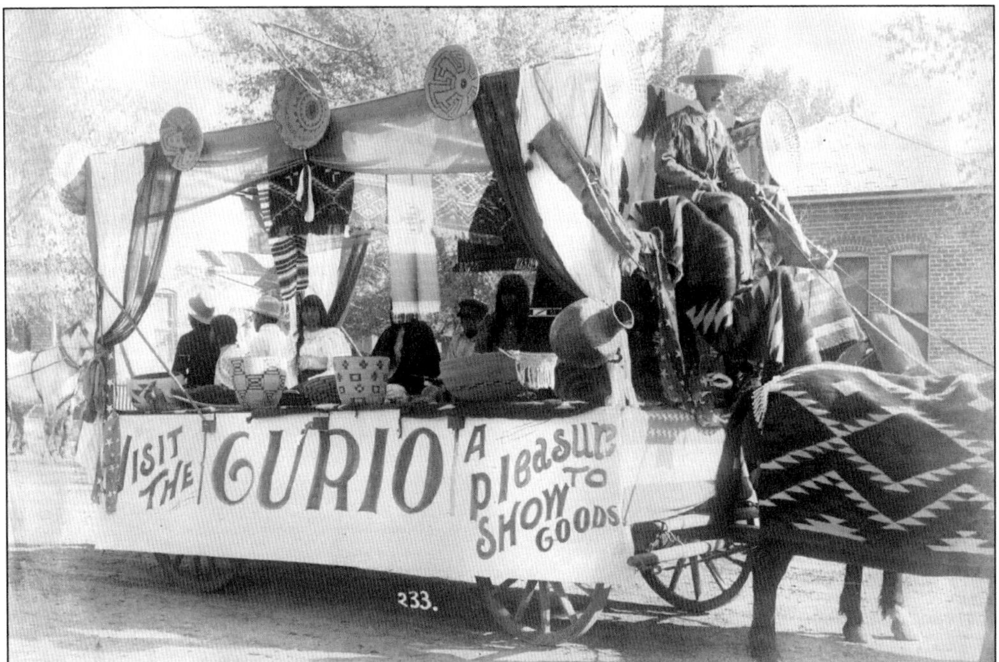

The Phoenix Indian and Cowboy Festival parade float for "The Curio," dealers in "Mexican and Indian Curios, and prehistoric goods," located at 145 West Jefferson. (Silver print, A. F. Messinger photographer, c. 1899. Collection of the author © vintagephoto.com.)

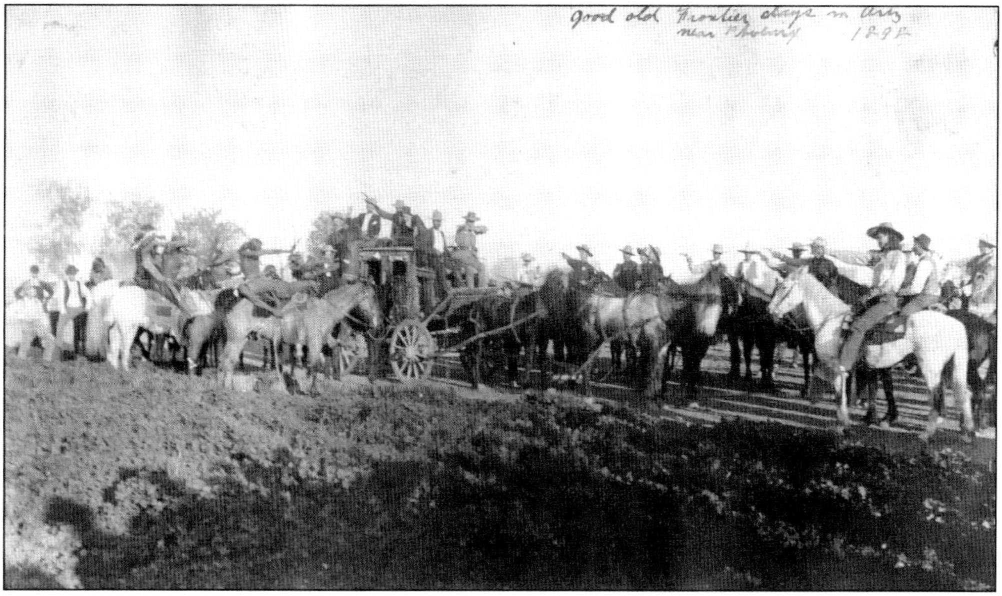

A mock stagecoach hold-up was staged in conjunction with the Phoenix Indian and Cowboy Festival. (Silver print, A. F. Messinger photographer, c. 1899. Collection of the author © vintagephoto.com.)

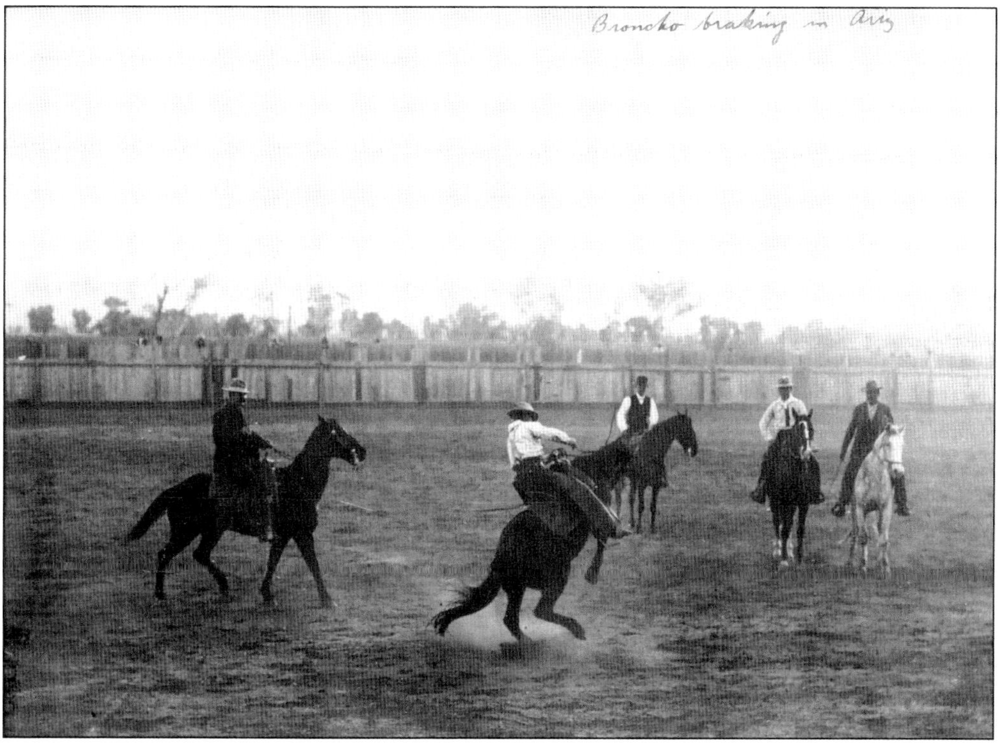

The prominence of ranching and cattle in the Salt River Valley made rodeos, winter carnivals, and parades popular events. Photographer F. A. Hartwell captures a bronco in mid-buck at the Phoenix Indian and Cowboy Festival. (Silver print. F. A. Hartwell photographer, c. 1899. Collection of the author © vintagephoto.com.)

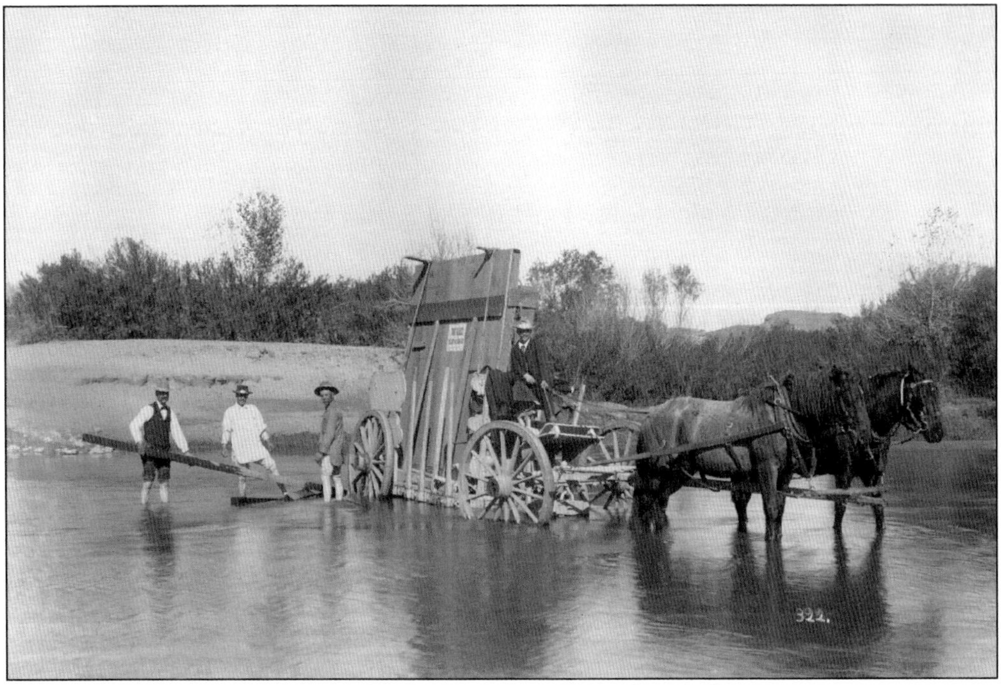

This group is trying to free a mired freight wagon at an unidentified river crossing in Maricopa County. (Silver print, A. F. Messinger photographer, *c.* 1899. Collection of the author © vintagephoto.com.)

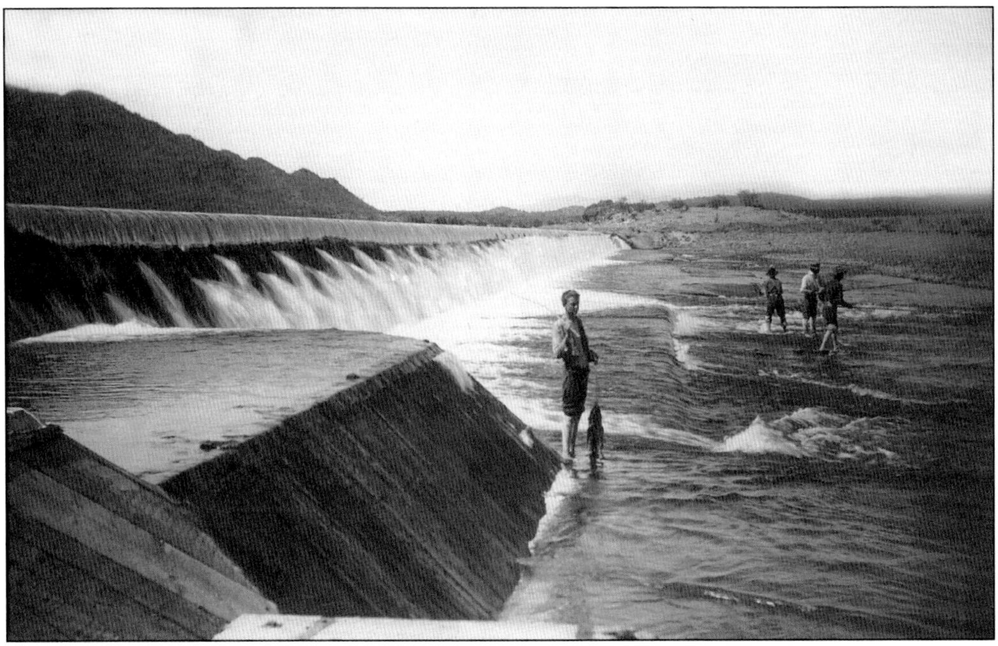

Water was always popular for recreation in arid Arizona. In this image, a group of boys fish near the head gate of the Arizona Canal on the Salt River east of Phoenix. (Boudoir cabinet card, F. A. Hartwell photographer, *c.* 1898. Collection of the author © vintagephoto.com.)

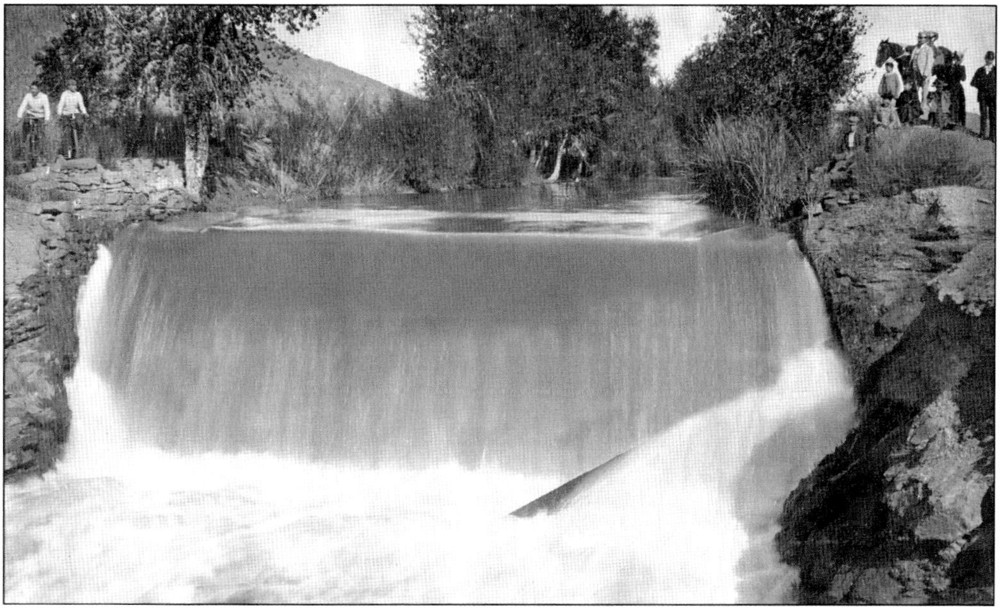

Arizona Falls, formed by a natural drop on the Arizona Canal (near Fifty-sixth Street and Indian School Road today), was another popular picnic destination near Phoenix. It was site of the first hydroelectric plant in Phoenix in 1902. Later, it became popular tourist destination visitors to the nearby Ingleside Inn. (Silver print, Frank A. Hartwell photographer, *c.* 1898. Collection of the author © vintagephoto.com.)

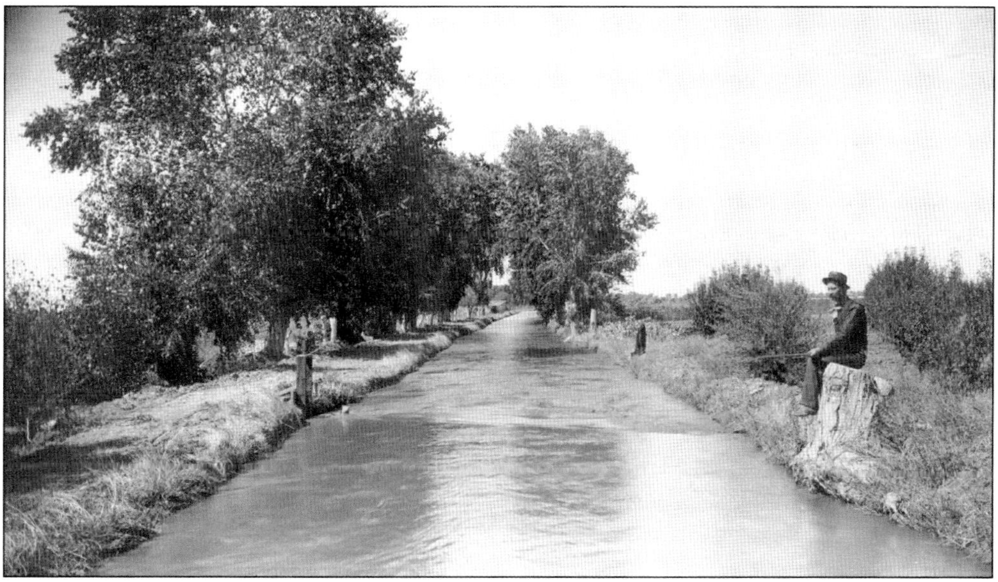

The canals and irrigation ditches that crisscrossed the Salt River Valley also provided recreational opportunities and were part of the a small town rural environment of the time. Fish from the Salt and Verde rivers passed into the canals and became sources of food and pleasure to Phoenicians like this unidentified man who relaxes and fishes from a cottonwood tree stump. (Albumen boudoir cabinet card, Frank A. Hartwell photographer, *c.* 1898. Collection of the author © vintagephoto.com.)

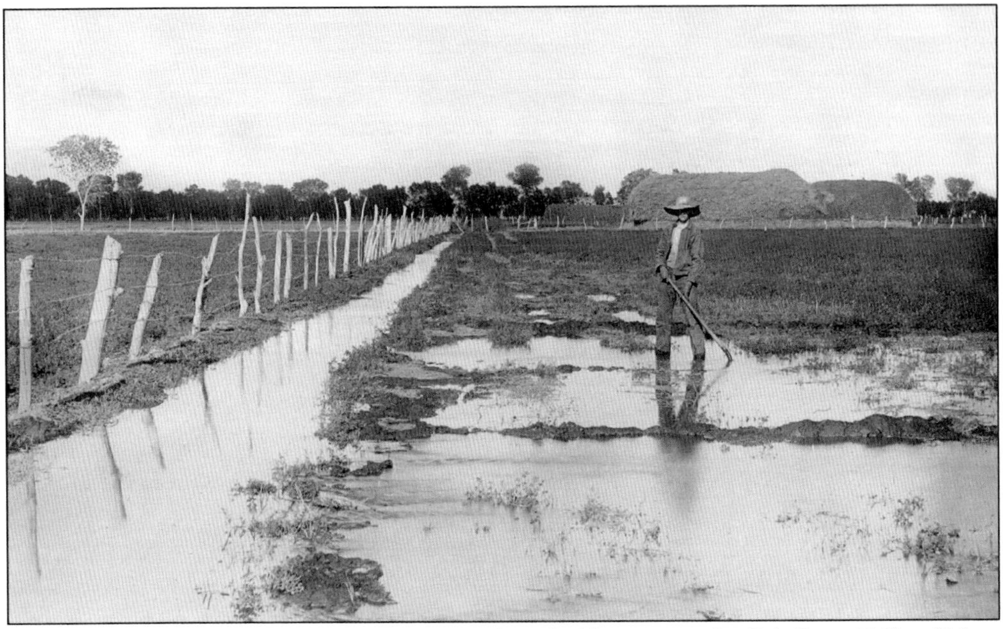

A typical agricultural irrigation scene at an unidentified location in the Salt River Valley. (Silver print, A. F. Messinger photographer, c. 1899. Collection of the author © vintagephoto.com.)

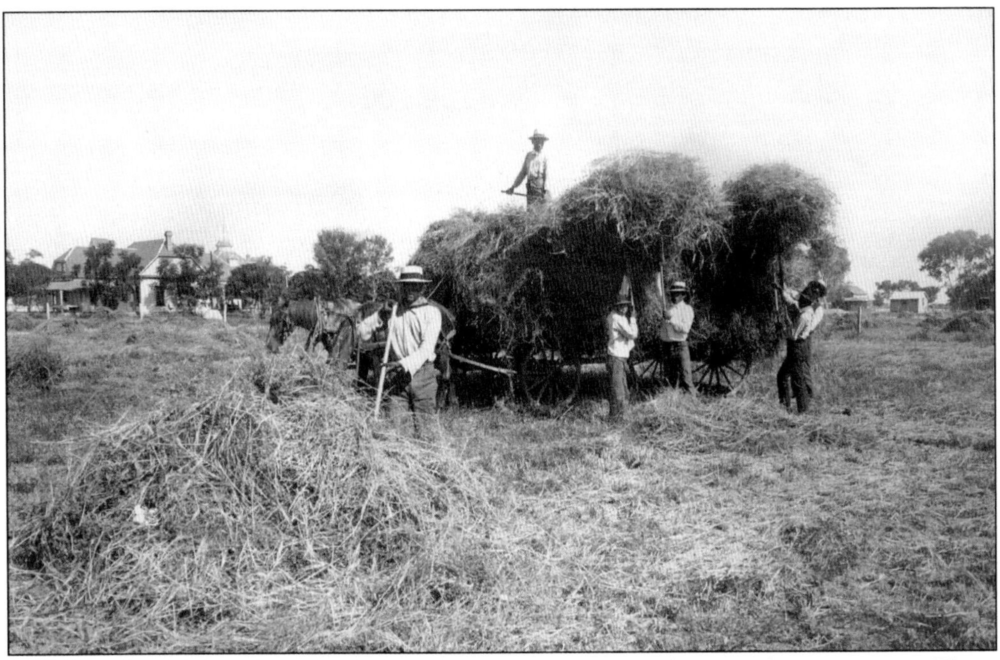

The Phoenix India School included a working farm among its educational opportunities. These upperclassmen are harvesting a bumper crop of alfalfa. (Silver print, A. F. Messinger photographer, c. 1900. Collection of the author © vintagephoto.com.)

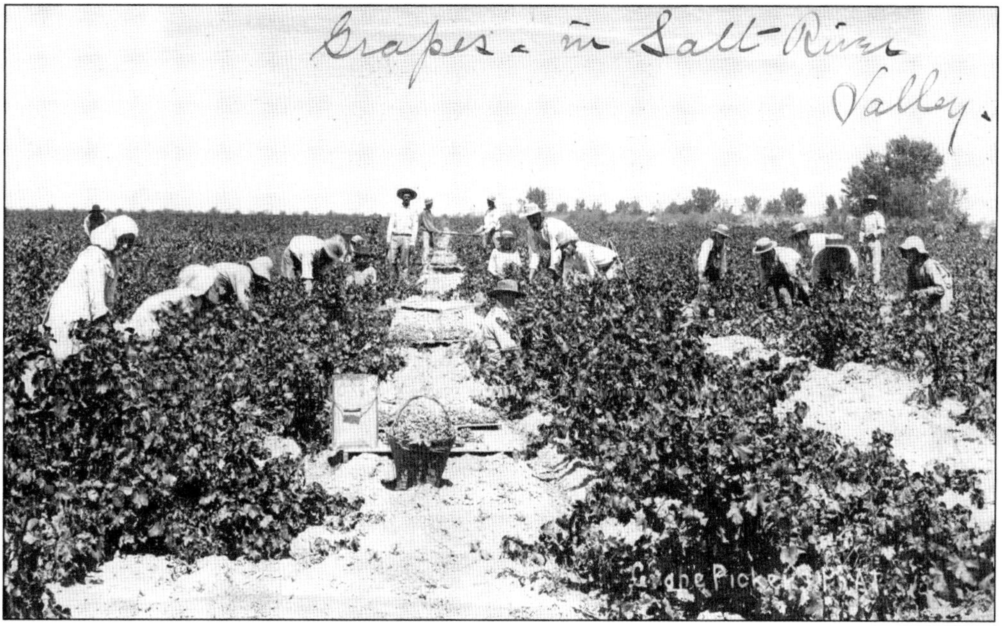

Harvesting grapes at an unidentified Salt River Valley farm. (Boudoir cabinet card, F. A. Hartwell photographer, *c.* 1898. Collection of the author © vintagephoto.com.)

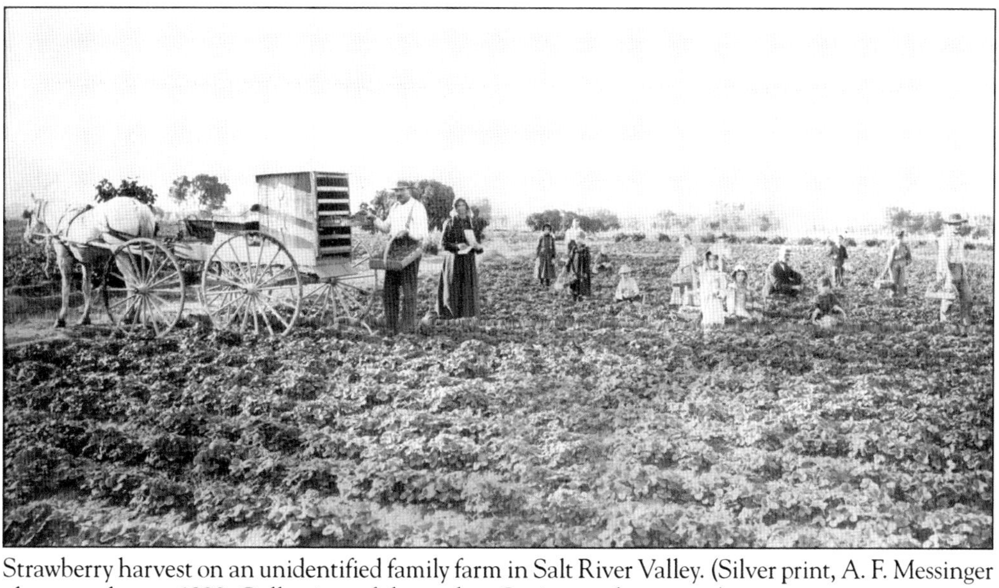

Strawberry harvest on an unidentified family farm in Salt River Valley. (Silver print, A. F. Messinger photographer, *c.* 1899. Collection of the author © vintagephoto.com.)

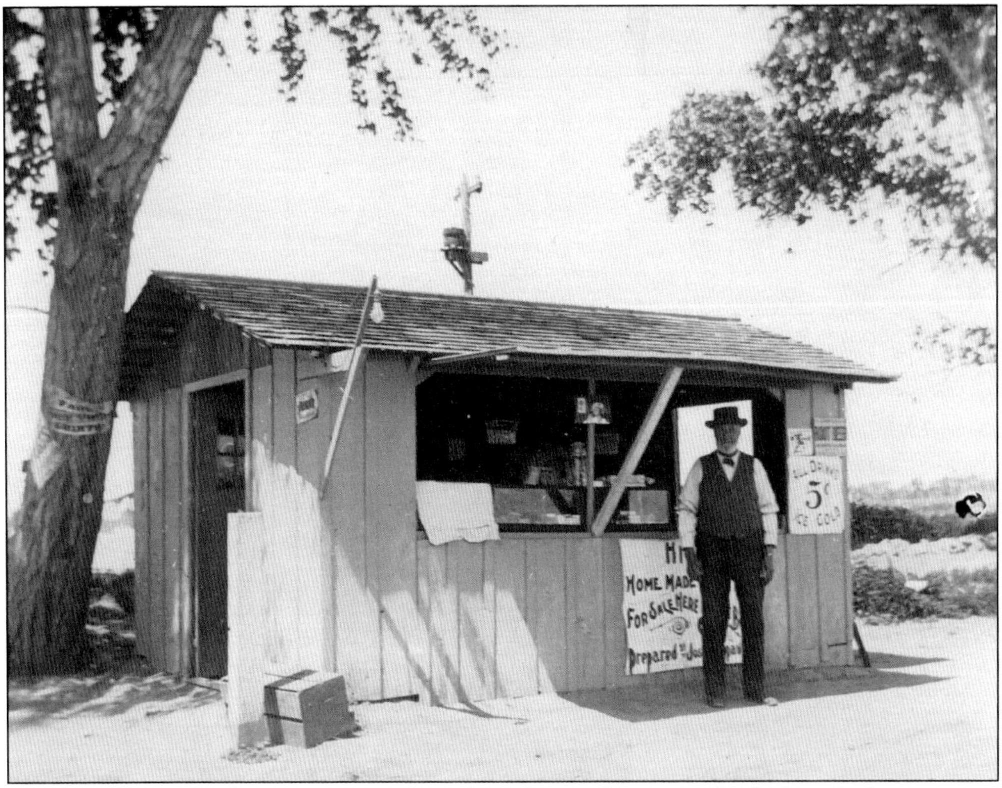

In another example of Arizona entrepreneurship, this gentleman established a refreshment stand on Center Street, north of Thomas. His innovation was to charge tolls for traffic, but Center Street was soon opened to free public travel. (Silver print, photographer unknown, *c.* 1898. Collection of the author © vintagephoto.com.)

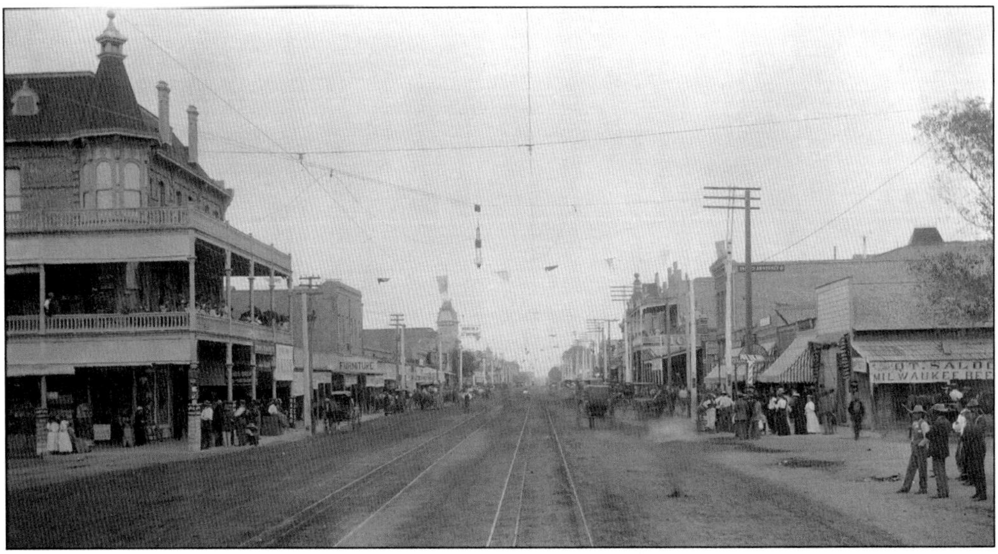

Looking south down Center Street with the Cotton Building on the left and before construction of the Porter building that will be built on the west side of the street. (Boudoir cabinet card, F. A. Hartwell photographer, *c.* 1897. Collection of the author © vintagephoto.com.)

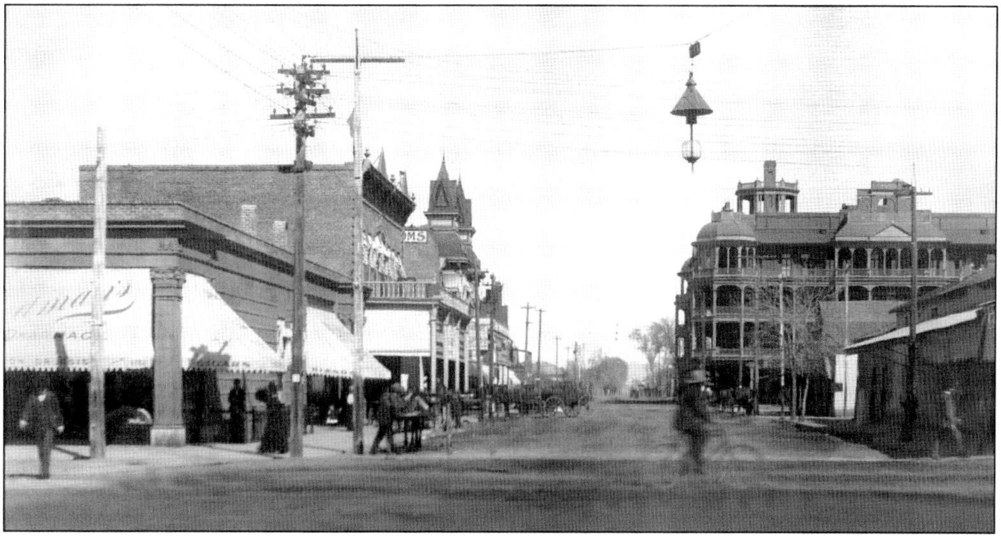

Looking north on Centre Street from Washington Street, Goodman's Pharmacy (successor to the Garden City Drugstore) at 2 West Washington is on the left. The Adams Hotel is on the northwest at right rear, opposite the Anderson Block on the southwest corner of Center and Adams. (Silver print, A. F. Messinger photographer, c. 1899. Collection of the author © vintagephoto.com.)

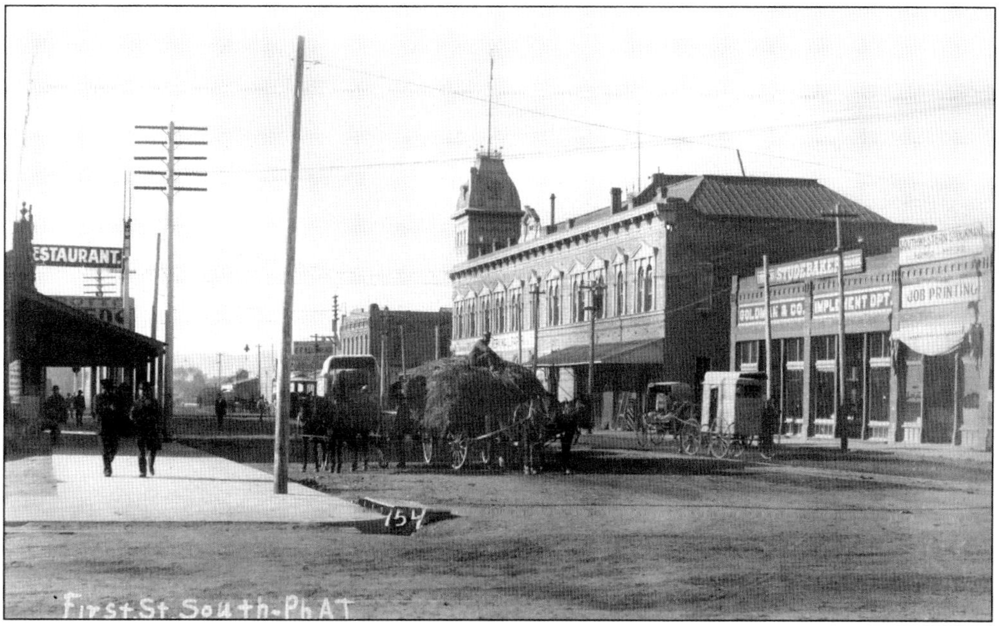

The view looking south on First Street from toward Washington with South Mountain in the background. The Grotto Restaurant at left was at 11–13 North First Street. The Cotton Building at the northwest corner of Center and Washington is center right. The Goldman and Company main store at 2–10 East Washington was operated by Charles, Leo, Max, and Rube Goldman, the Implement Department (at the right) was on First Street. (Silver print, A. F. Messinger photographer, c. 1899. Collection of the author © vintagephoto.com.)

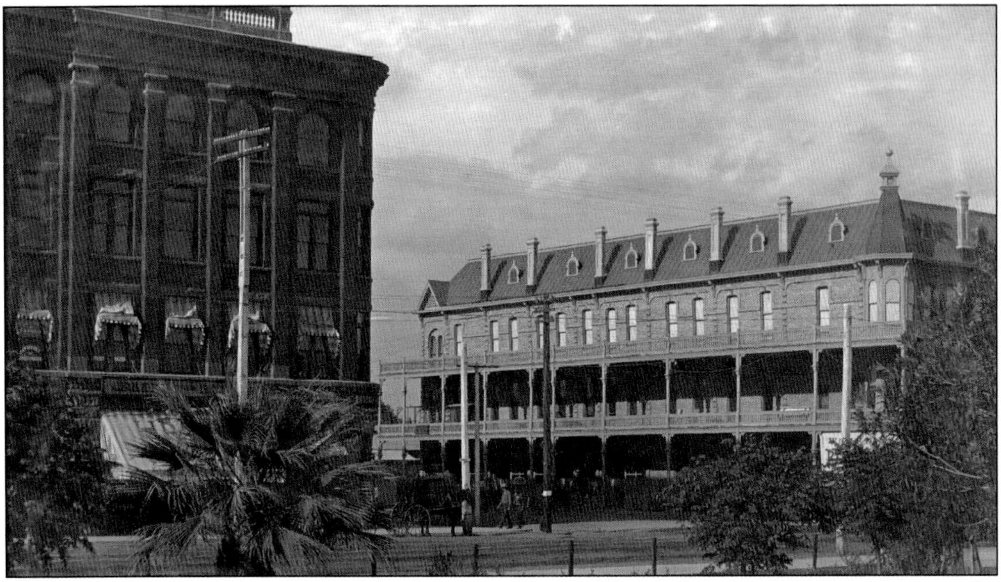

Looking northeast at the corner of First Avenue and Washington shows the Fleming Block on the northwest corner and the Monihon Building on the northeast corner. (Silver print, A. F. Messinger photographer, *c.* 1899. Collection of the author © vintagephoto.com.)

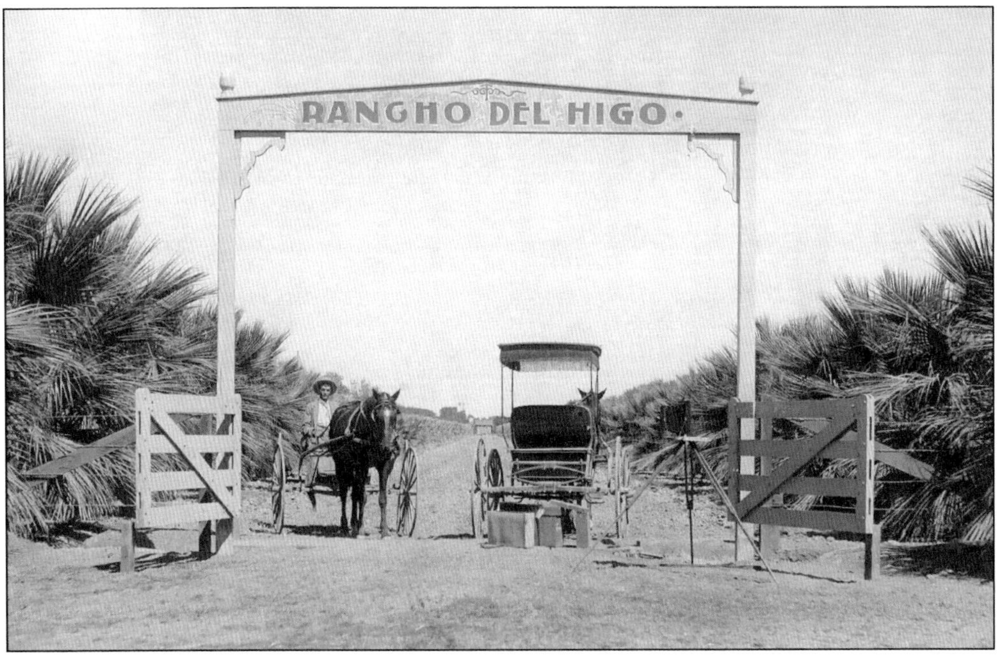

Entrepreneurial photographers traveled throughout the Salt River Valley with their large-view cameras, tripods, and related equipment. Messinger and Altenburgh made an unusual image that shows their carriages and photographic equipment while working on location at "Rancho Del Higo," a fig farm in northeast Phoenix. (Albumen boudoir cabinet card, Messinger and Altenburgh photographers, *c.* 1898. Collection of the author © vintagephoto.com.)

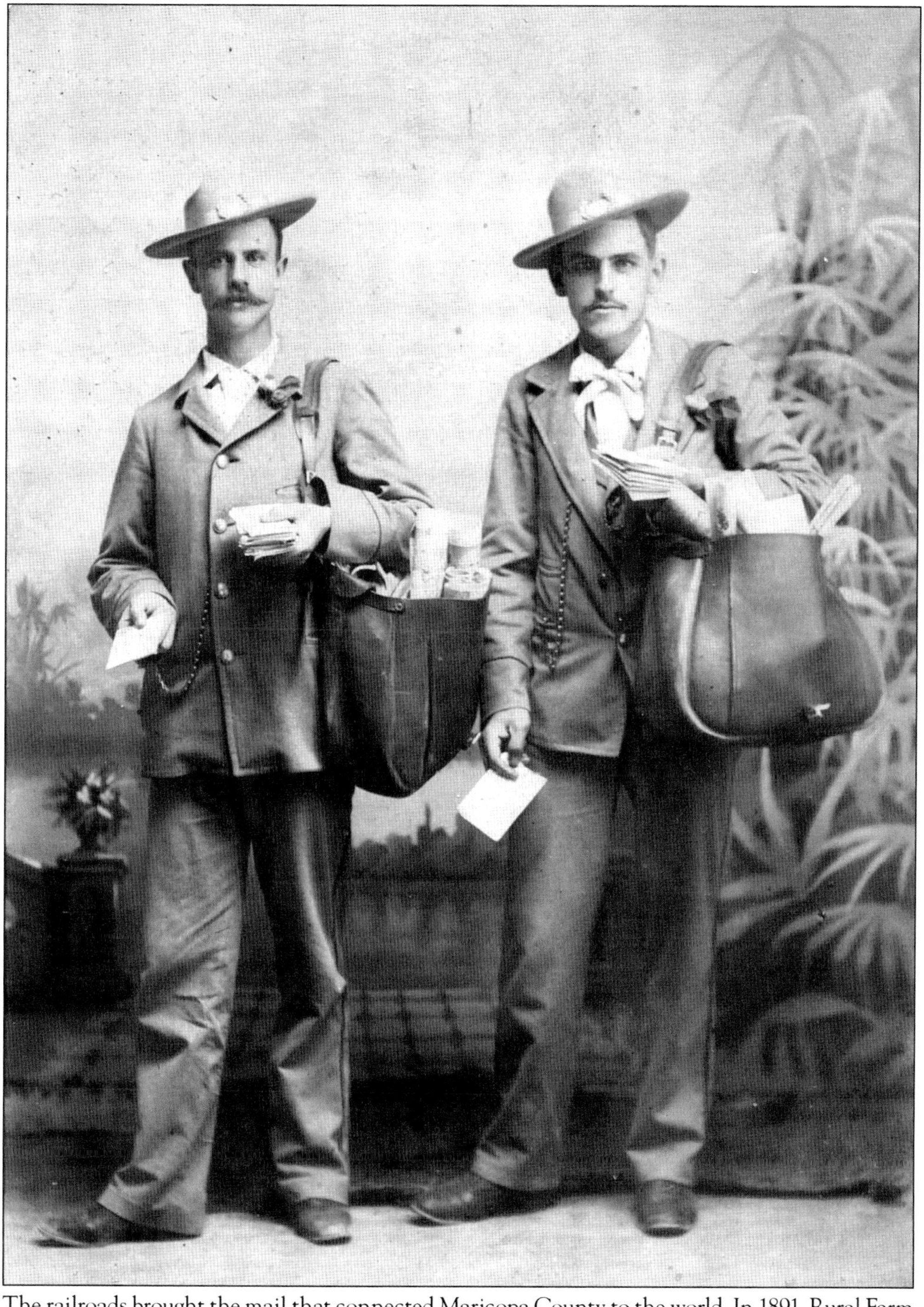

The railroads brought the mail that connected Maricopa County to the world. In 1891, Rural Farm Delivery was established, providing regular mail delivery to the ranches and farms throughout Maricopa County. These unidentified postal carriers served Phoenix and pose as if delivering the mail with their mailbags and uniforms. (Cabinet card, J. P. Rhodes photographer, c. 1900. Collection of the author © vintagephoto.com.)

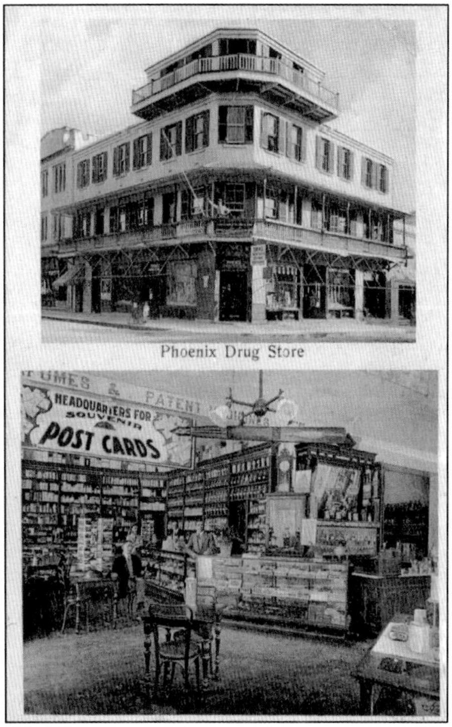

Postcards saw an explosion in popularity at the beginning of the 20th century. Printed and photographic postcards documented life on the farms and ranches, and in the towns and cities of Maricopa County. The Phoenix Drug Company (above) promoted itself as the "headquarters for Souvenir Post Cards" in a banner above their postcard racks. (Printed postcard produced for the Phoenix Drug Company, *c.* 1908.)

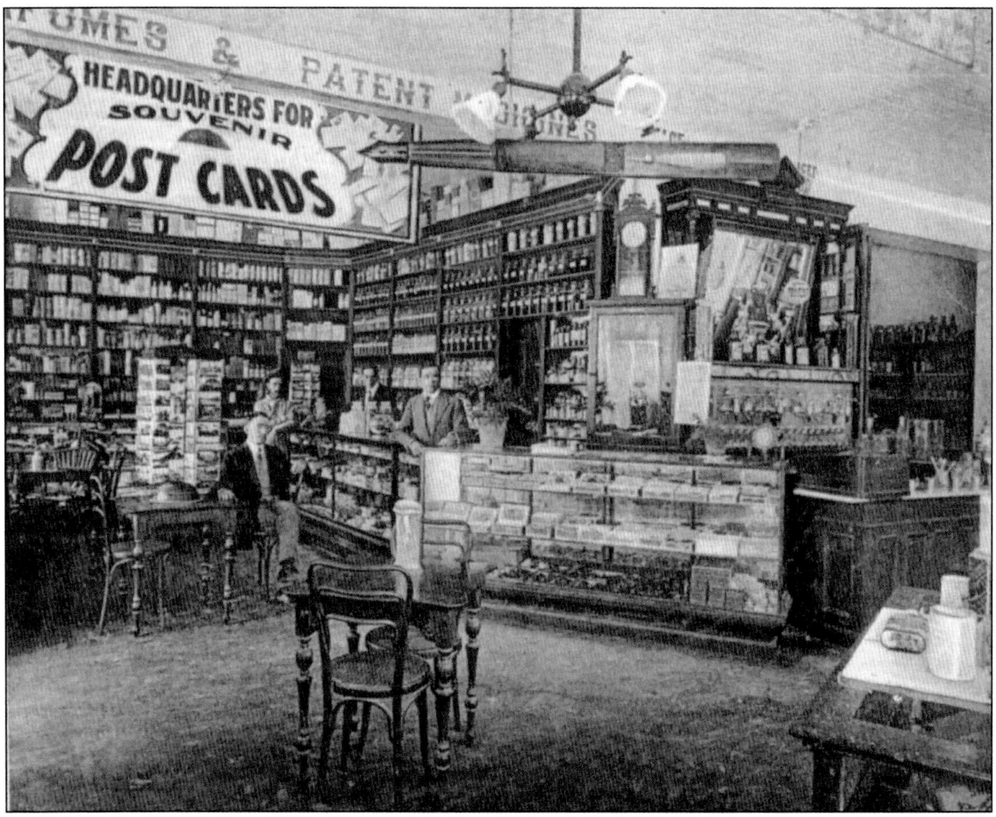

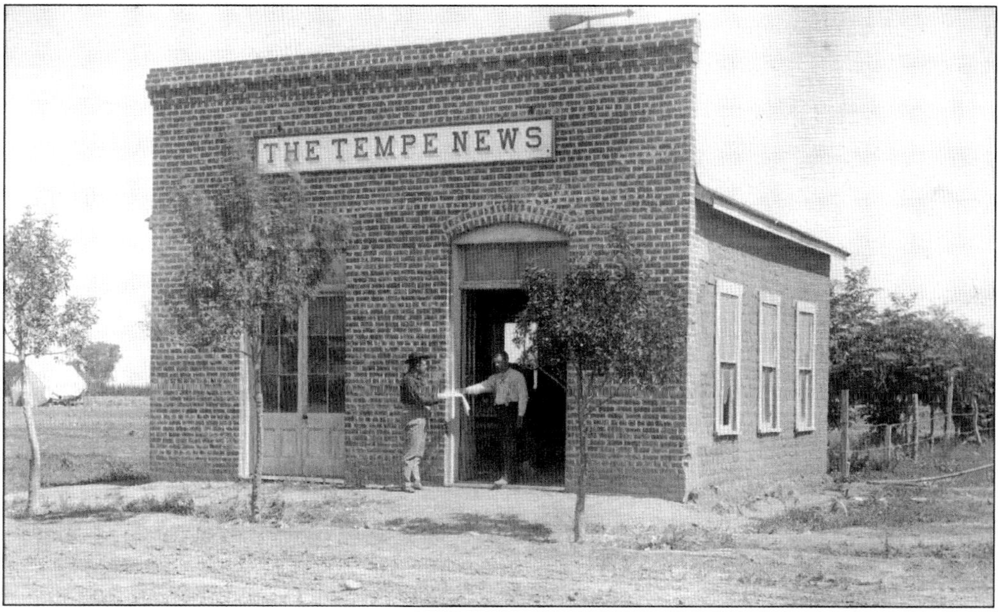

The *Salt River Valley News* was renamed the *Tempe News* in 1887. The original office was on the second floor of an adobe building above the blacksmith and carpentry shops at Hayden's Mill. A few years later, the paper moved to its own building on Fifth Street, near Mill. Curt Miller began his career publisher in 1887, and continued to operate the weekly paper for the next 55 years. (Boudoir cabinet card, Phoenix View Company photographer, c. 1898. Collection of the author © vintagephoto.com.)

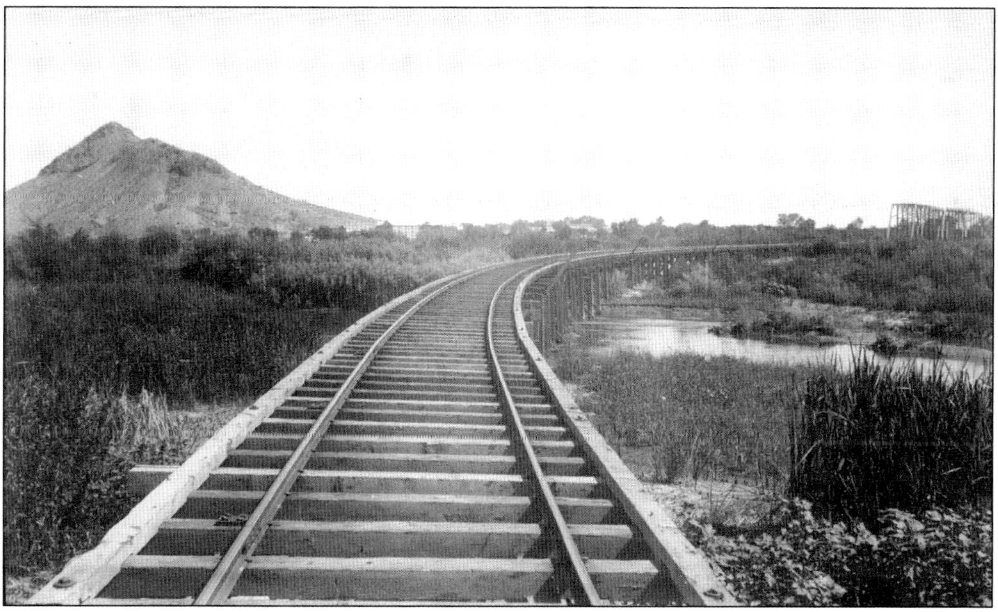

Track on the Salt River Bridge was completed in June 1887 and was extended north and west to Phoenix, which was reached by the railroad on July 4, 1887. The passenger trip between Phoenix and Tempe took approximately 40 minutes. (Boudoir cabinet card, photographer unknown, c. 1900. Collection of the author © vintagephoto.com.)

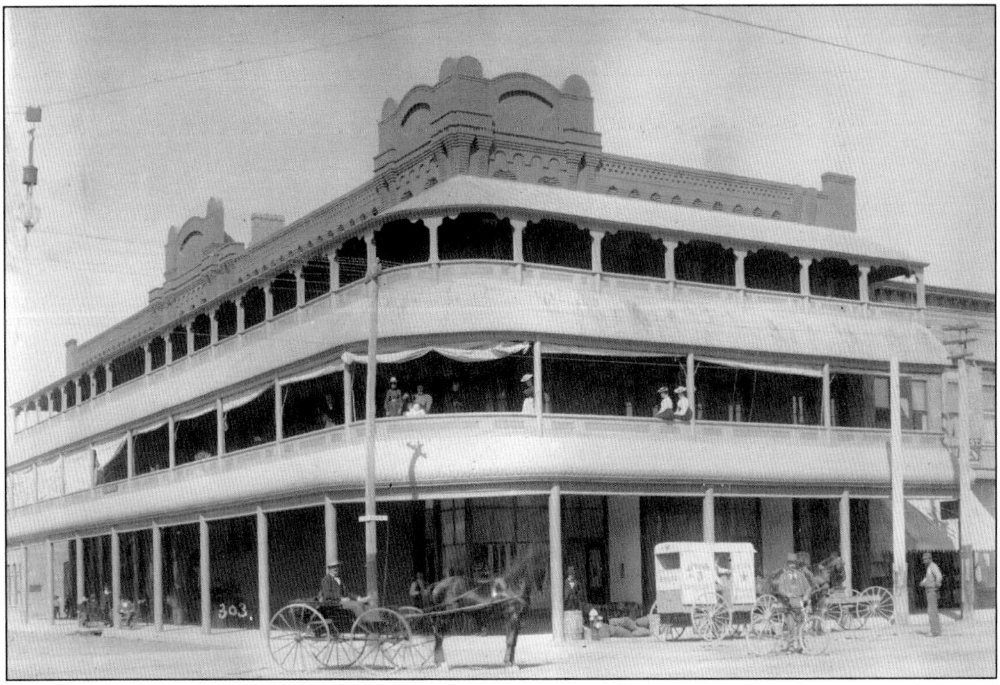

The Ford Hotel, one of the premier accommodations in Phoenix, was located at Washington and Second Avenue. The outdoor sleeping porches were common fixtures in the days before air conditioning. (Silver print, photographer unknown, c. 1900. Collection of the author © vintagephoto.com.)

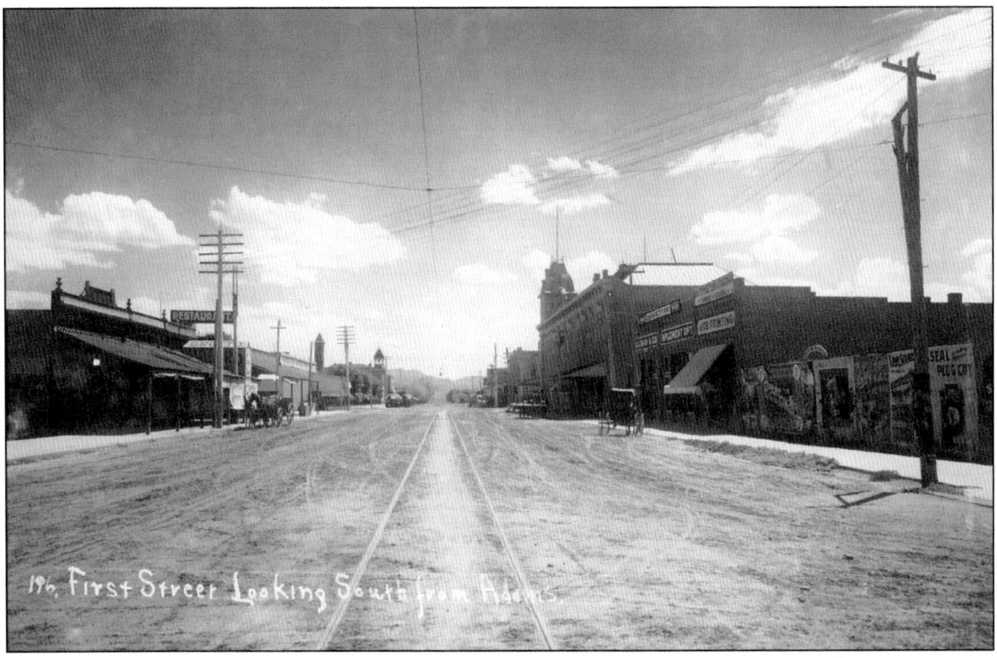

First Street in Phoenix is pictured looking south along the trolley tracks from Adams Street. At left, the Grotto Restaurant is visible at 11–13 North First Street. On the right is the Arizona Republican Job Printing at 38–40 East Adams. (Silver print, photographer unknown, c. 1900. Collection of the author © vintagephoto.com.)

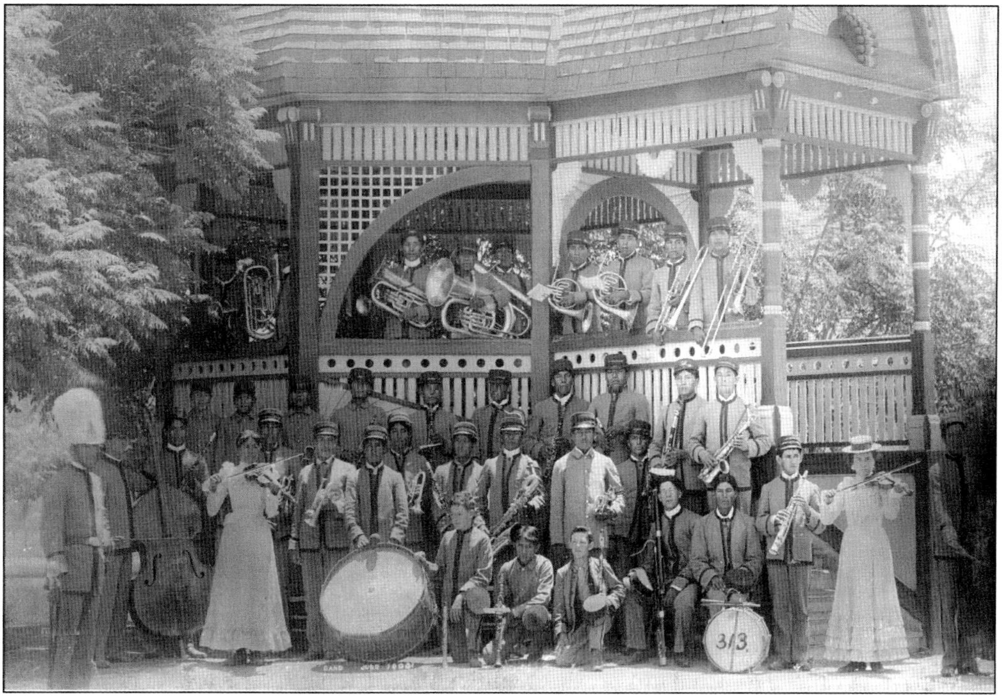

The Phoenix Indian School Band poses in front of the gazebo on the grounds of the Phoenix Indian School. (Silver print, A. F. Messinger photographer, c. 1900. Collection of the author © vintagephoto.com.)

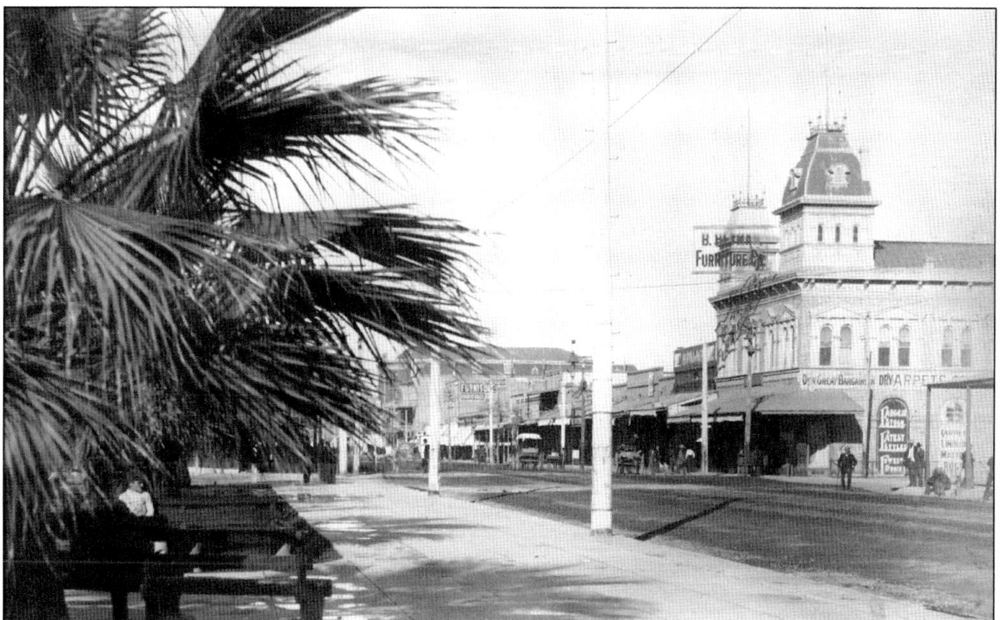

This view looks west down Washington Street from City Hall Plaza. The Heyman Furniture Company at right is in the Anderson Building (later the Berryhill Building) on the northwest corner of First Street and Washington. (Silver print, A. F. Messinger photographer, c. 1899. Collection of the author © vintagephoto.com.)

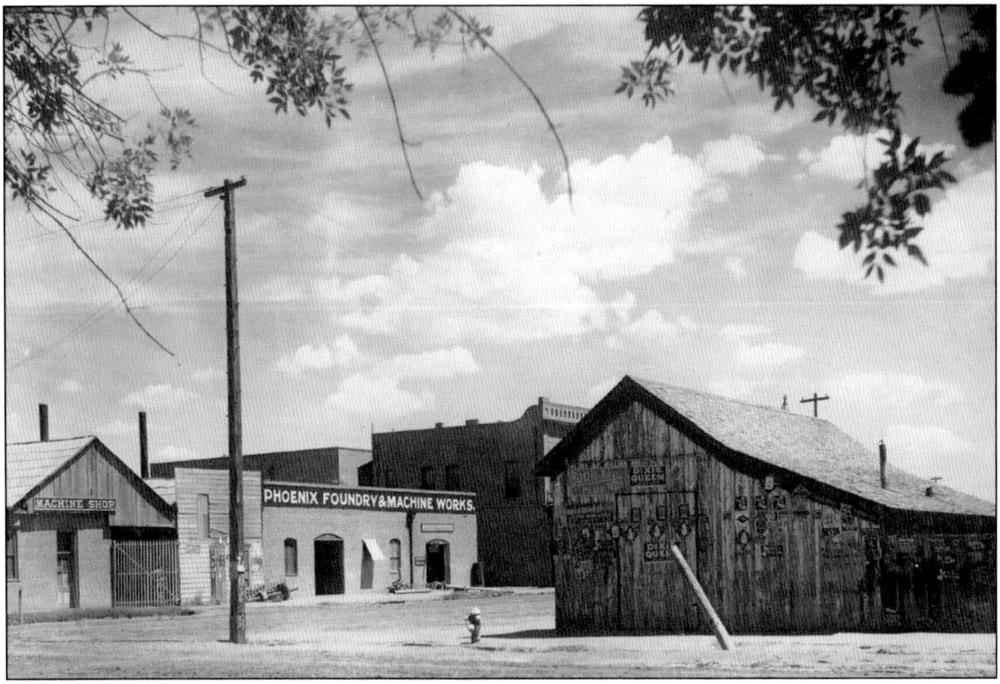

The Phoenix Foundry and Machine Works was located at 25–31 North Second Street. (Silver print, A. F. Messinger photographer, c. 1900. Collection of the author © vintagephoto.com.)

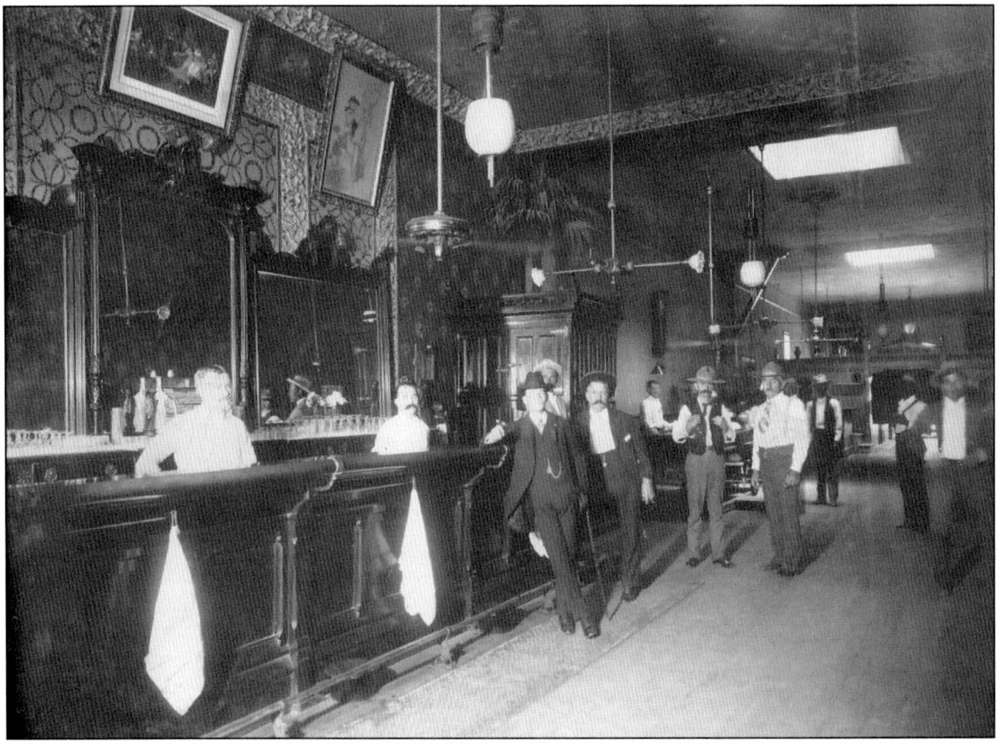

An unidentified Phoenix bar room interior, c. 1899. (Silver print, A. F. Messinger photographer. Collection of the author © vintagephoto.com.)

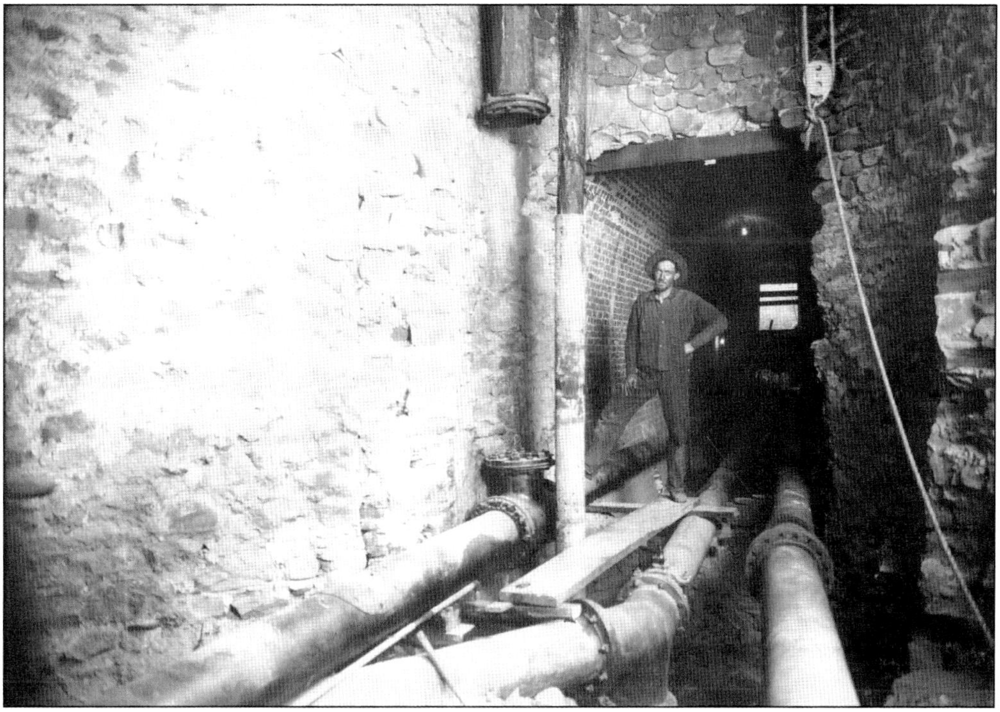

Maintenance of the underground water system that ran beneath the Phoenix business district. (Silver print, A. F. Messinger photographer, *c.* 1898. Collection of the author © vintagephoto.com.)

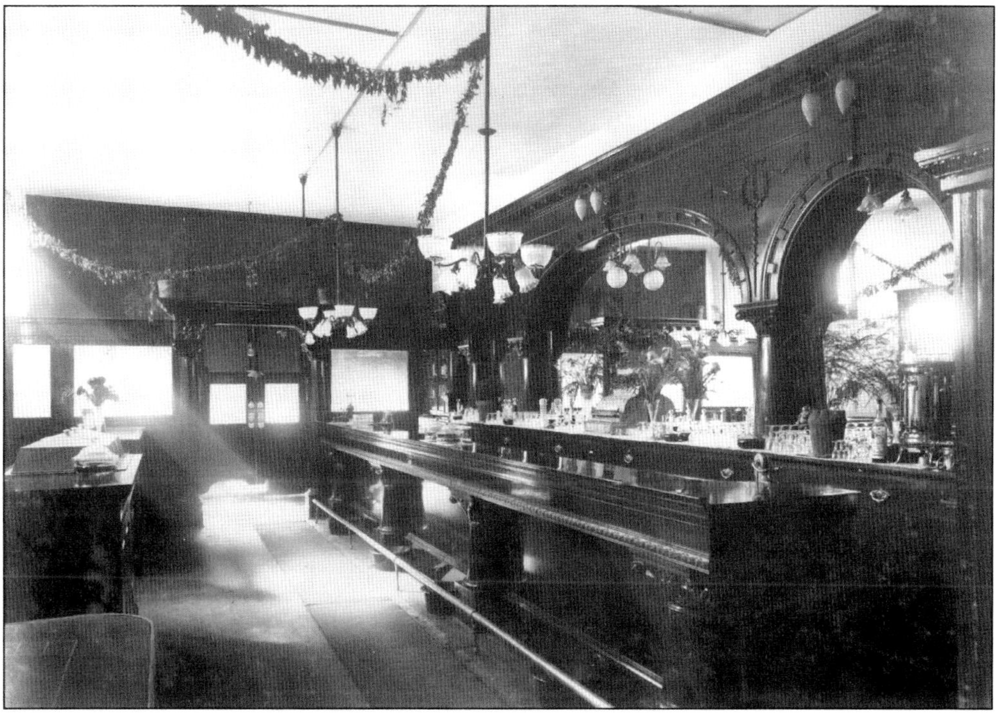

Sunlight cuts through the interior of an unidentified Phoenix barroom, *c.* 1900. (Silver print, A. F. Messinger photographer. Collection of the author © vintagephoto.com.)

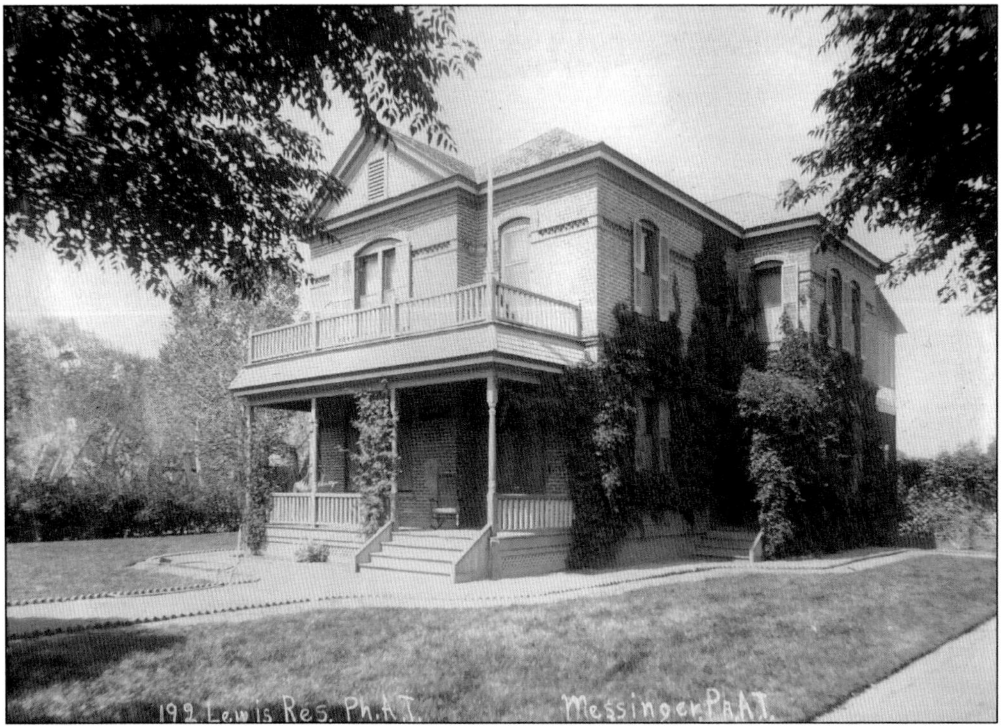

The residence of R. Allyn Lewis on Center Street, about two blocks north of McDowell Road. (Silver print, A. F. Messinger photographer, *c.* 1900. Collection of the author © vintagephoto.com.)

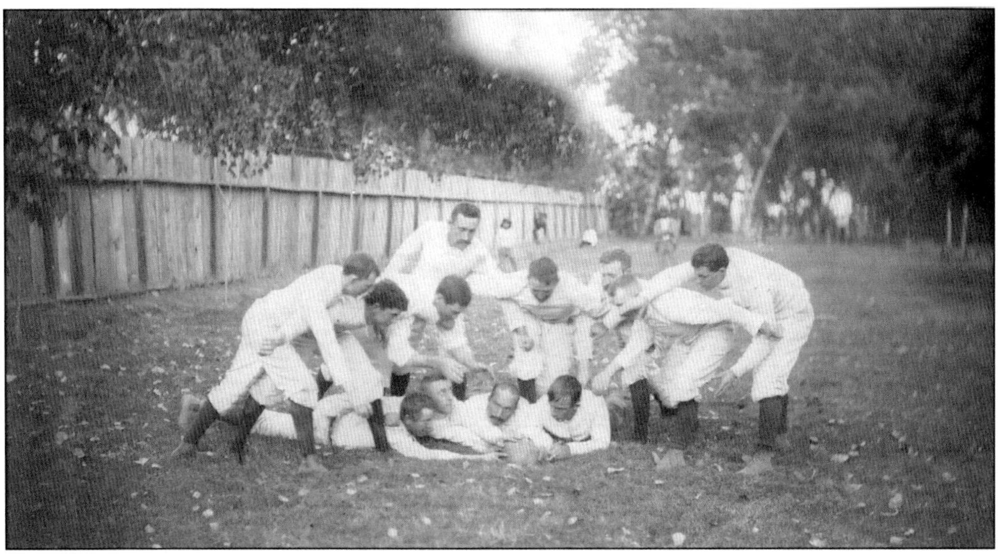

Phoenix soon boasted many of the accouterments of larger cities, such as theaters and an opera house. The members of the Phoenix Athletic Club pose in a rugby scrim in a time before the domination of baseball and football as national pastimes. (Boudoir cabinet card, F. A. Hartwell photographer, *c.* 1900. Collection of the author © vintagephoto.com.)

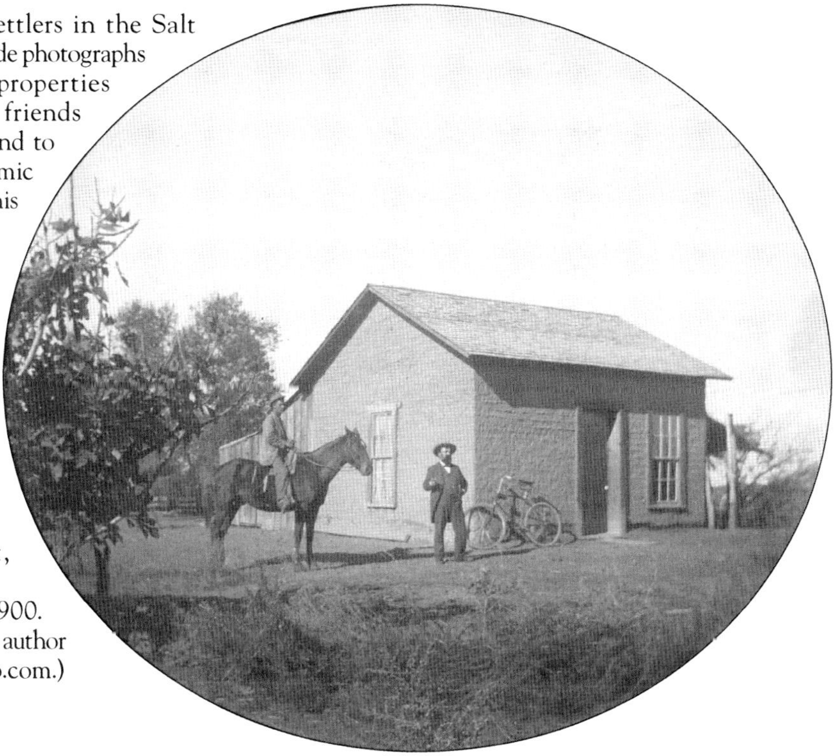

Many proud settlers in the Salt River Valley made photographs of their new properties to share with friends and relatives and to promote economic development. This unidentified Tempe ranch owner makes a statement about his refinement by posing with both horse and bicycle in front of his new adobe home. (Silver print, photographer unknown, c. 1900. Collection of the author © vintagephoto.com.)

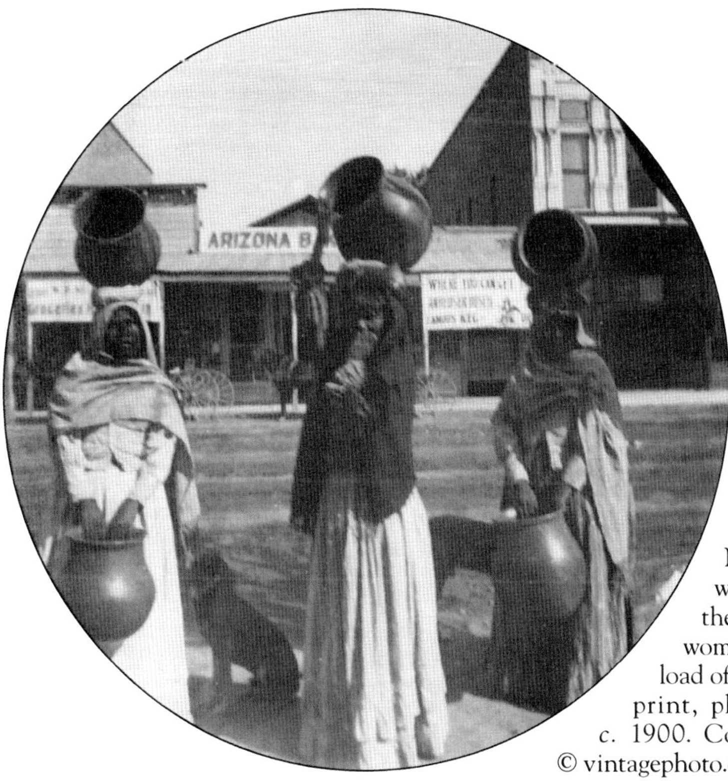

Native American women were commonly seen on the streets of Phoenix. These women stop to pose with their load of Ollas in Phoenix. (Silver print, photographer unknown, c. 1900. Collection of the author © vintagephoto.com.)

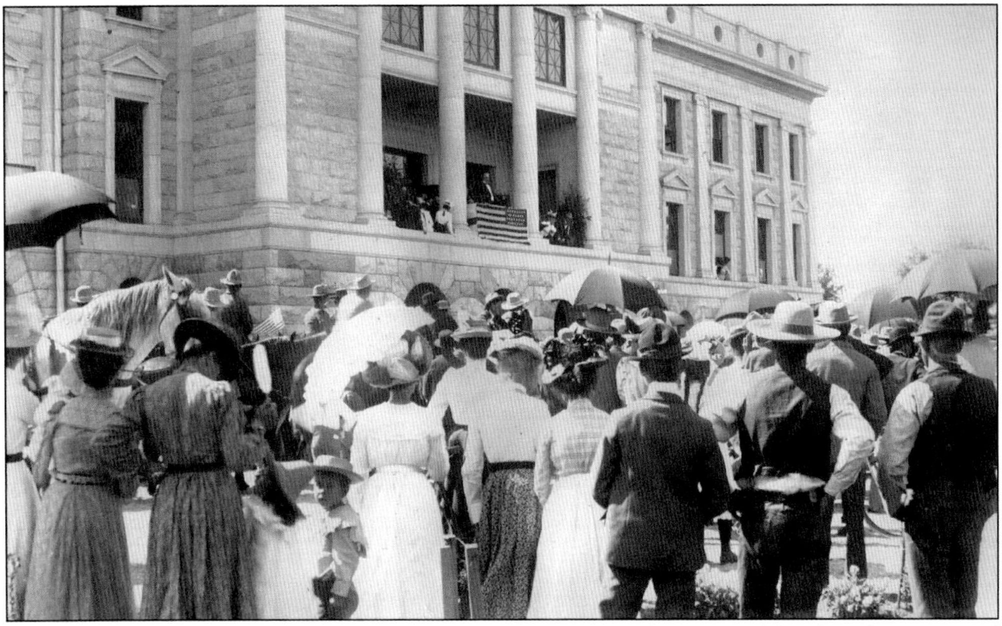

In 1889, M. H. Sherman and Marcellus E. Collins donated a tract of land at the west end of Washington Street for construction of an Arizona Capital building in Phoenix. George Houton Smith was engaged to create a garden on the capitol grounds. Tom Lovell was hired as contractor for the building in 1900. The completed Arizona Capital was dedicated by Gov. Nathan O. Murphy on February 25, 1901. (Silver print, photographer unknown. Collection of the author © vintagephoto.com.)

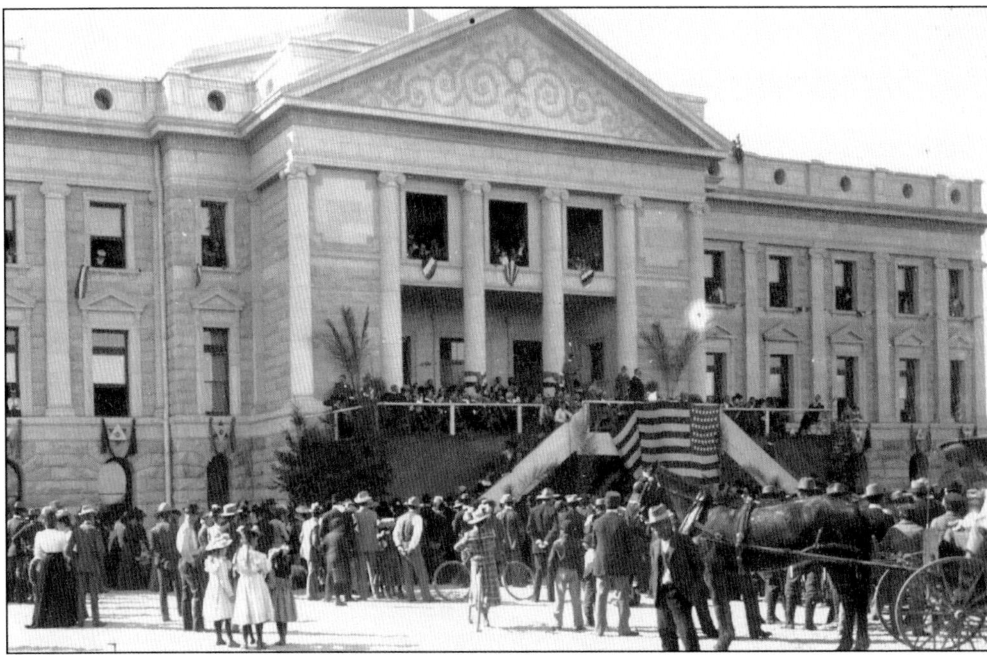

This A. F. Messinger silver print shows an unidentified speaker at the territorial capital during the visit of President McKinley, before his trip to the Congress Mines north of Phoenix in early May 1901. Silver print, A. F. Messinger photographer. Collection of the author © vintagephoto.com.)

Six

1902–1907

The need for water and growing demand for electrical power led to a major innovation and a lasting landmark in Central Arizona. In 1902, farmers organized the Salt River Valley Water Users Association joining the 12 independent canal companies to coordinate water resources. In 1904, planning with the federal government created Roosevelt Dam just below the junction of the Salt and Verde rivers. In western Maricopa County, the Buckeye Irrigation Company was bonded in 1907 to expand irrigation from the Gila River.

Roosevelt Dam construction began in 1905 and fueled East Valley growth. The boom began in Mesa in which served as the railhead for supplies. Mesa added a new depot, three blocks of businesses, two stockyards, another hotel, and an ice plant. Mesa soon boasted all the trappings of a modern city, an opera house, hotels and restaurants, saloons, drugstores, dry goods, a bank and its own newspaper.

The dam provided an incentive for continued growth in the East Valley. The dam was also a major experiment in harnessing hydroelectric power to create electricity. Construction of Roosevelt Dam was completed in just six years, and the project was dedicated on March 18, 1911. Pres. Theodore Roosevelt traveled to Arizona making speeches in Phoenix and Tempe en route to the Dam dedication.

On October 29, 1902 the Maricopa and Phoenix Railroad Bridge at Tempe collapsed under Engine No. 6 and three freight cars, leaving a Pullman car teetering precariously at the end of the remaining span. Amazingly none of the passengers were injured. Construction crews put up a temporary bridge and restored the important railroad route in just two days.

The original Tempe Union Depot building burned in 1903. A new station that served passengers of the Phoenix and Eastern Railroad replaced it. The new building was located west of Mill Avenue, at the base of the Tempe Butte just north of Fifth Street. Initially horse-drawn wagons provided transportation from the depot, but they were soon replaced by automobiles and trucks.

Phoenix businessman William J. Murphy had accumulated large tracts of land in the western Salt River Valley. Murphy partnered with two scientists from the University of Arizona to explore growing sugar beets in Maricopa County. By 1903, Murphy's investors from Michigan and New Jersey, the Eastern Sugar Company, constructed a tremendous brick sugar factory in Glendale that was completed in 1905 and still stands today.

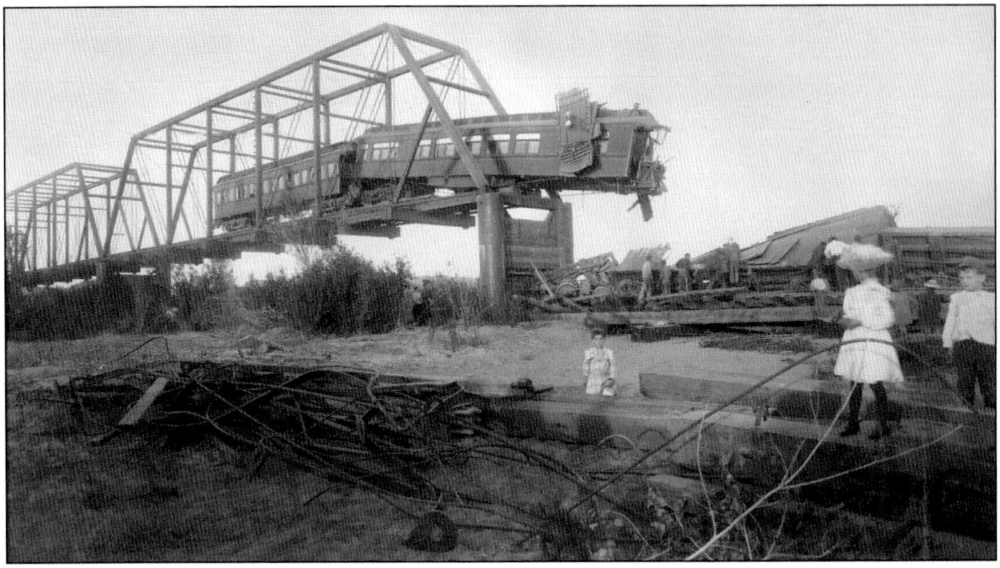

On October 29, 1902, the Maricopa and Phoenix Railroad Bridge at Tempe collapsed under Engine No. 6 and three freight cars, leaving a Pullman car teetering at the end of the remaining span. Amazingly, none of the passengers were injured. They walked back across the bridge and were taken to Tempe by wagon. The temporary bridge repair took only two days. (Silver print, A. F. Messinger photographer. Collection of the author © vintagephoto.com.)

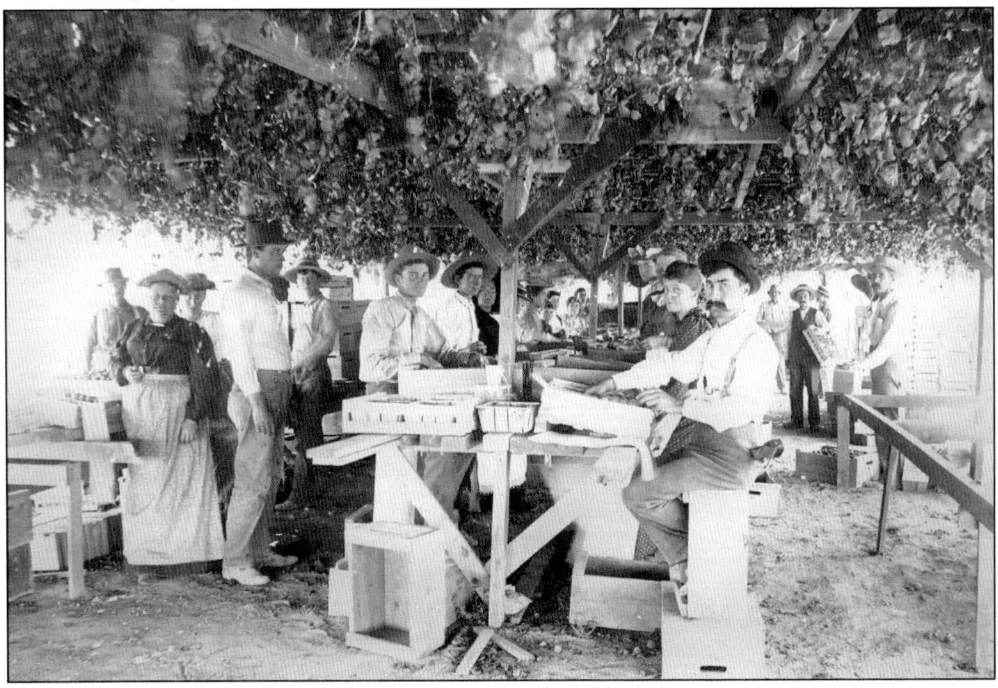

Farmers in the Salt River Valley grew a number of winter crops, which were picked, packed, and shipped to markets in the East by rail. Crops varied widely and included corn, wheat, oats, barley, pink beans, Irish potatoes, watermelons, cantaloupe, peaches, apricots, plums, pears, blackberries, strawberries, tomatoes, and cabbage. (Silver print, A. F. Messinger photographer, c. 1901. Collection of the author © vintagephoto.com.)

Boosters of the Salt River Valley used every opportunity to promote agriculture and demonstrate the uniqueness of the landscape. This view looking north from South Mountain shows the impact of irrigation on the valley, framed by an iconic Saguaro cactus. This image became part of educational materials offered by the Keystone View Company, who produced and distributed and thousands of copies. (Stereograph, published by the Keystone View Company, c. 1903. Collection of the author © vintagephoto.com.)

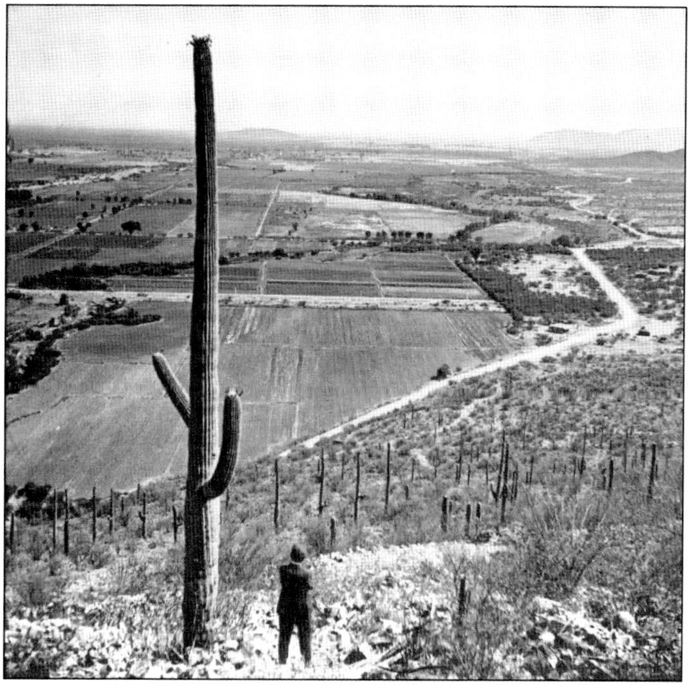

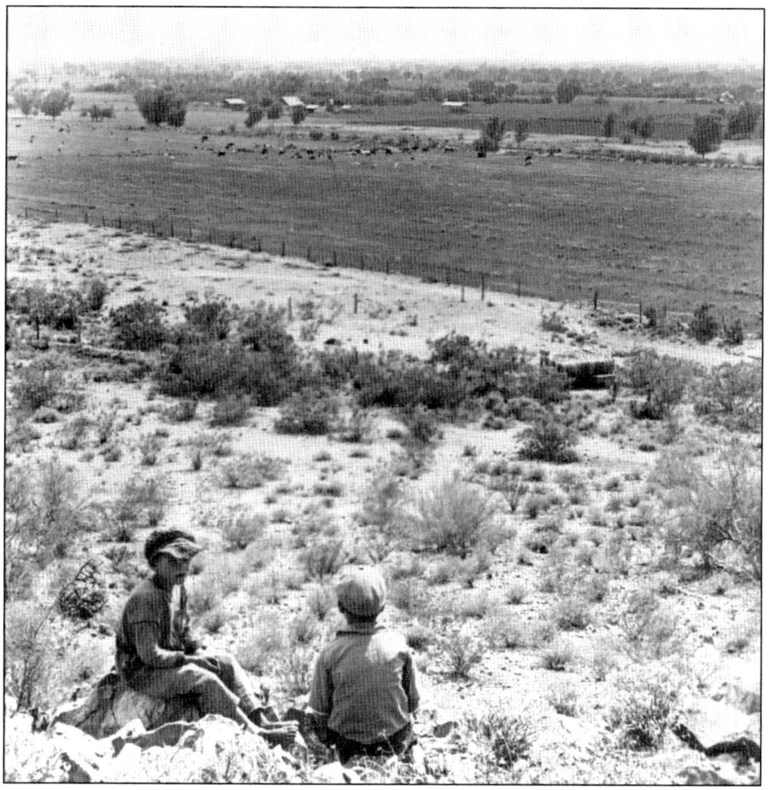

This image published by Underwood and Underwood shows the view looking northwest over the farm fields of the Salt River Valley from the foothills of South Mountain. (Stereograph, Underwood and Underwood publishers, c. 1903. Collection of the author © vintagephoto.com.)

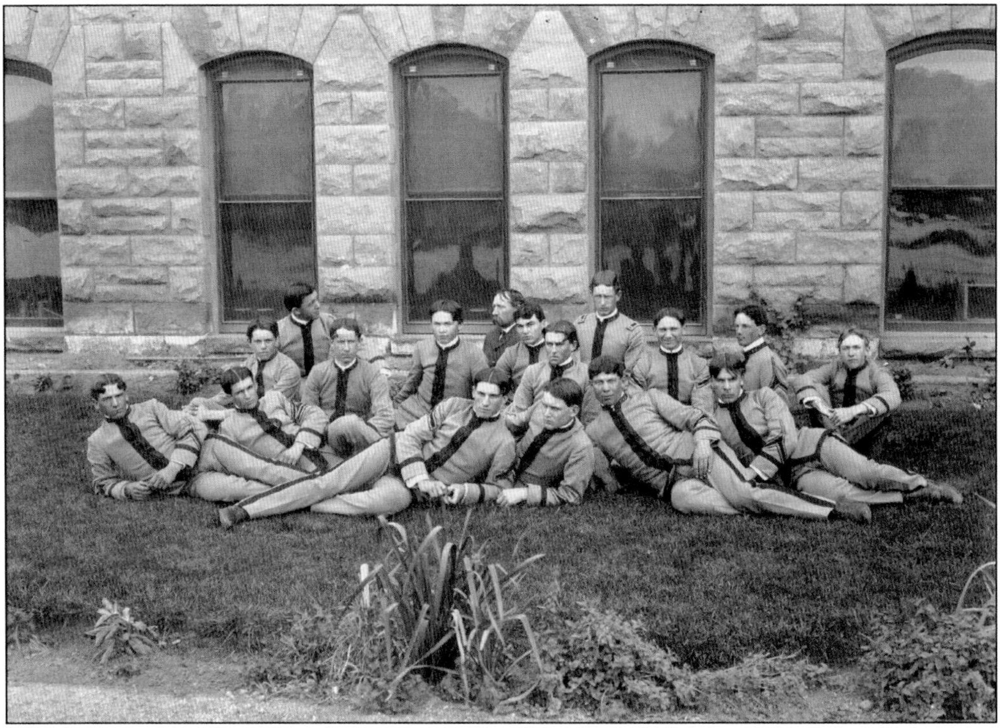

In 1885, the Arizona Territorial Normal School (now Arizona State University) was founded in Tempe. This informal group of male student military cadets poses next to Old Main at the Tempe Normal School. By this time, the school had grown to about 245 students. (Silver print, F. A. Hartwell photographer, *c.* 1903. Collection of the author © vintagephoto.com.)

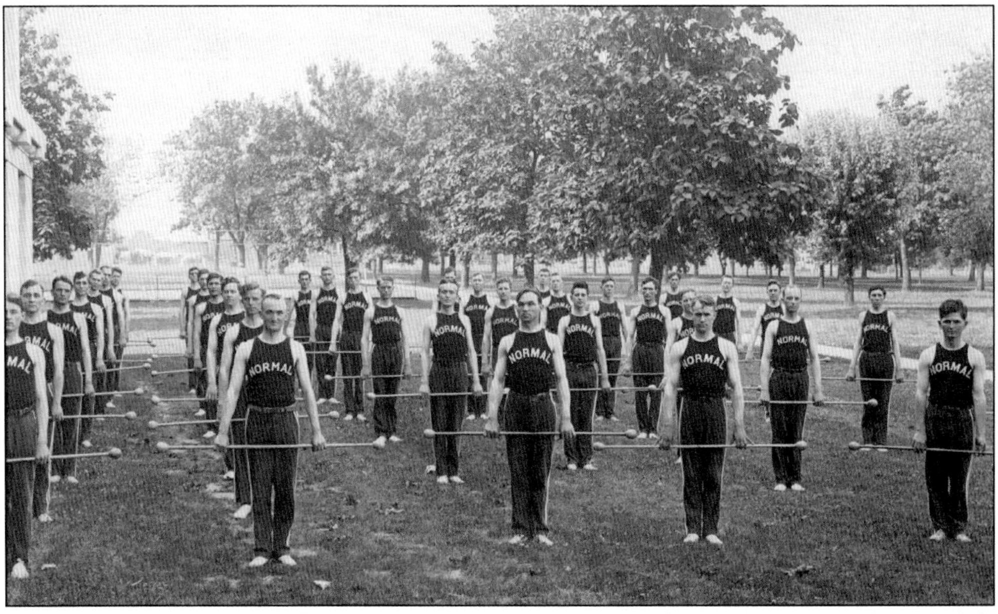

The little teachers school had both upperclassmen ("Normals") and underclassmen ("Sub-normals"). The upper class men's gymnastics class poses in the quad adjacent to Old Main. (Real photographic postcard, photographer unknown, *c.* 1907. Collection of the author © vintagephoto.com.)

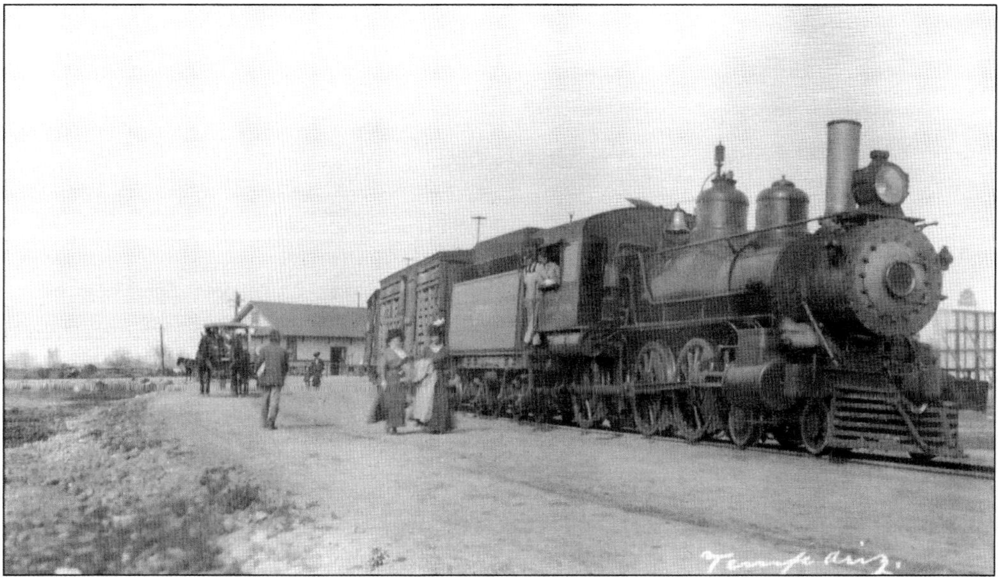

The train to Mesa leaving from the Maricopa and Phoenix Railroad depot on Fifth Street at the base of the Tempe Butte. (Real photographic postcard, photographer unknown, *c.* 1908. Collection of the author © vintagephoto.com.)

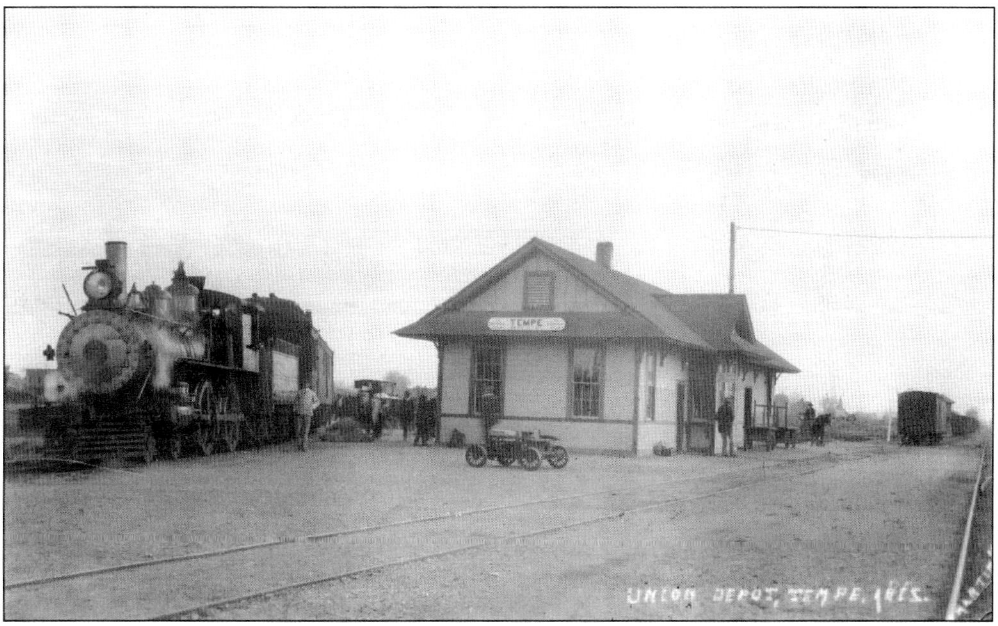

Union Depot Building's original location was north of Fifth Street and west of Mill. Two trains a day went between Phoenix and Tempe. Looking south at the Railroad Station for the Maricopa & Phoenix and Salt River Railroad Company at Third Street in Tempe. The train from Mesa is on the left, and the rails that lead to Maricopa on the right. Beginning on November 13, 1893. The Hunsaker stagecoach would carry passengers from the Tempe Depot to Mesa until the Phoenix, Tempe, and Mesa Railroad was established on December 9, 1895. (Real photographic postcard, photographer unknown, *c.* 1908.)

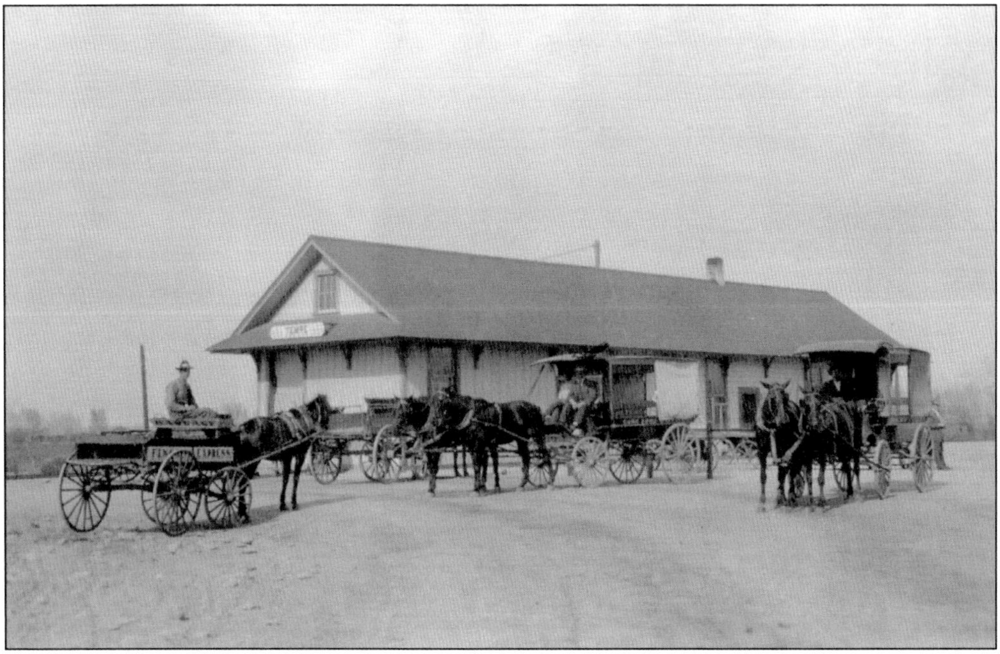

The original Tempe Depot burned in 1903 and was replaced by a new station for the Phoenix and Eastern Railroad. The new building was located west of Mill Avenue, at the base of the Tempe Butte just north of Fifth Street. Initially, horse-drawn wagons provided transportation from the depot. (Real photographic postcard, photographer unknown, *c.* 1905. Collection of the author © vintagephoto.com.)

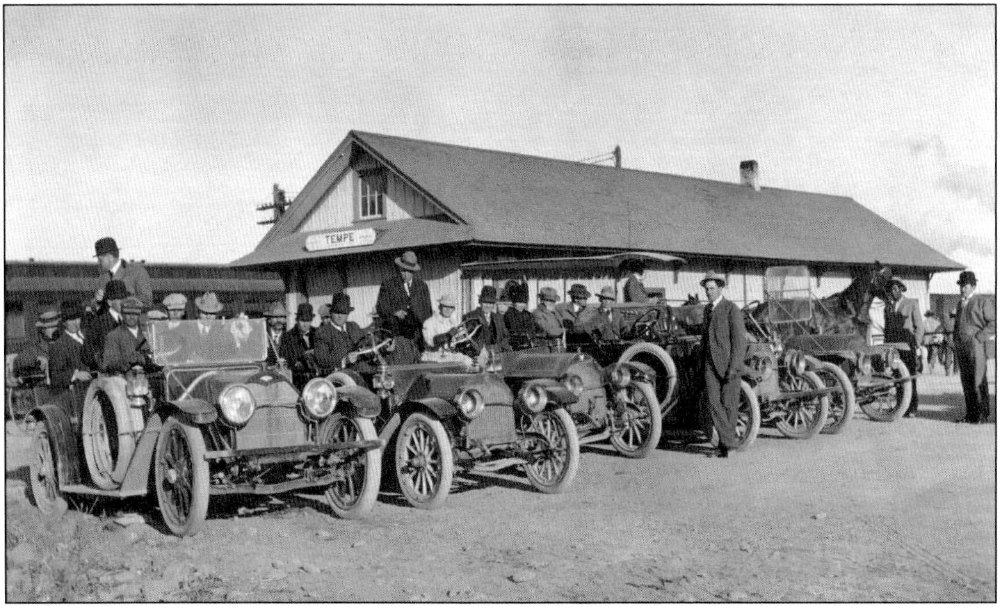

A few years later, automobiles replaced the wagons and carriages working from the Tempe depot. (Real photographic postcard, photographer unknown, *c.* 1910. Collection of the author © vintagephoto.com.)

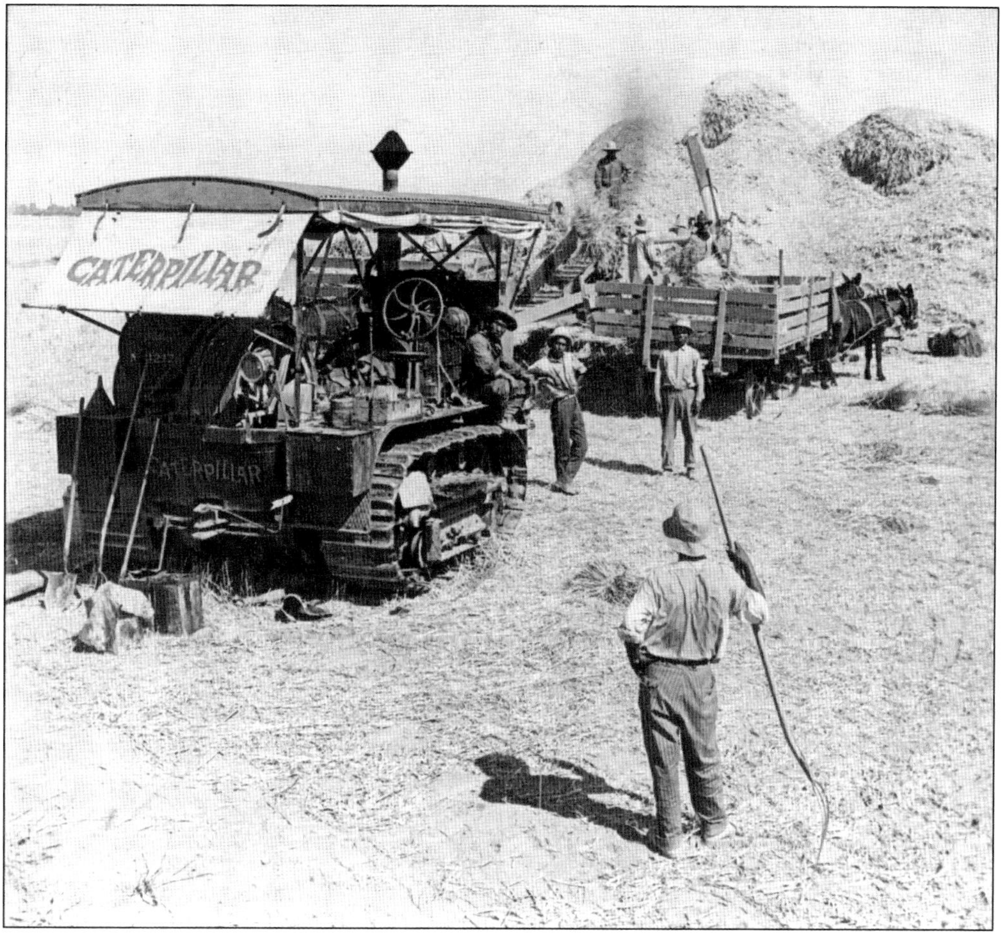

Mechanization of agriculture increased scale and improved productivity. This early Caterpillar tractor working on a field in the Slat River Valley was unique enough to become the subject of a nationally marketed stereograph. (Stereograph, Underwood & Underwood publishers, c. 1905. Collection of the author © vintagephoto.com.)

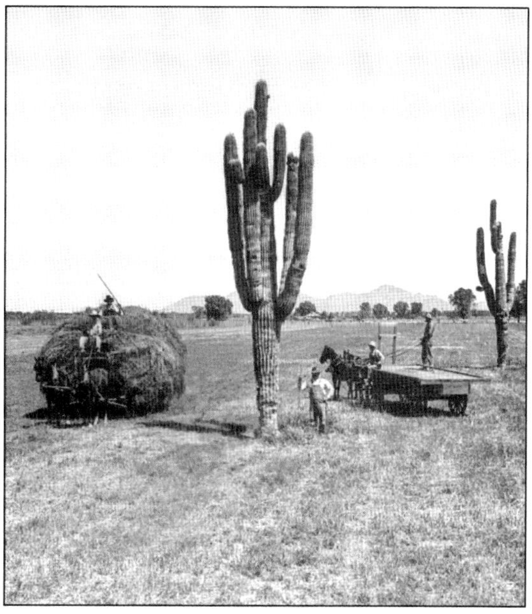

Alfalfa was a popular forage crop in the Salt River Valley. Irrigation led to rapid growth of farming, here so rapid they planted around the Saguaro, which became both obstacles and photo opportunities during harvest season. (Stereograph, photographer unknown, c. 1905. Collection of the author © vintagephoto.com.)

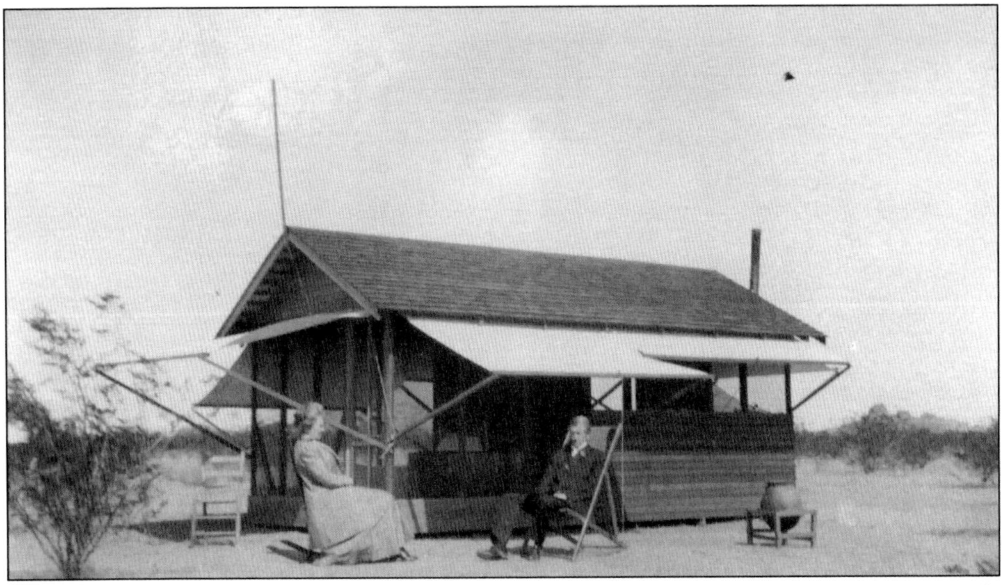

The mild weather, low cost, and familiarity from the mining camps throughout the Territory made tents popular for health seekers and as temporary homes for new visitors. In 1903, the abundance of tent dwellers led Phoenix to pass an ordinance banning them within city limits. (Cyanotype real photographic postcard, Ralph R Doubleday photographer, c. 1910. Collection of the author © vintagephoto.com.)

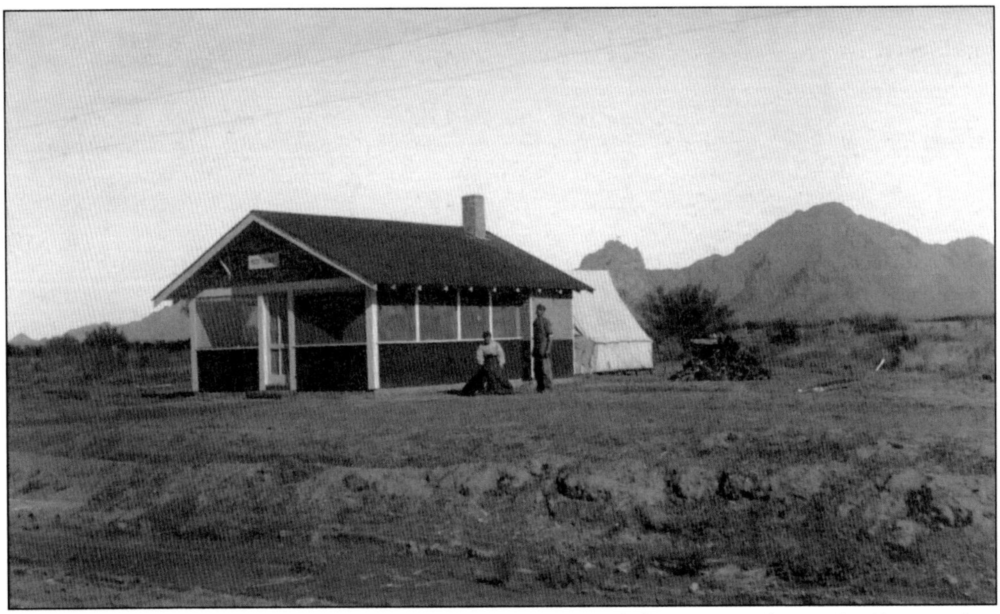

These settlers southwest of Camelback Mountain replaced their original tent dwelling with a simple frame structure they named "Poco Tiempo." (Real photographic postcard, photographer unknown, c. 1910. Collection of the author © vintagephoto.com.)

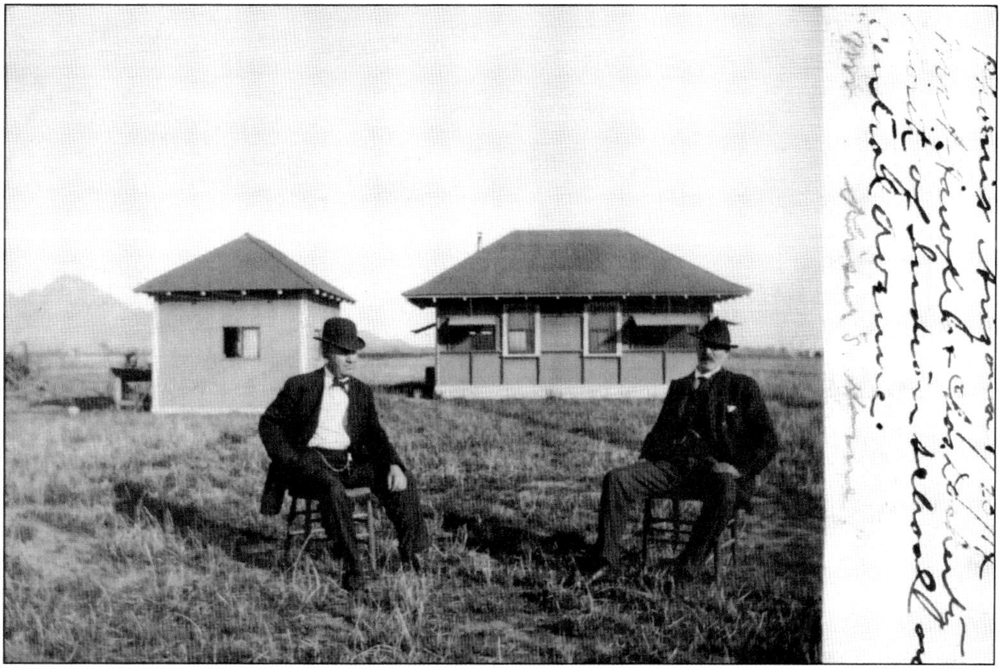

Two gentlemen pose in front of their new homestead north of the Phoenix Indian School with Piestewa Peak in the background. (Real photographic postcard, photographer unknown, *c.* 1908. Collection of the author © vintagephoto.com.)

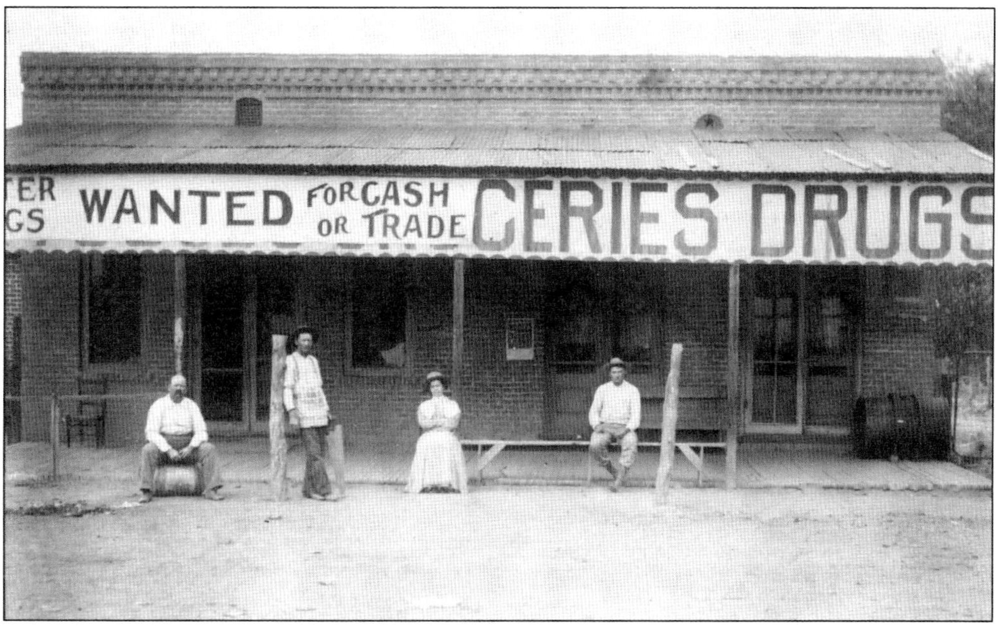

The New England Land Company originally established Glendale on 360 acres in the Northwest Valley in 1892. The principal early residents were members of the Church of the Brethren from Illinois. A visitor to the 1907 Arizona Territorial Fair sent this real photographic postcard of an unidentified Glendale grocery store. (Real photographic postcard, photographer unknown, *c.* 1907. Collection of the author © vintagephoto.com.)

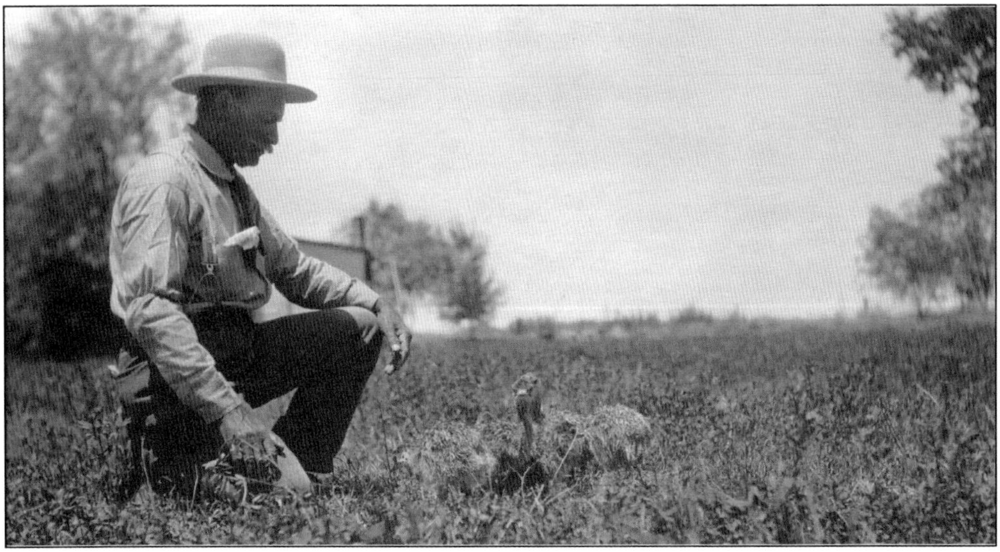

Ostrich plumes were in great demand for hats and as fashion accessories. Phoenix had several successful ostrich farms and became a major producer, breeding chicks and selling feathers. By 1914, the Salt River Valley had over 6,000 birds on farms in Phoenix, Glendale, and Tempe. (Silver prints, photographer unknown, *c.* 1907. Collection of the author © vintagephoto.com.)

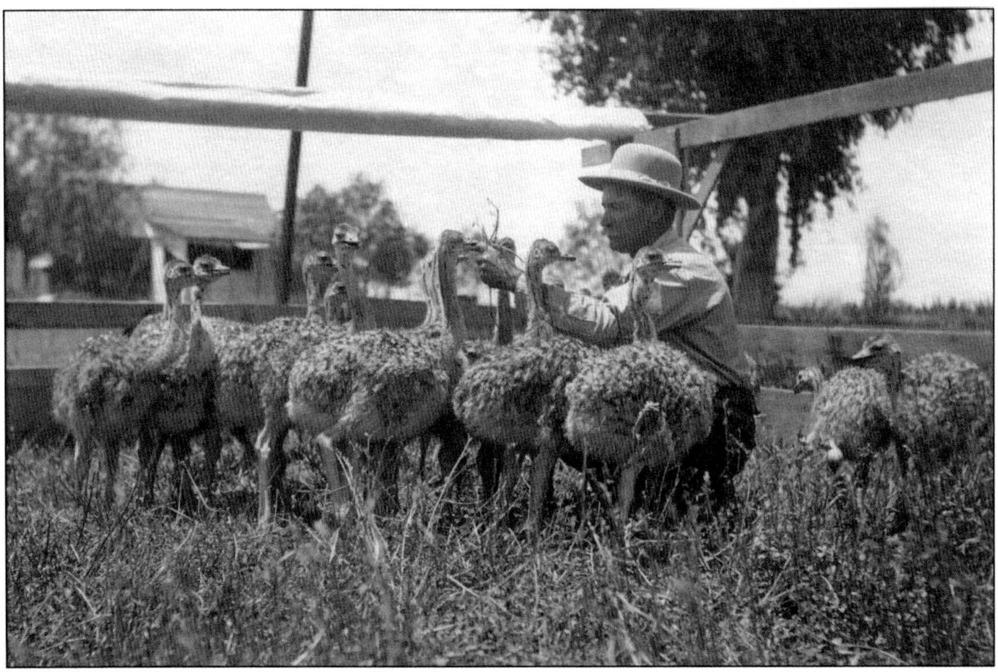

Seven

1908–1910

Flooding washed out the Arizona Dam that diverted water from the Salt River about 22 miles northeast of Phoenix, in April 1905 and again in 1906. This disrupted the water supply and had serious consequences throughout the Salt River, since virtually every farmer and rancher relied on the canals to irrigate their crops. Construction of a new diversion facility, the 1,000-foot-long, 29-foot-high Granite Reef Dam, began in 1906 and was completed two years later.

Maricopa County provided an ideal climate for technologies emerging at the start of the 20th century. Steam and gasoline powered tractors and harvesting equipment were purchased and tested. Balloons were exhibited at the 1908 and 1909 Territorial Fairs in Phoenix and brave attendees could take tethered rides high above the fairgrounds. To demonstrate the power and reliability of the automobile and help highlight need for a cross-country road system, a race from Los Angeles to Phoenix, the Cactus Derby, was established in 1908. The annual race continued until 1914 and helped create demand for developing roads in the West, as it focused international attention on Arizona each fall.

In 1910, over half of the automobiles registered in Maricopa County were in Phoenix, which had about 382 licensed autos. By 1914, when the Cactus Derby ended, auto registrations in Maricopa County had grown almost 800 percent, to over 5,000 vehicles.

Los Angeles and Phoenix were also catalysts in early aircraft development, hosting the first aviation meets in America. The Dominguez Hills meet in Los Angeles was first, in January 1910. Phoenix followed a month later on February 10–12, 1910. Hotels filled and schools closed for the event. Records were set for flights as two Curtis planes raced a White touring car and motorcycle in front of huge crowds at the Territorial Fairgrounds. The planes moved on to fly in Tucson, and the success of these early events helped Arizona become a popular location for aviation development.

The Adams Hotel quickly built a reputation as one of the best hotels in the Southwest. Its gazebo-like turret became a local landmark that appeared in thousands of postcards and promotional brochures. But the Adams was made of wood, and its high ceilings open floor plan and turret made it susceptible to fire. On May 17, 1910, the Adams burned to the ground in a spectacular fire that was, luckily, contained and prevented from spreading across downtown Phoenix.

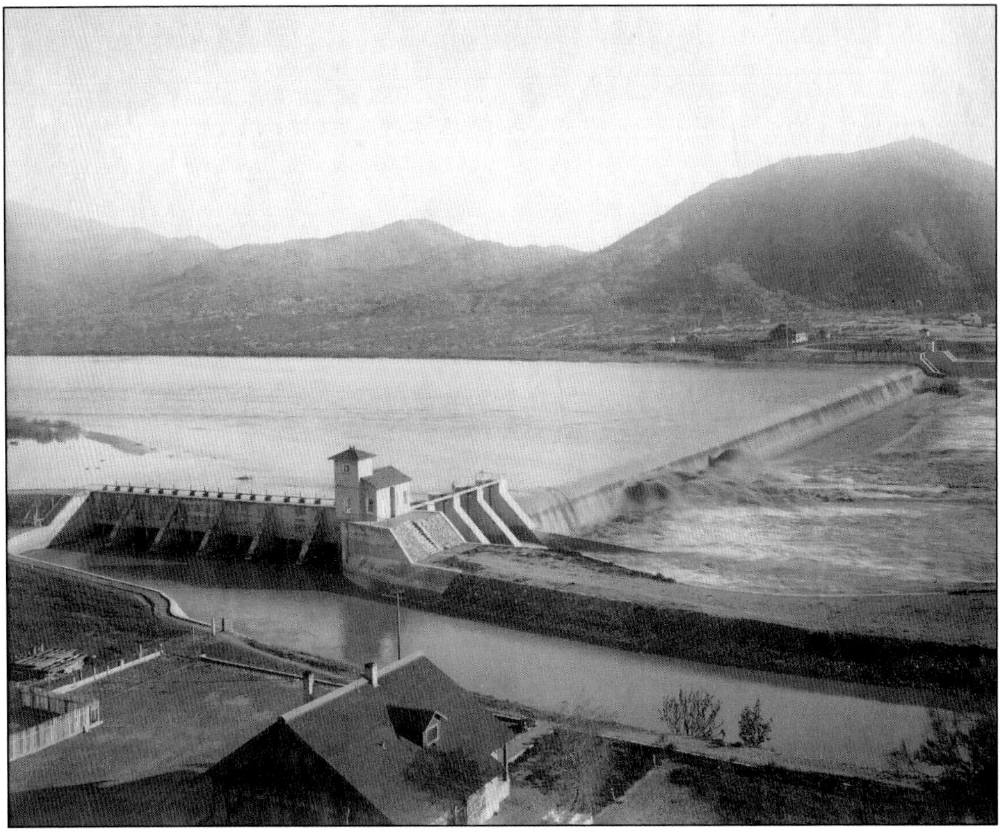

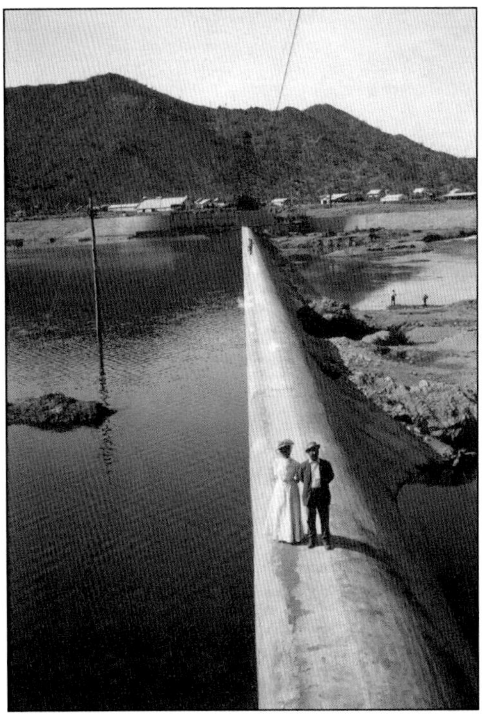

Granite Reef Dam was built on the Salt River 22 miles northeast of Phoenix to divert water into the canals of the Salt River Valley. The dam was completed in 1909 and was 1,000 feet long and 29 feet high. (Silver print, photographer unknown, *c.* 1910. Collection of the author © vintagephoto.com.)

Northeast of Mesa, Granite Reef Dam quickly became a destination for day trips from Phoenix. This couple poses on the top of the dam during low water flow. (Real photographic postcard, photographer unknown, *c.* 1910. Collection of the author © vintagephoto.com.)

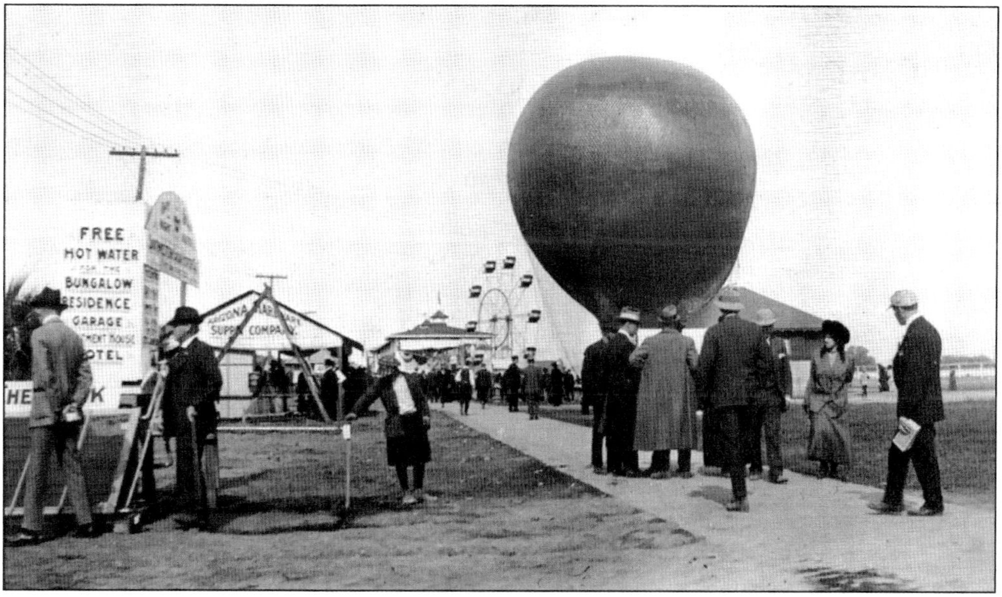

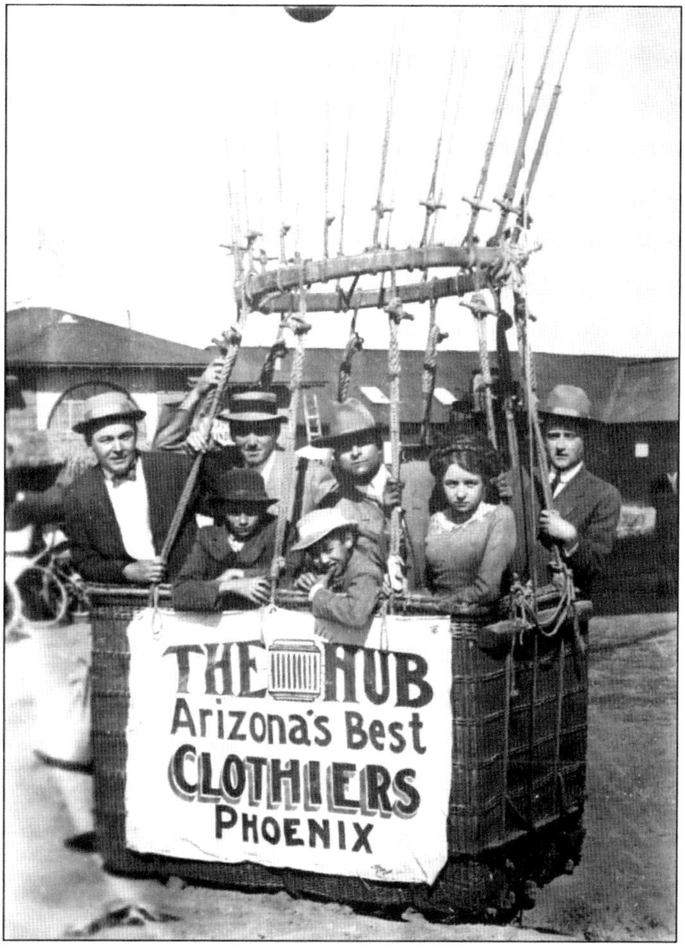

At the 1909 territorial fair in Phoenix, Otha O'Dell offered the wealthy and adventurous tethered balloon trips above the fairgrounds and provided a new forum for local advertising. (Real photographic postcards, photographers unknown, c. 1909. Collection of the author © vintagephoto.com.)

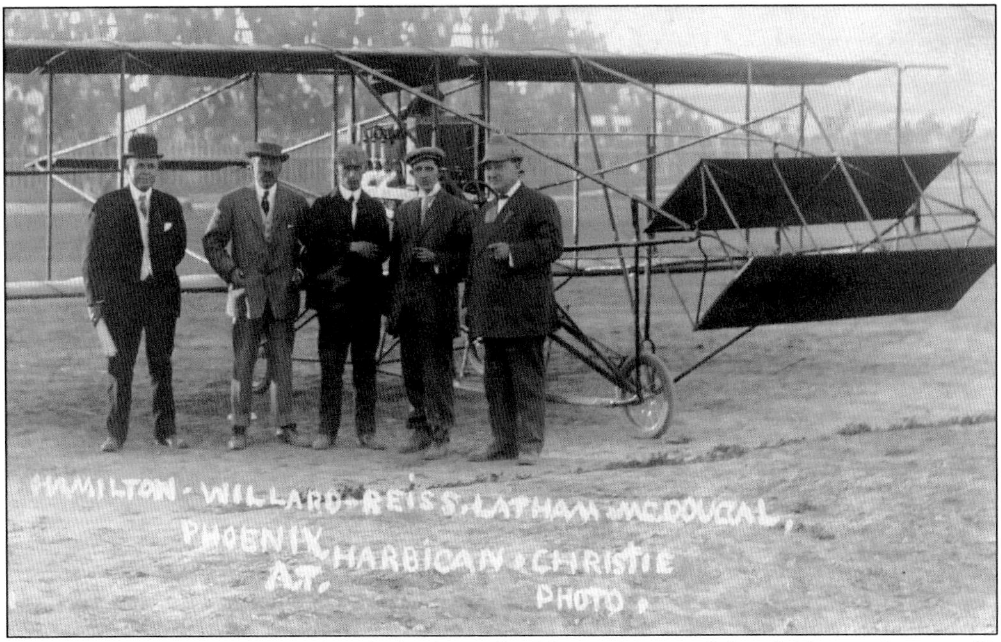

Pilots Charles Hamilton (center) and Charles Willard (second from right) with Phoenix boosters H. I. Latham, Mr. Reis, and Mr. McDougal, posed in front of the four-cylinder Curtiss "Golden Flyer" biplane at the Aero Meet at the Phoenix Fairgrounds on February 10, 11, and 12, 1910. (Photographic postcard, Harrigan and Christie photographers. Collection of the author © vintagephoto.com.)

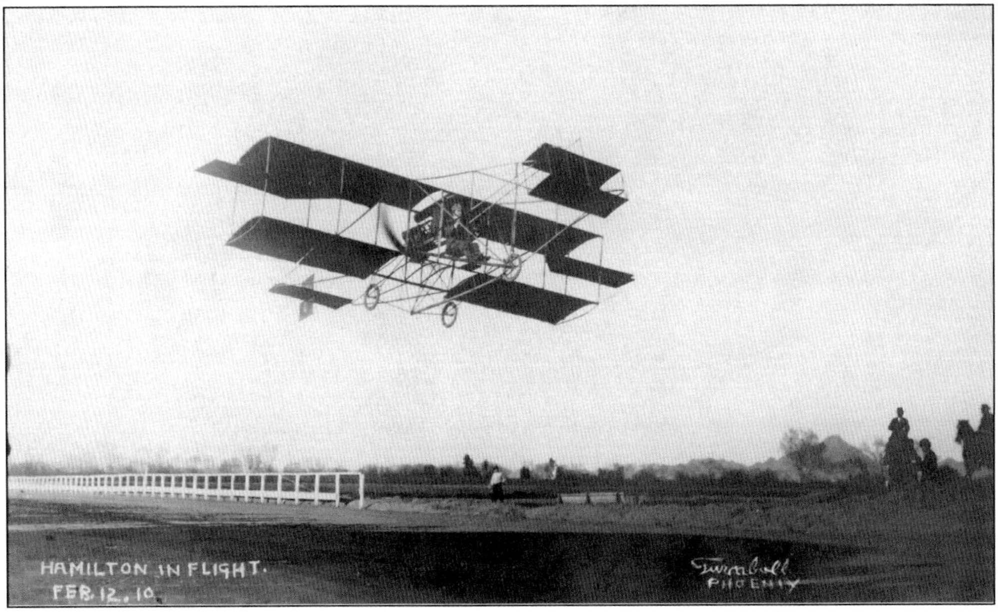

Phoenix was home of the second aviation meet in America, a month after the first at Dominguez Hills, California, on February 12–14, 1910. Two aviators, Charles Willard and Charles Hamilton, flew Curtis planes at the Phoenix fairgrounds. The planes raced each other, a Curtis motorcycle, and White touring car. Several records were set, and the event put Arizona on the map as an aviation test bed, with its mild winters and wide-open spaces. (Real photographic postcard, photographer unknown. Collection of the author © vintagephoto.com.)

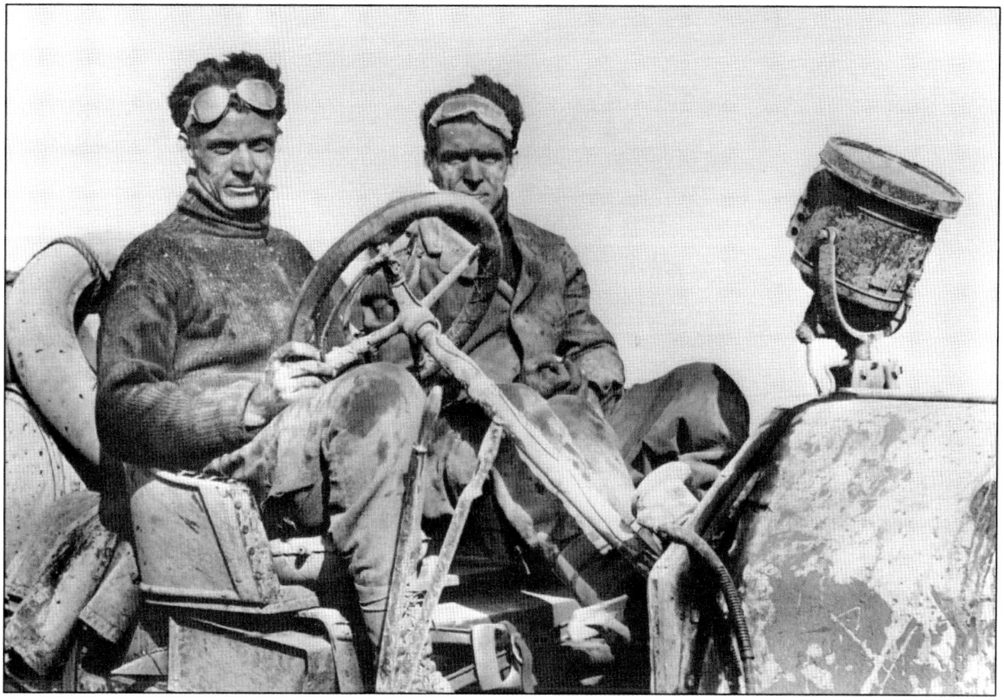

The Nikrent brothers Joe (driver) and Louis (mechanic) are pictured in their Buick at the end of the 1909 Cactus Derby. This image has often been misidentified as being Barney Oldfield in a later race. Note the inflatable cushion that replaced the upholstered seat as well as the single spotlight. (Silver print, photographer unknown, *c.* 1913. Collection of the author © vintagephoto.com.)

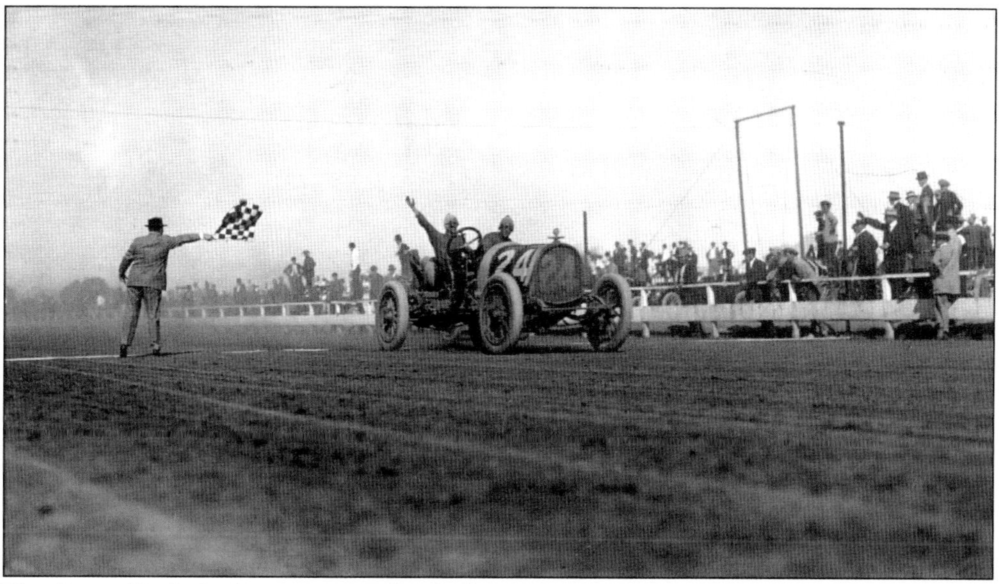

The Cactus Derby built a reputation for challenging automobile racing and testing in the harsh desert environment. The race became a sales tool for tires, cars, and automobile accessories. After the Derby ended, auto racing remained popular. This race car gets the checkered flag as it crosses the finish line at the Fairgrounds racetrack in Phoenix. (Real photographic postcard, photographer unknown, *c.* 1915. Collection of the author © vintagephoto.com.)

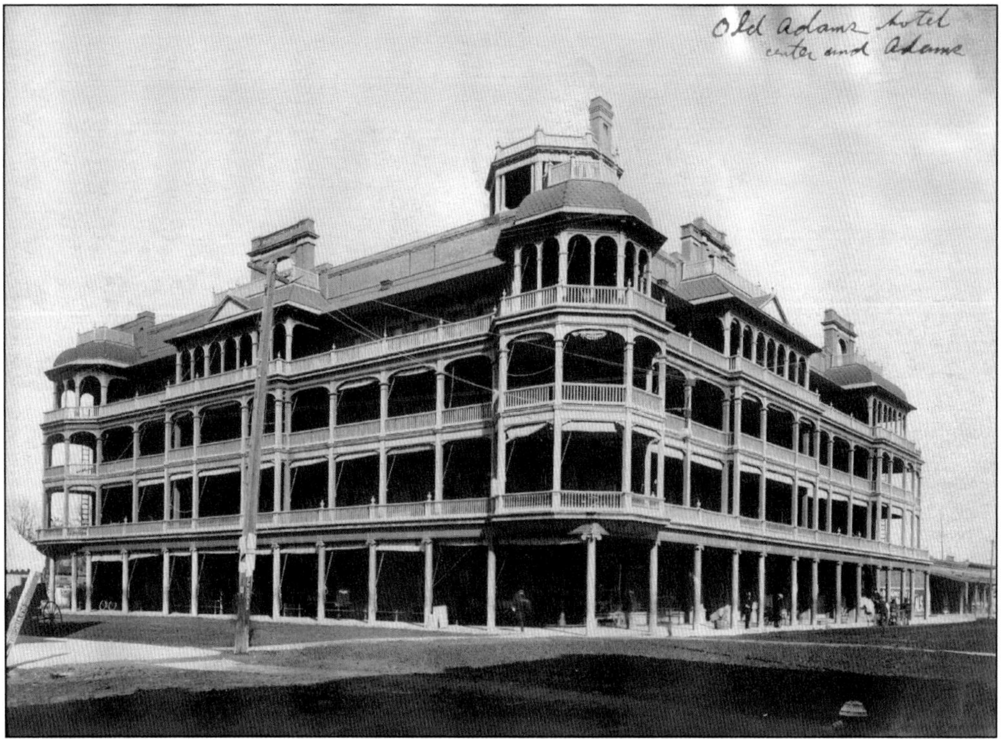

The first Adams Hotel was completed in December 1896 at the corner of First Avenue and Washington in Phoenix. Distinctive, decorative architectural features included the wooden turret and cupola that burned dramatically when the hotel caught fire on May 17, 1910. (Silver print, F. A. Hartwell photographer, c. 1898. Collection of the author © vintagephoto.com.)

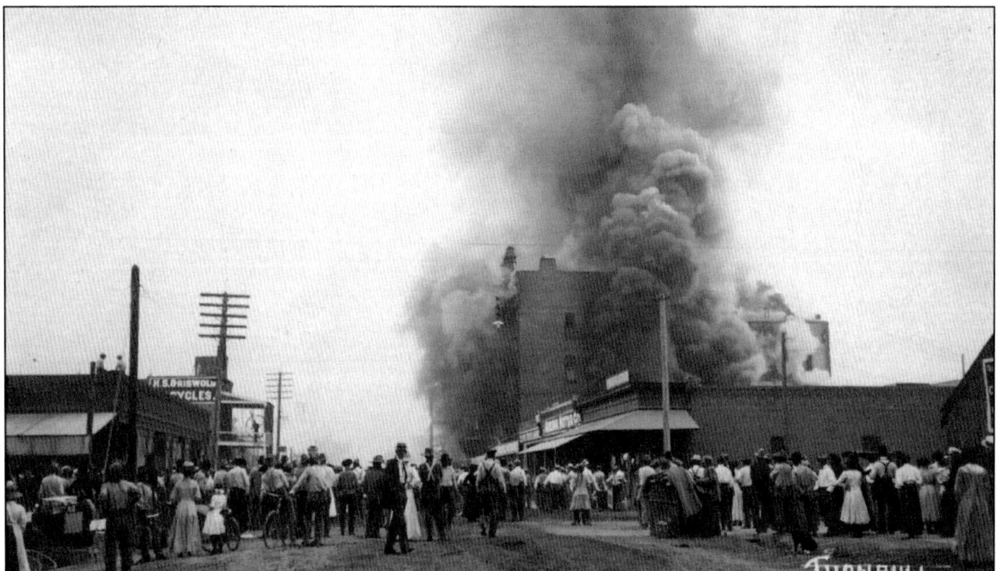

This view north down Center Street shows the crowd watching the Adams Hotel fire in 1910. (Real photographic postcard, Robert A. Trumbull photographer. Collection of the author © vintagephoto.com.)

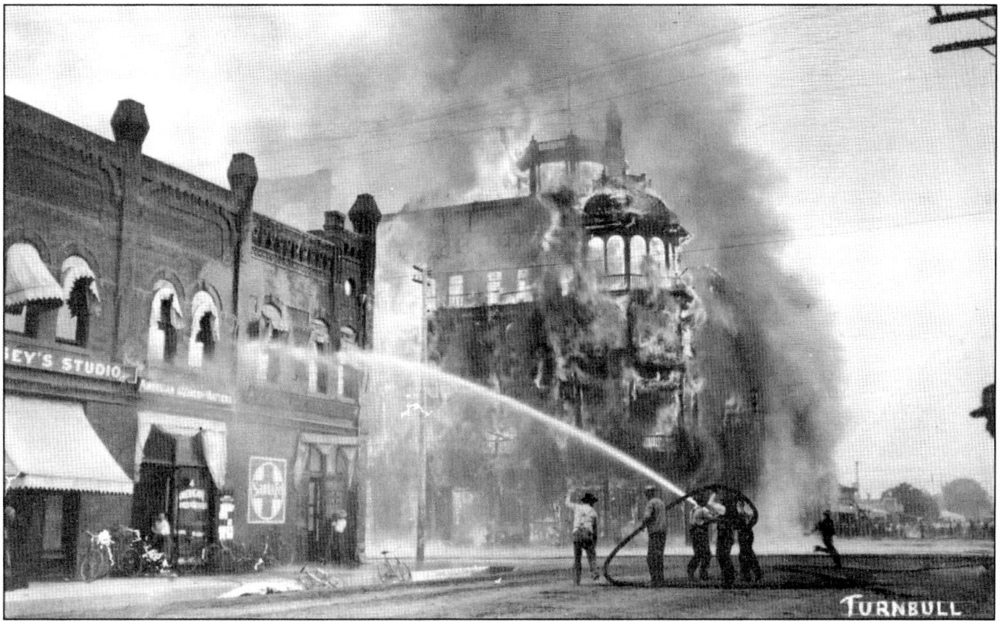

Firemen hose down buildings adjacent to the burning Adams Hotel to try to prevent the fire from spreading throughout downtown Phoenix. (Real photographic postcard, Robert A. Trumbull photographer, c. 1910. Collection of the author © vintagephoto.com.)

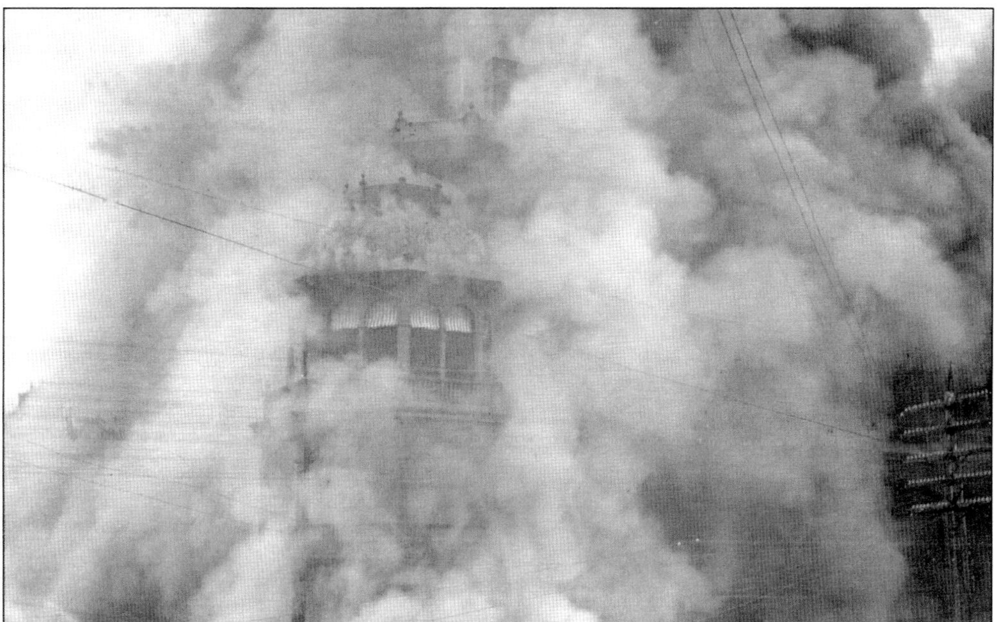

This postcard shows the turret of the Adams Hotel engulfed in smoke as the hotel burned to the ground on May 17, 1910. (Real photographic postcard, photographer unknown. Collection of the author © vintagephoto.com.)

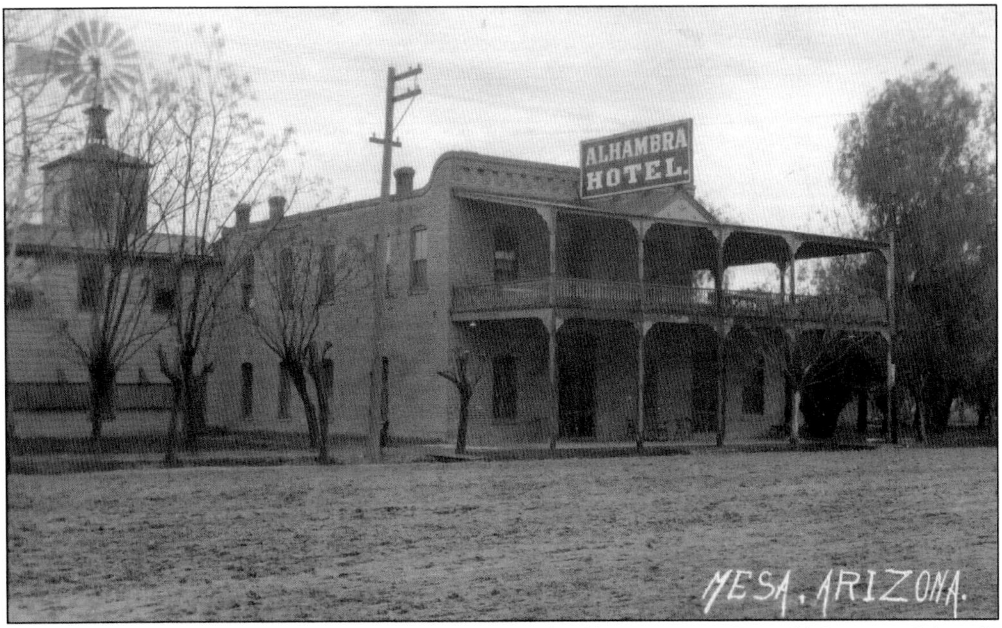

The original Alhambra Hotel was a two-story brick building at 43 McDonald Street in Mesa. It was completed in November 1894 at a cost of $4,000. In 1921, the structure burned and was rebuilt. It was later renamed the Pioneer Hotel. (Real photographic postcard, photographer unknown, c. 1910. Collection of the author © vintagephoto.com.)

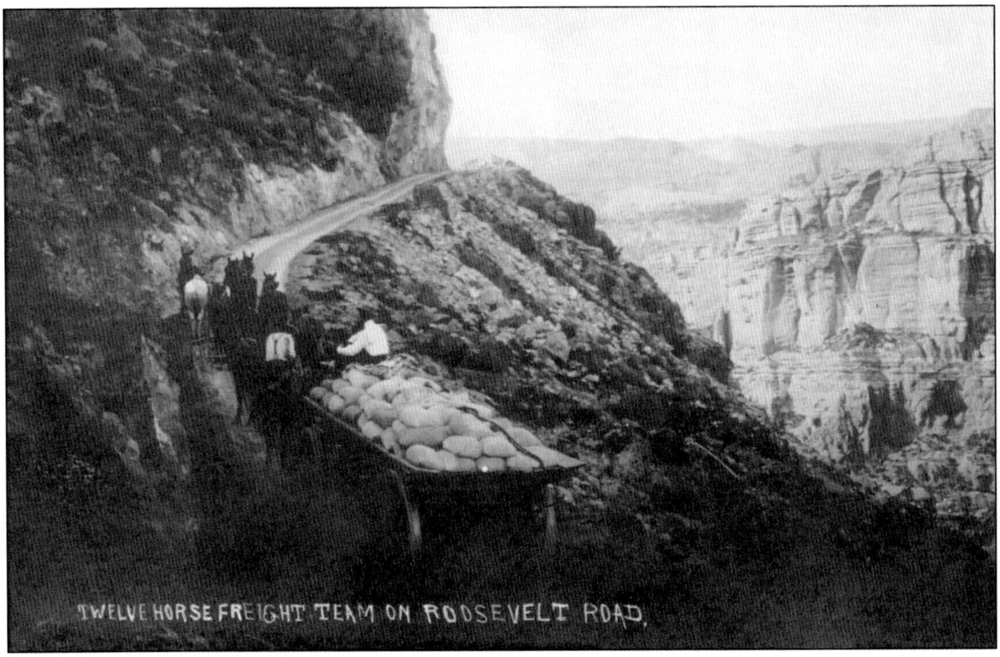

The wagon route from Mesa to the Roosevelt Dam was primitive and torturous. Thousands of wagonloads of cement and equipment had to be hauled along what later became the Apache Trail. (Real photographic postcard, photographer unknown, c. 1908. Collection of the author © vintagephoto.com.)

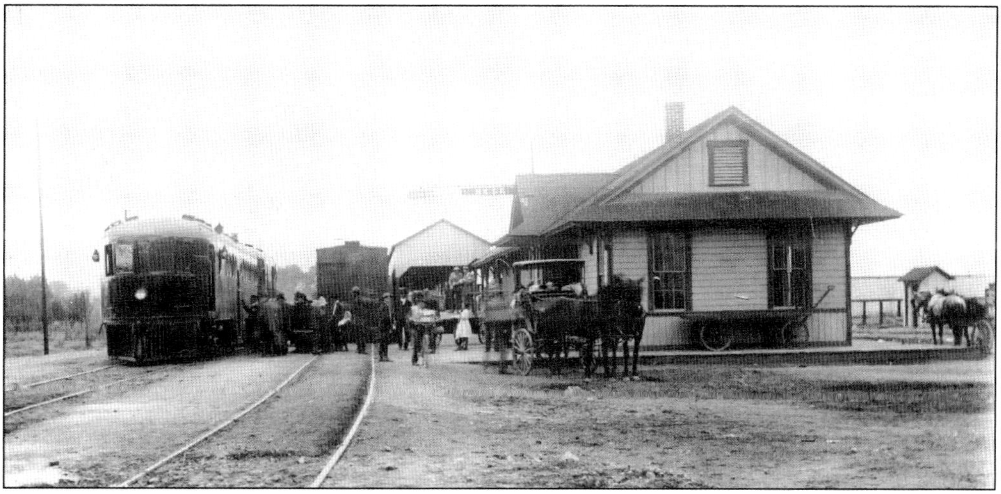

The first railroad arrived in Mesa in 1895, linking the town with Tempe and Phoenix, which had now become only 45 minutes away. The Southside Depot for the Phoenix and Eastern Railroad was built in 1903 between Center and Sirrine on Third Street. (Real photographic postcard, photographer unknown, c. 1910. Collection of the author © vintagephoto.com.)

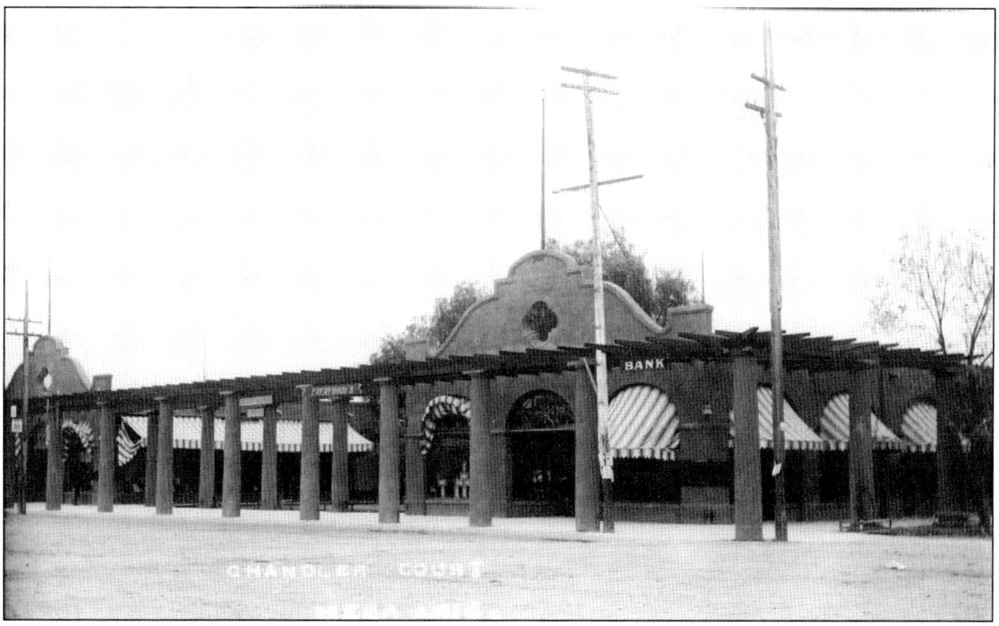

Chandler Court on the northwest corner of Main and MacDonald Streets was the first office complex in Mesa and the first building with evaporative cooling in Arizona. (Real photographic postcard, photographer unknown, c. 1910. Collection of the author © vintagephoto.com.)

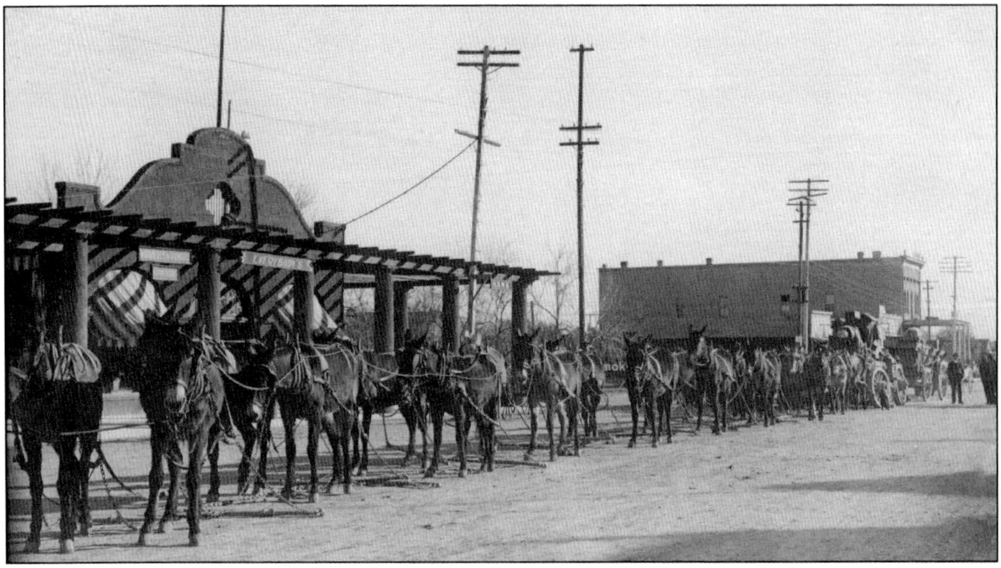

A freight team with rotor for the hydroelectric generators being installed at Roosevelt Dam posed in front of Chandler Court on Main Street in Mesa, February 1910. (Real photo postcard, photographer unknown. Collection of the author © vintagephoto.com.)

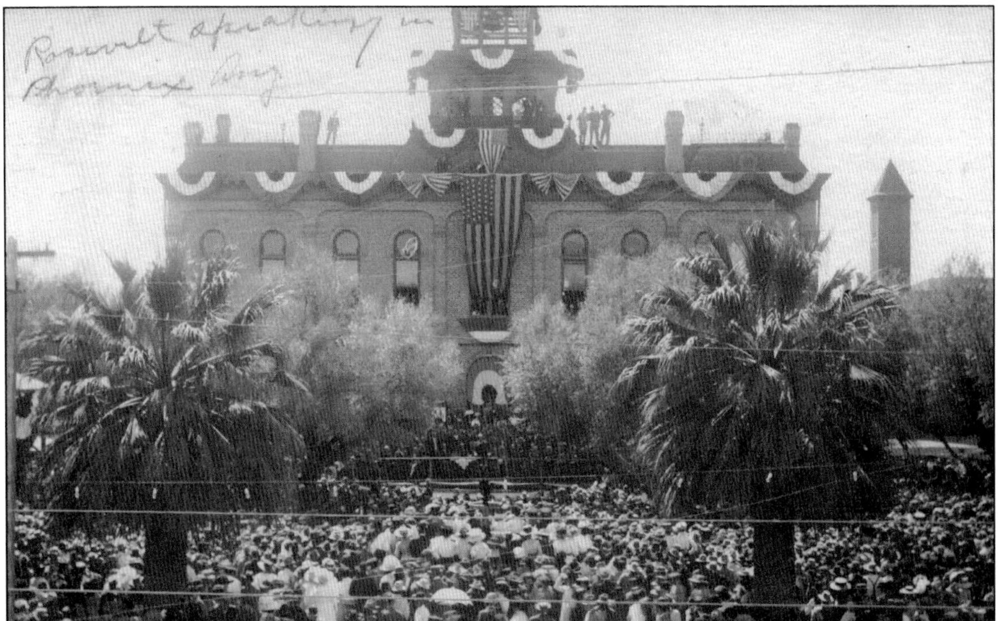

Theodore Roosevelt traveled to Phoenix for the dedication of Roosevelt Dam. The construction of Roosevelt Dam began in 1905 and fueled growth of the East Valley. In particular Mesa, which served as the railhead for supplies for Dam construction saw tremendous impact from the project. The dam was also a major experiment in harnessing hydroelectric power to create electricity. Roosevelt dam was completed just six years later, and was dedicated on March 18, 1911. Pres. Theodore Roosevelt stopped to make speeches in Phoenix and Tempe en route to the Dam dedication. (Real photographic postcard, photographer unknown. Collection of the author © vintagephoto.com.)

Eight

1911–1914

The trolley routes in Phoenix continually expanded as developers added new tracts and the suburbs grew. By 1911, the Phoenix Railway Company operated the Phoenix, Orangewood and Glendale trolley lines, running from: Central Phoenix to the Fairgrounds along Grand Avenue; north on Second and Fifth Avenues; north on Third Street to the Phoenix Indian School then east to Twelfth Street and Fairmont; west on Pierce to Tenth Street then north to Sheridan; and east along Washington to a loop at Sixteenth Street. Trolley tickets ranged from 25¢ to Orangewood to 50¢ to Glendale.

For decades, travelers crossing Maricopa County had only a few options to cross the Salt River. The River divided the County and the city of Phoenix and flowed much of the year, and early travelers went to Tempe to cross at Hayden's Ferry. Railroad bridges provided another crossing option, but casual travel was not easy until 1911, when the Center Street Bridge was built across the Salt River. The Center Street Bridge supported pedestrian and carriage traffic across the river.

Another bridge across the Salt River began construction in 1911. A side street just west of the Mill Avenue in Tempe was chosen as the best location for a bridge in the East Valley. The site provided bedrock for bridge piers, and was one of the narrowest crossings of the river. The Territorial Control Board approved the Ash Avenue Bridge using a repeating arch design.

Prison reformer and Gov. George W. P. Hunt directed that prisoners from the Territorial Prison build the bridge. To soothe Tempe residents' concerns, Hunt promised to resign if any prisoners escaped. Though 15 prisoners tried to escape, all were quickly recaptured and Hunt avoided having to live up to his promise. The Ash and Center Street bridges quickly became popular, and soon carried automobile and truck traffic across Maricopa County.

On May 17, 1912, Dr. Alexander John Chandler began selling lots in his planned community. Chandler came to Arizona as the territory's first veterinary surgeon, then became a pioneer in developing irrigation systems, and eventually controlled over 18,000 acres as one of the valley's largest landowners. Chandler's vision for his community included a hotel and park lined by businesses to create a central town square. The Hotel San Marcos, complete just a year and a half later, further boosted the growth of Chandler.

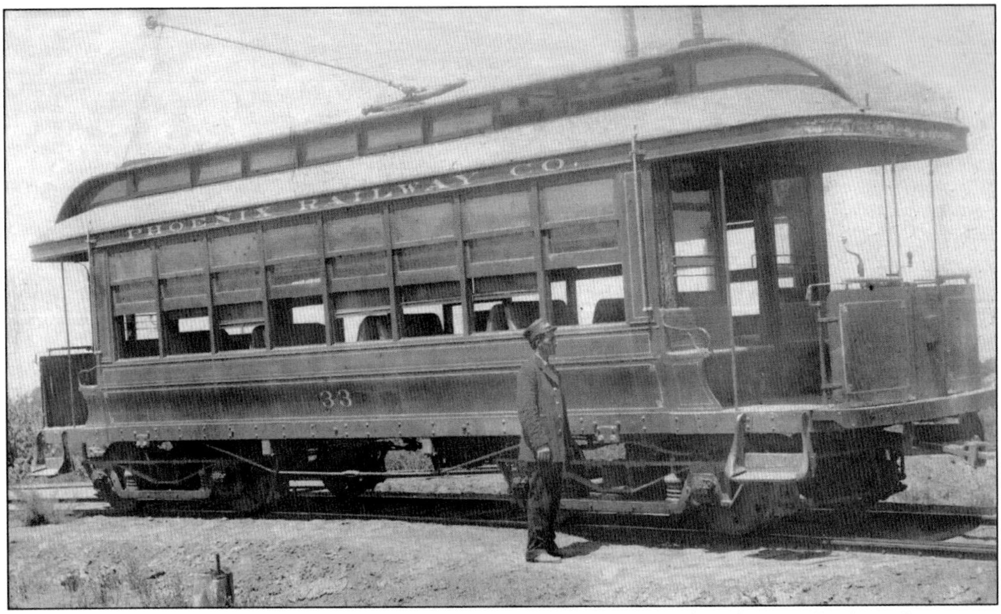

Phoenix streetcars were electrified in September 1893, and by 1911 the Phoenix Railway Company operated the Phoenix, Orangewood, and Glendale lines. Tickets ranged from 25¢ to Orangewood to 50¢ to Glendale. Car 33 was brought to Phoenix from Los Angeles in 1911 and seated 40. The trolley car is pictured near Fairmont and Third Street. (Real photographic postcard, photographer unknown, *c.* 1913. Collection of the author © vintagephoto.com.)

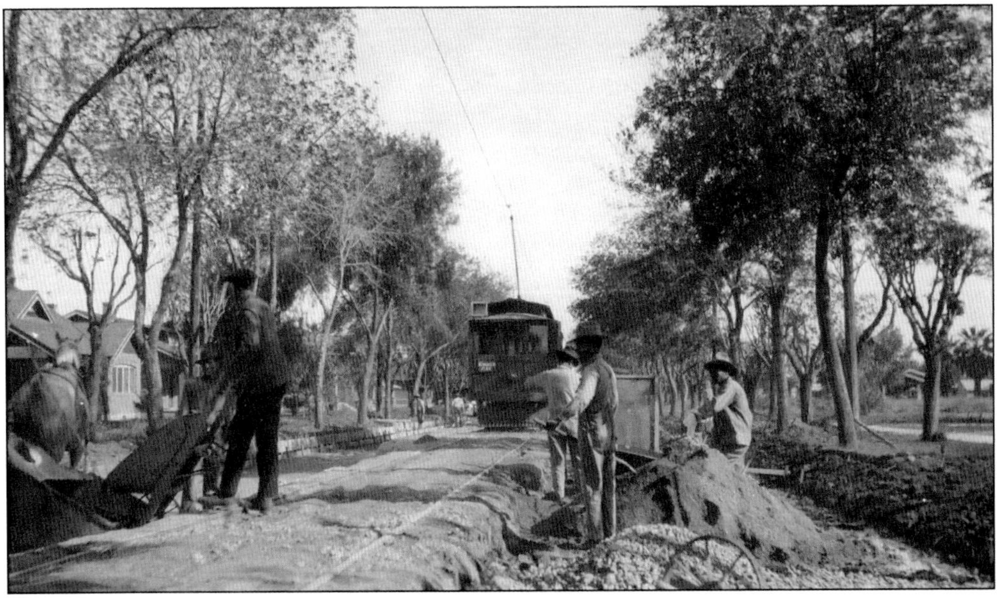

As the city limits of Phoenix grew and suburban towns developed, the Phoenix Street Railway continued to grow. The streetcars carried crews and materials as the construction extended the rail lines. (Silver print, photographer unknown, *c.* 1915. Collection of the author © vintagephoto.com.)

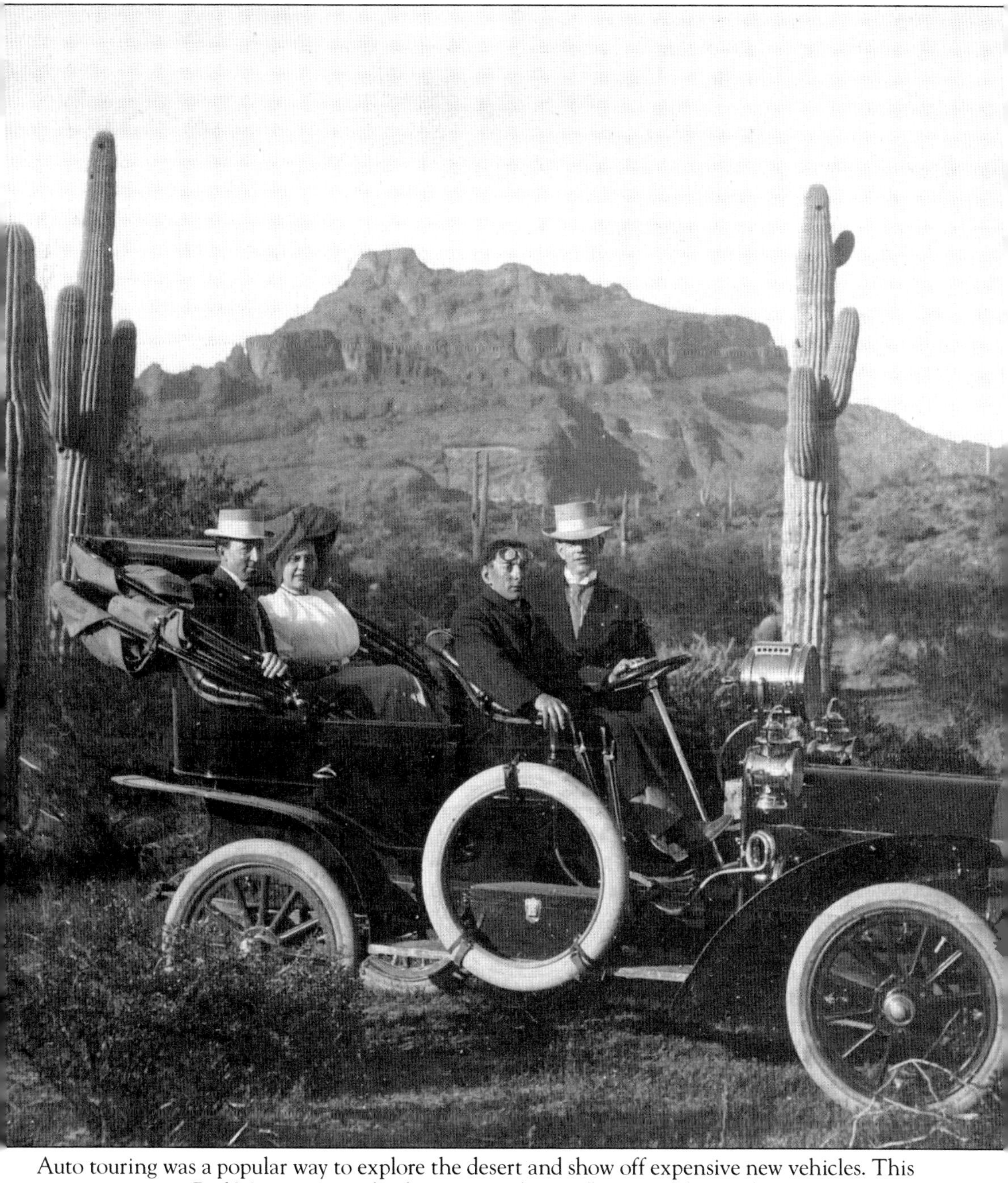

Auto touring was a popular way to explore the desert and show off expensive new vehicles. This group poses near Red Mountain north of Mesa near the confluence of the Verde and Salt Rivers. Someone in this view was a photographer who sent this amateur stereograph in for a critique. On the reverse it states that it is well composed, but a bit too posed. (Stereograph, photographer unknown, c. 1912. Collection of the author © vintagephoto.com.)

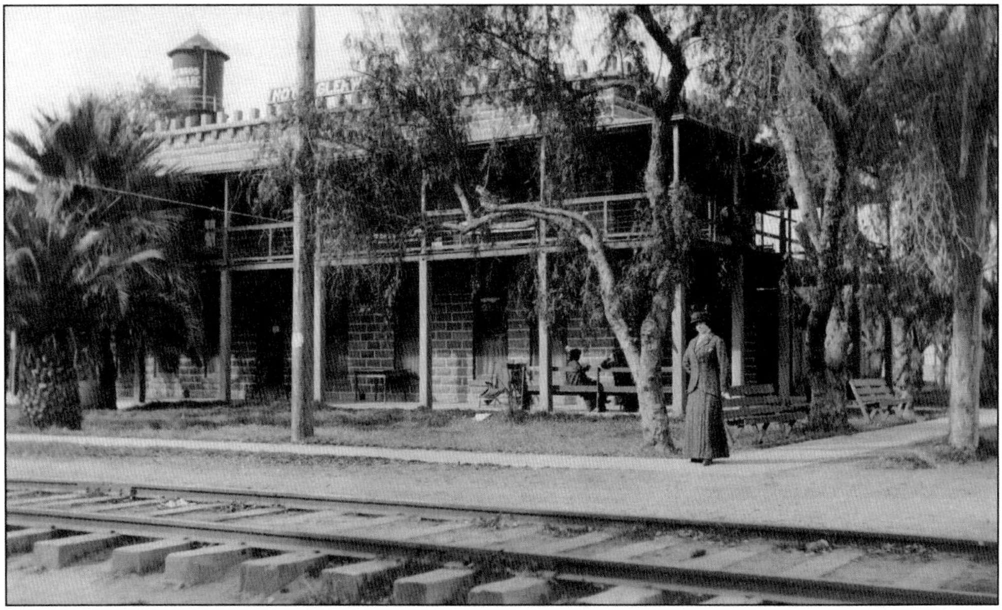

The Hotel Glenwood was one block north of the Santa Fe Depot in Glendale, at the terminus of the Glendale interurban trolley car line from Phoenix. A. W. Bennett, the proprietor, real estate dealer, and mayor of Glendale, offered American and European plans and "white cooks (and) all outside rooms with verandas." (Real photographic postcard, photographer unknown, c. 1912. Collection of the author © vintagephoto.com.)

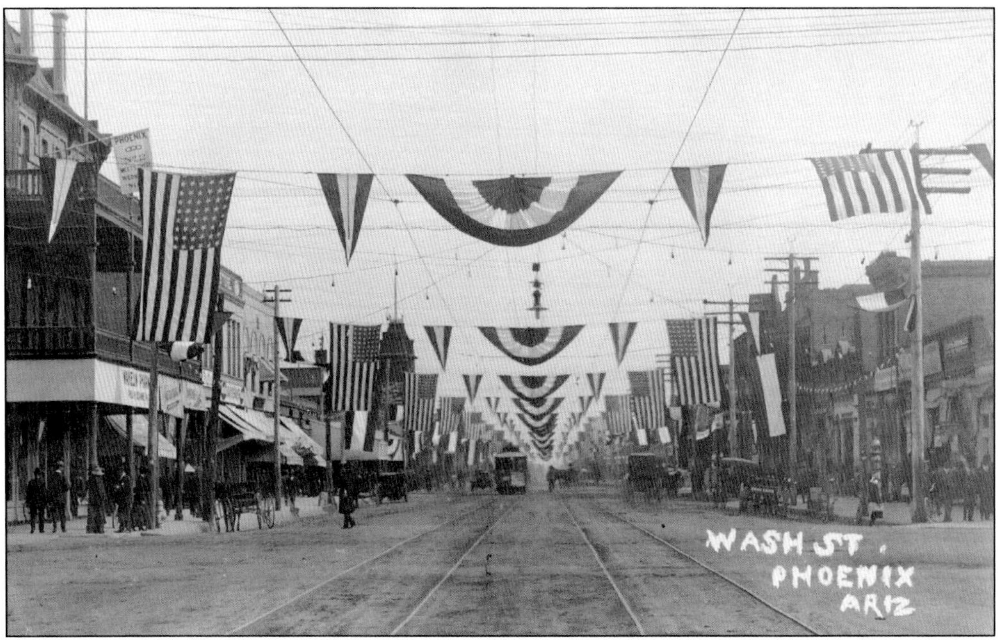

Pictured here is the Phoenix Railway Company line on Washington Street, likely decorated for an Independence Day celebration. (Real photographic postcard, photographer unknown, c. 1911. Collection of the author © vintagephoto.com.)

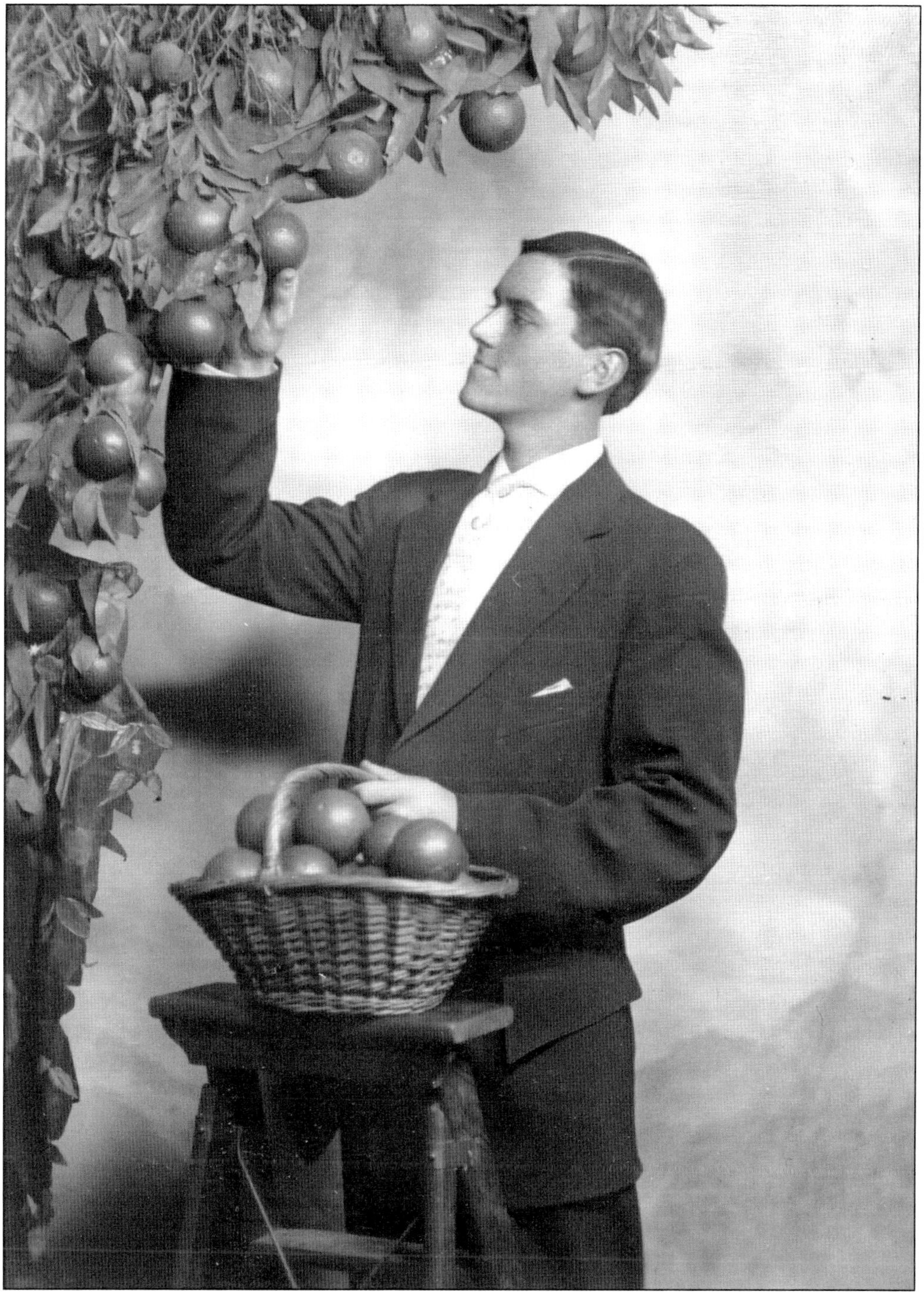

Citrus was ideally suited to the irrigated fields and climate of the Salt River Valley and quickly became a significant crop. Later Arizona became noted for the 4 Cs—cattle, copper, climate, and citrus. (Real photographic postcard, photographer unknown, *c.* 1910. Collection of the author © vintagephoto.com.)

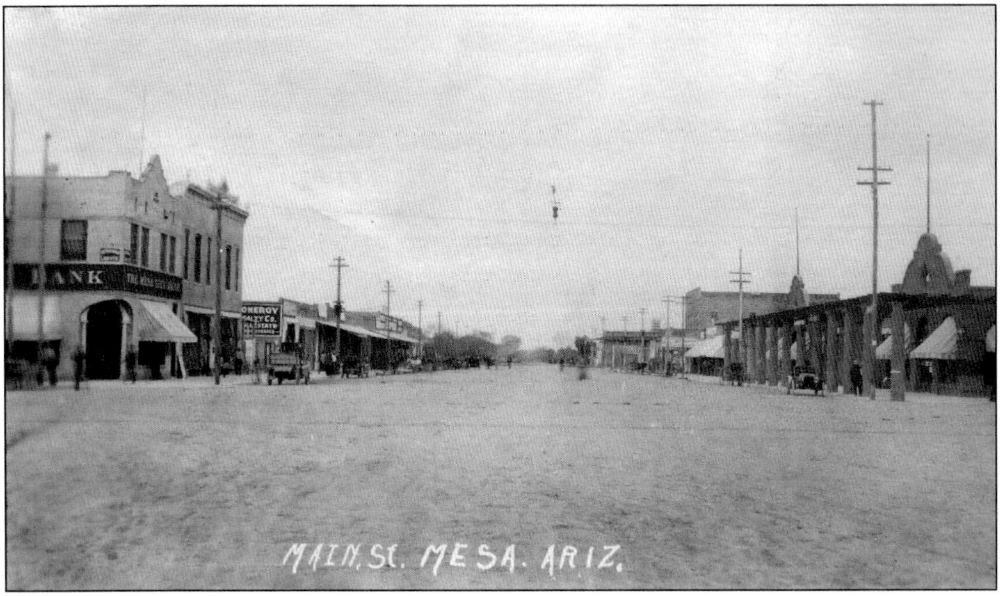

Looking west up Main Street in downtown Mesa from McDonald Street, Chandler Court is on the right. Like most valley cities, even the main streets were unpaved. (Real photographic postcard, photographer unknown. c. 1911. Collection of the author © vintagephoto.com.)

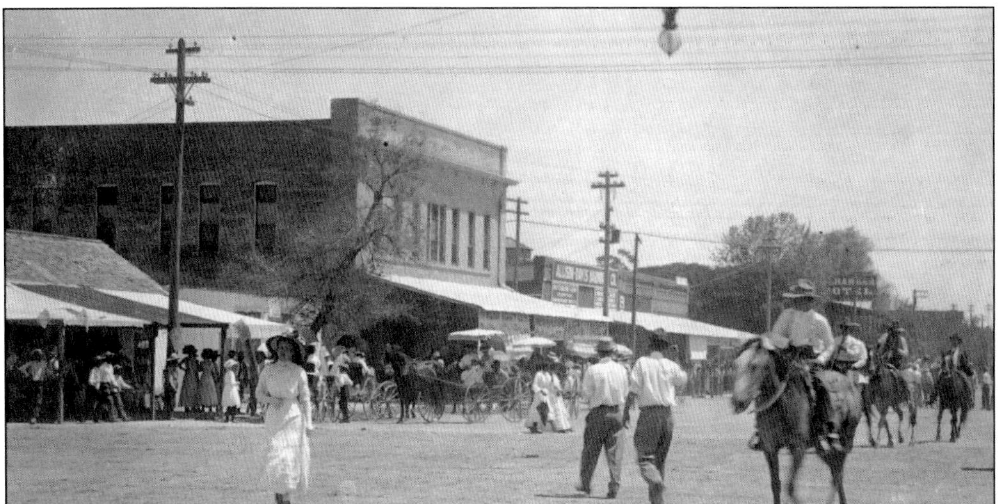

One of the landmark buildings in downtown Mesa was the Le Sueur-Gibbons building that catered to the construction of Roosevelt Dam. Built on the site of the Zeno Cooperative Mercantile on the southwest corner of Main and Macdonald Streets. It is visible at the rear of this busy summer scene in downtown Mesa. (Real photographic postcard, c. 1912. Collection of the author © vintagephoto.com.)

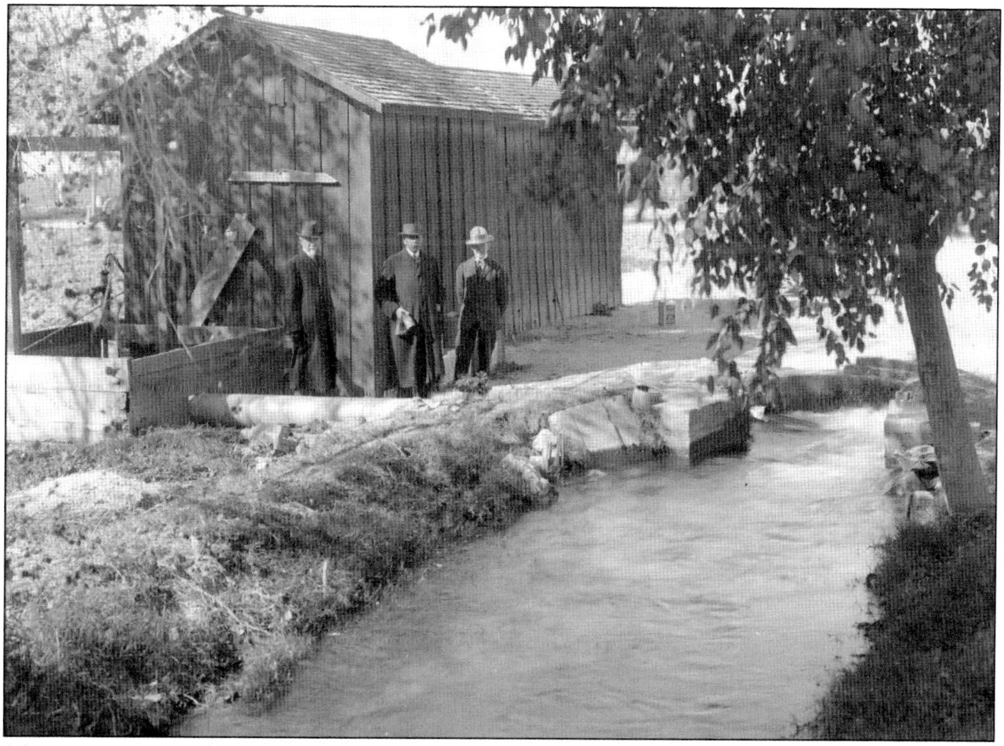

Like most early canals in the Salt River Valley, the Mesa Canal evolved from the historic Hohokam irrigation system. Begun soon after the arrival of Mormon pioneers in 1878, the canal fostered the development of agriculture in the area including some of the finest early vineyards in the Territory. (Silver print, photographer unknown, c. 1914. Collection of the author © vintagephoto.com.)

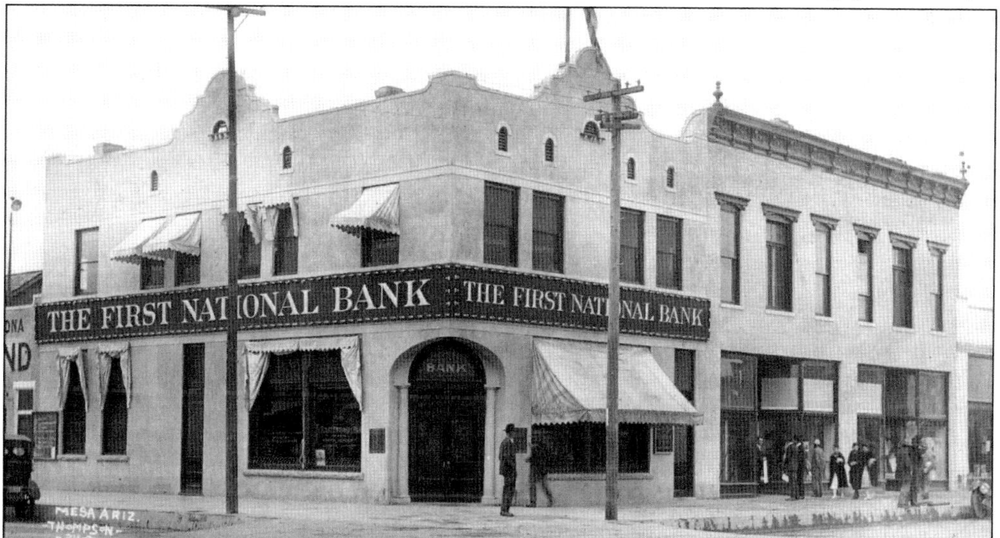

The Mesa City Bank was founded at the corner of Main and McDonald Streets in 1893 by Dr. E. W. Wilbur and C. F. Crouse and became the First National Bank in 1918. The bank was key to development of Mesa and the Eastern Salt River Valley. (Real photographic postcard, Thompson photographer. Collection of the author © vintagephoto.com.)

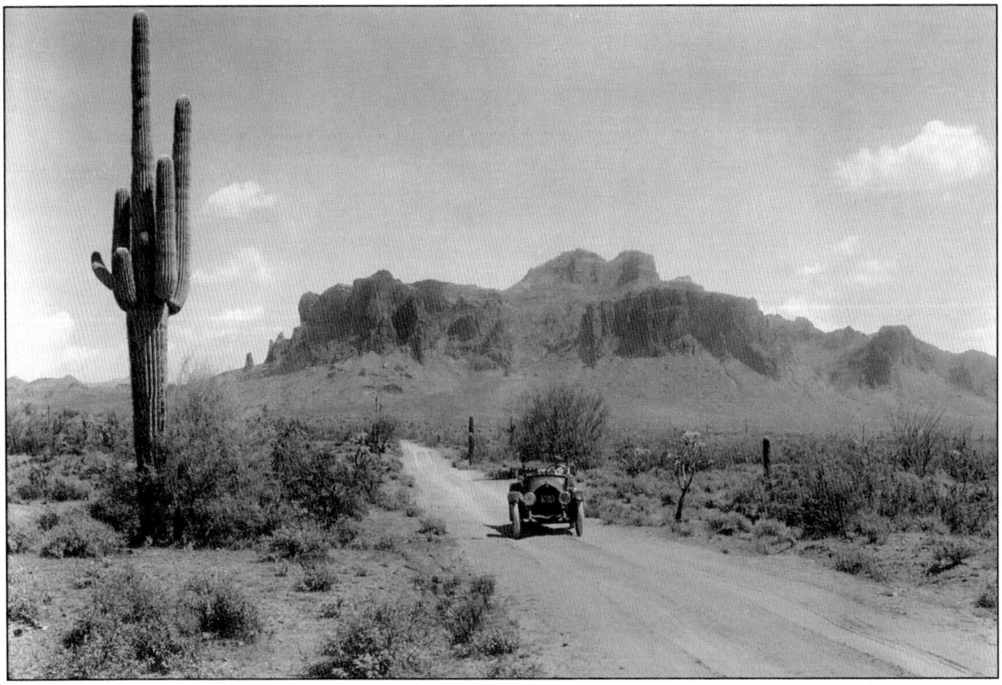

The Arizona National Reserve Route, or Apache Trail, became a popular automobile excursion. Here a driver poses by a Saguaro cactus on the east side of the Superstition Mountains near Apache Junction. (Hand colored silver print, photographer unknown, c. 1918. Collection of the author © vintagephoto.com.)

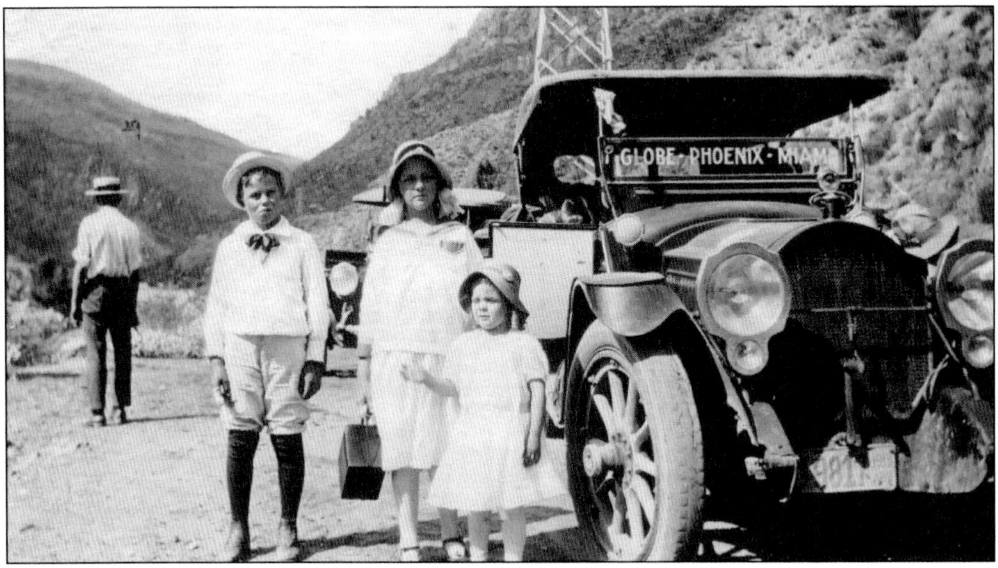

Santa Fe contracted with the Globe-Phoenix stage line to take an eight-hour trip along the Arizona National Reserve Route. Travelers stayed in the Dominion Hotel in Globe then drove to the Apache Lodge at Roosevelt Dam for lunch, then to Fish Creek Station, and on through Tempe to Phoenix, where they boarded a Pullman car to take them on to Los Angeles. (Silver print, photographer unknown, c. 1915. Collection of the author © vintagephoto.com.)

Nine

1914–1918

The construction road to Roosevelt Dam became the popular Arizona National Reserve Route, and later became known as the Apache Trail. The Trail was primitive and automobile travel was slow. A natural water source, Fish Creek had been discovered by the King Woolsey expedition through the Superstition Mountains in 1864, and became a stop en route between Mesa and Roosevelt Dam during its construction. As traffic increased after completion of the dam, Fish Creek Station provided a popular stop to gas up and repair autos.

Cotton had been a minor crop in Arizona since Tempe farmer Felix Harwick won a $500 prize for growing the first commercial bale in Maricopa County in 1883. Cotton's importance grew dramatically in 1912, as about 150 acres of long staple Pima Cotton were planted as an experiment. Pima cotton produced a staple length of 1 1/3 inches and was touted as the toughest cotton available. The long fibers produced the strong thread and fabrics needed by the rapidly growing market for automobile and truck tires.

Arizona soon became a major supplier of Pima cotton. Three thousand acres of cotton were planted in 1914. In the East Valley, the Tempe Cotton Exchange brought in a ten-stand roller gin to process local cotton. Cotton prices dropped that year and so did plantings, to only about 2,000 acres. The cotton market recovered and 7,400 acres of cotton were planted in 1916. This grew to 72,000 acres in 1918, and reached 190,000 acres by 1920. Like most booms, the cotton craze soon peaked, then the bubble burst when cotton prices dropped dramatically in 1920.

The importance of canals and irrigation to Maricopa County residents led to a further consolidation of water resources in 1917. The Salt River Valley Water Users' Association gained control of the Roosevelt Dam, Granite Reef Dam, and the canals, laterals and ditches that constituted the Salt River Project. The canal system included the Arizona, old and new Crosscut, Eastern, Grand, South, Tempe, and Western canals.

The focus of armed conflict shifted from Pancho Villa and the Mexican Revolution along Arizona's southern border to Europe and World War I. The year 1918 saw the end of the war. The resulting drop in demand for copper and reduction from record prices of 37¢ a pound rippled through the Arizona economy. The impact was strongest in Arizona's mining communities, but Maricopa County also felt the impact of the postwar recession.

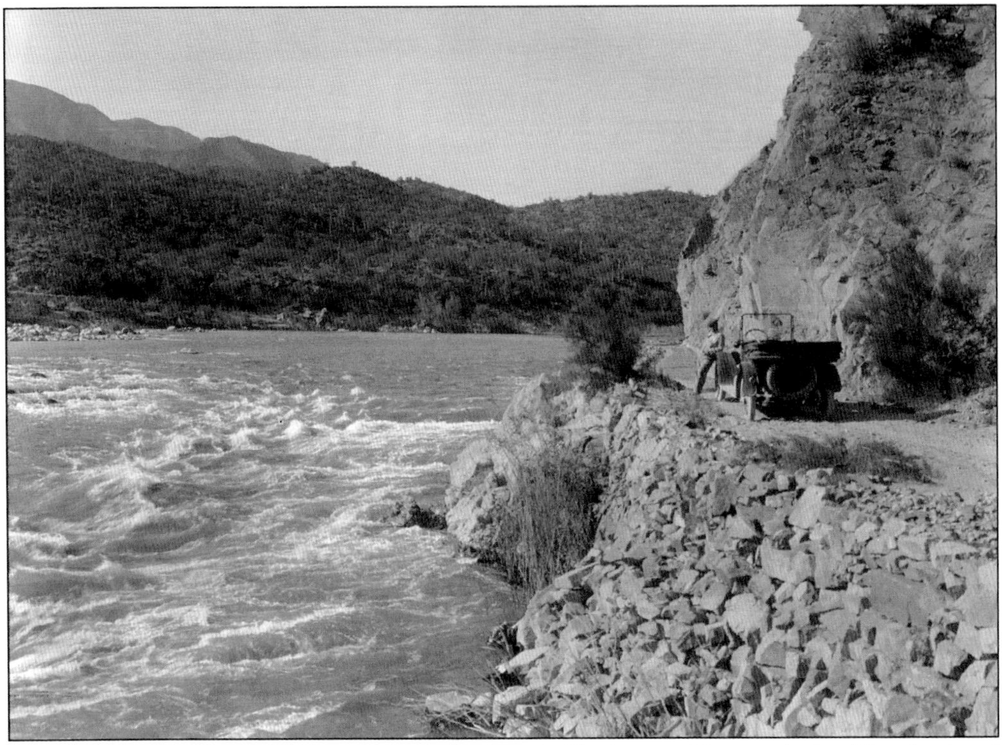

A contemplative moment captured along the Apache Trail east of Canyon Lake. (Hand colored silver print, photographer unknown, *c.* 1918. Collection of the author © vintagephoto.com.)

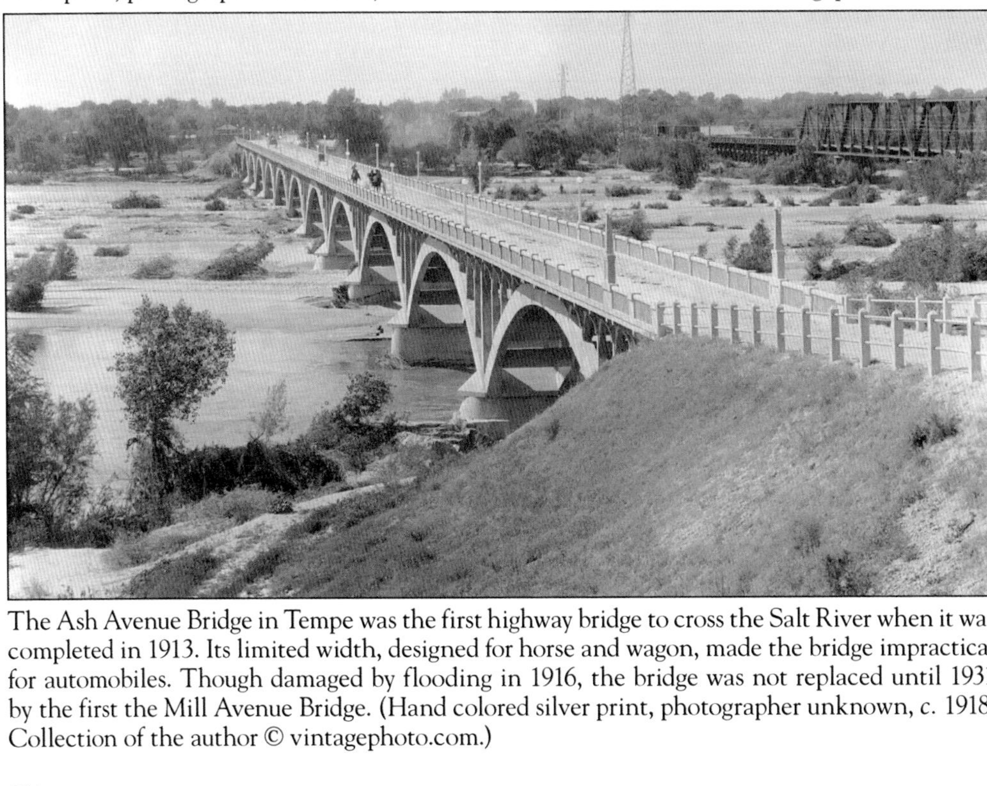

The Ash Avenue Bridge in Tempe was the first highway bridge to cross the Salt River when it was completed in 1913. Its limited width, designed for horse and wagon, made the bridge impractical for automobiles. Though damaged by flooding in 1916, the bridge was not replaced until 1931 by the first the Mill Avenue Bridge. (Hand colored silver print, photographer unknown, *c.* 1918. Collection of the author © vintagephoto.com.)

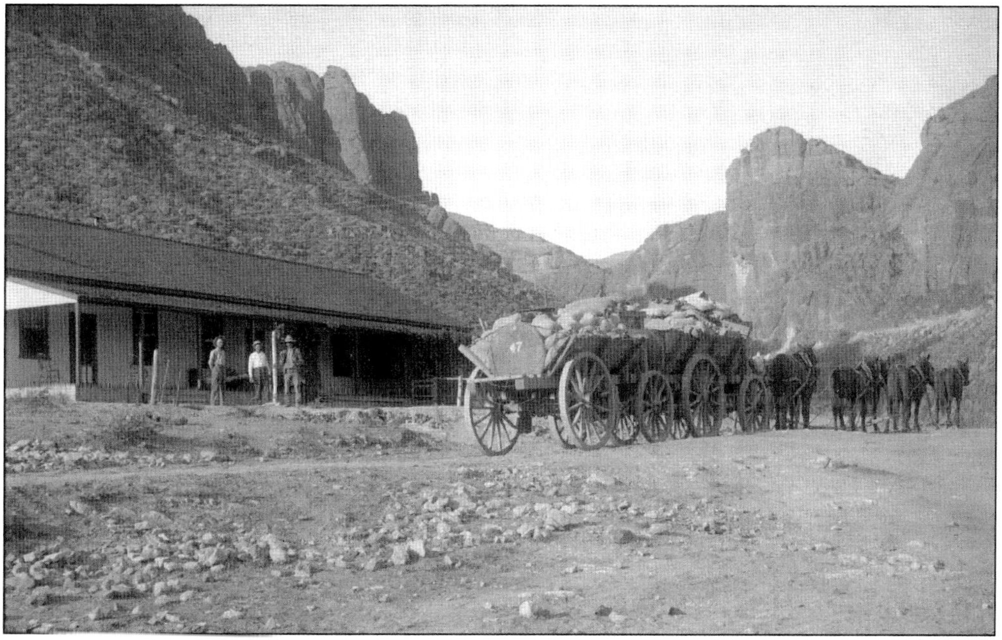

A heavily laden freight wagon train bound for the Roosevelt Dam construction site stopped at Fish Creek Station. (Silver print, photographer unknown, *c.* 1910. Collection of the author © vintagephoto.com.)

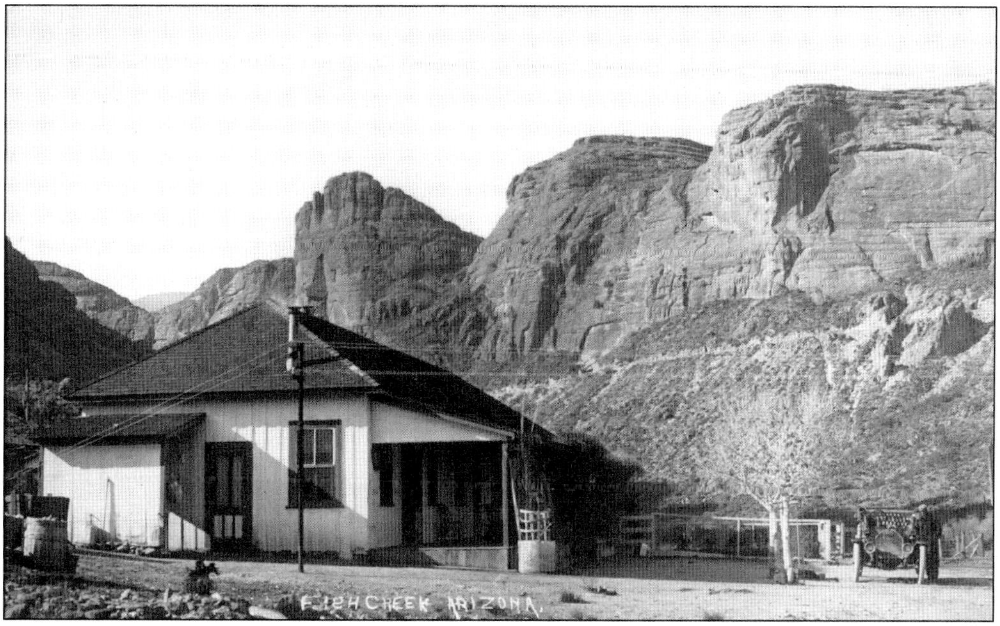

After construction of Roosevelt Dam, the Arizona National Reserve Route was used for automobile excursions and saw regular motor coach travel between Phoenix and Globe. Fish Creek Station provided gasoline and a stopping point along the route in the middle of the Superstition Mountains. (Real photographic postcard, photographer unknown, *c.* 1915. Collection of the author © vintagephoto.com.)

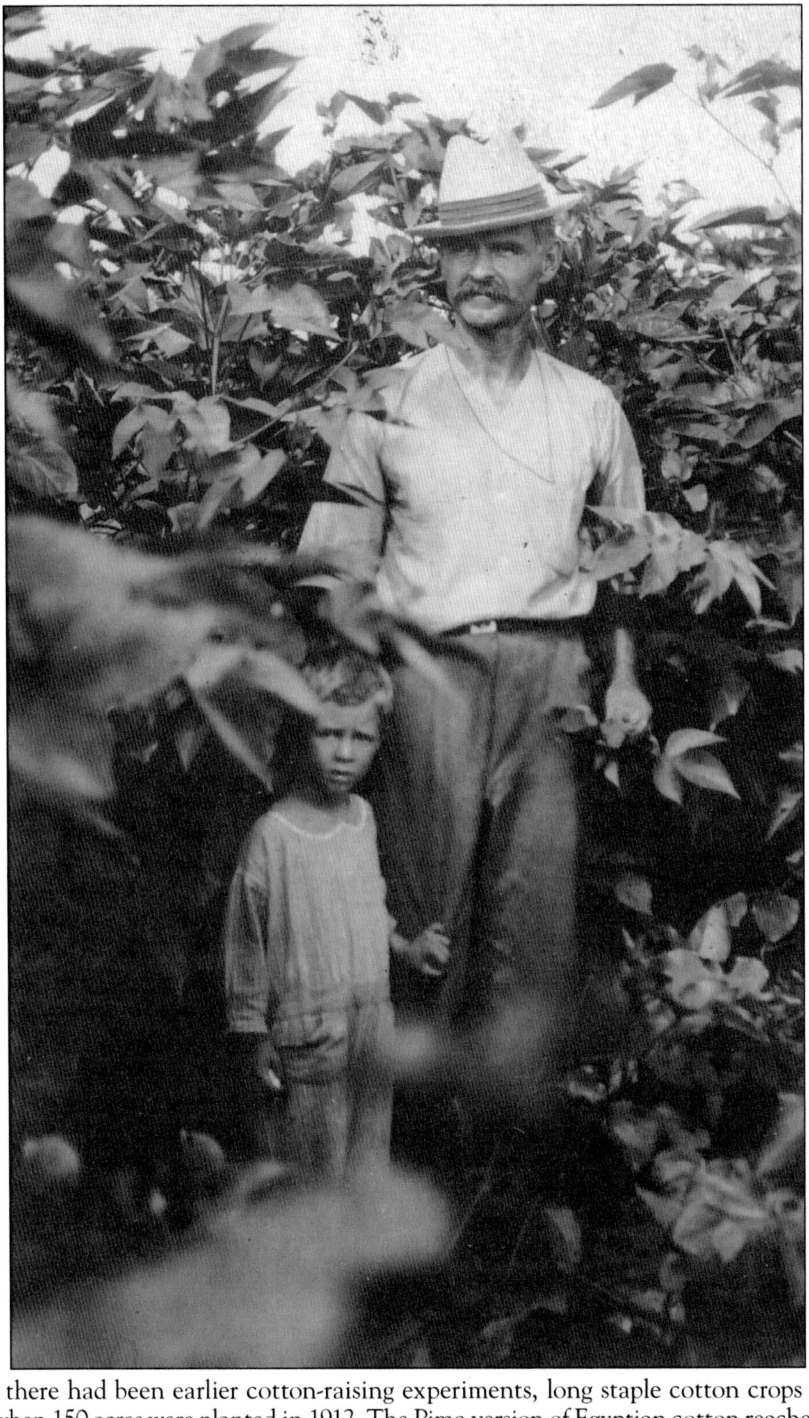

Though there had been earlier cotton-raising experiments, long staple cotton crops began in earnest when 150 acres were planted in 1912. The Pima version of Egyptian cotton reached a staple length of 1 1/3 inches and was the toughest and produced the best automobile tire thread and fabric in the world. By 1916, 7,400 acres of cotton were planted, and then grew to 72,000 in 1918, and 190,000 by 1920. The cotton boom burst when prices dropped in 1920. (Real photographic postcard, photographer unknown, *c.* 1918. Collection of the author © vintagephoto.com.)

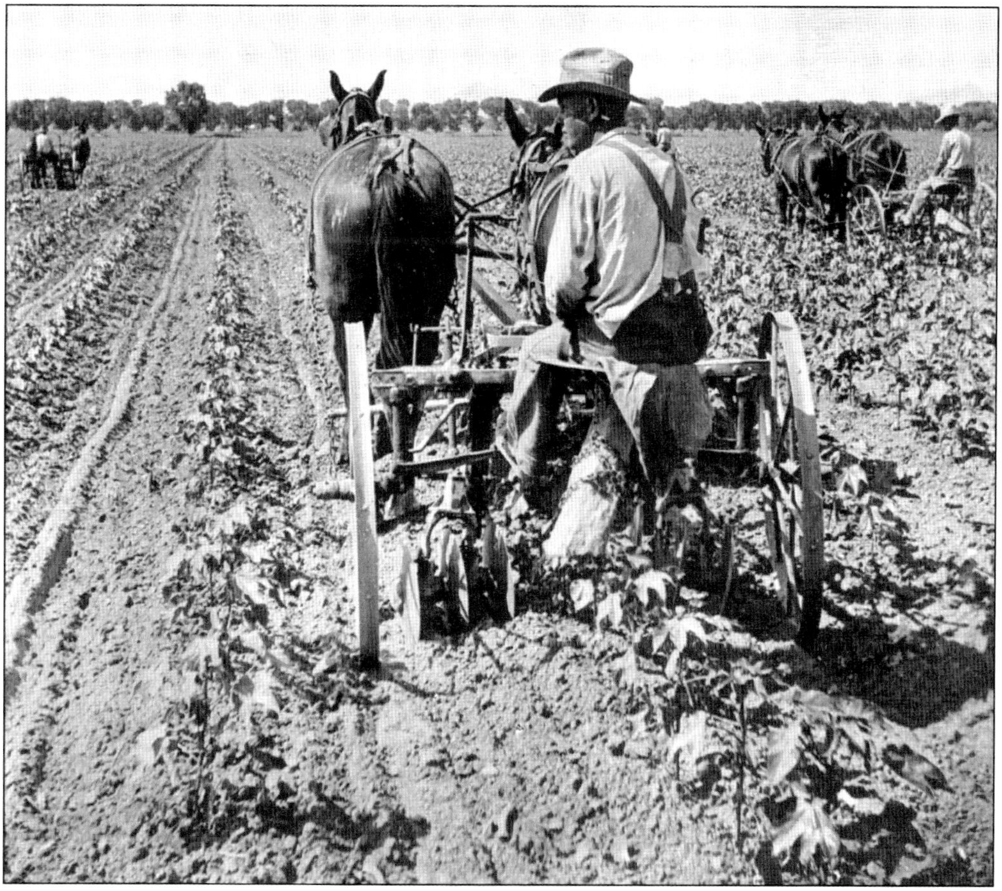

This unidentified cotton farmer uses a horse-drawn plough on a farm near Phoenix. (Stereograph, Keystone View Company publisher *c.* 1915. Collection of the author © vintagephoto.com.)

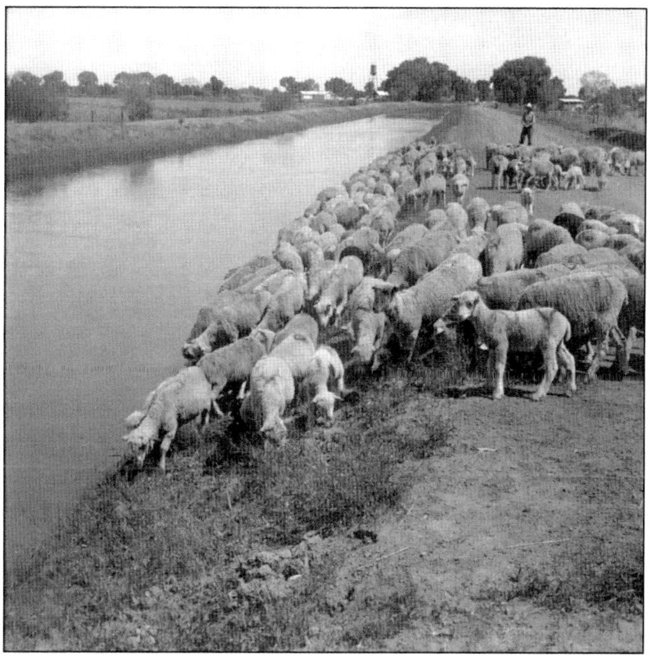

Sheepherders took their flocks to cooler high country for the summers but returned to the Salt River Valley in the fall. This flock is pictured along a canal near Tempe. (Stereograph, Keystone View Company publisher *c.* 1915. Collection of the author © vintagephoto.com.)

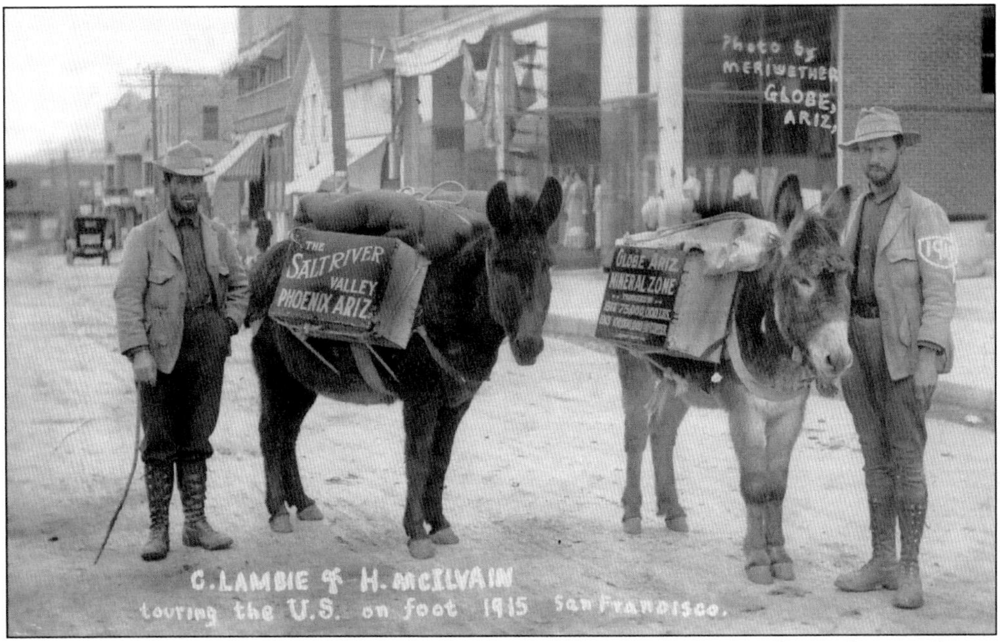

Cross-country walking became a craze early in the 20th century. C. Lambie and H. McIlvain, photographed in Globe en route to San Francisco, have added advertising, including a promotion for Phoenix and the Salt River Valley to their packs. (Real photographic postcard, Henry B. Merriweather photographer, c. 1915. Collection of the author © vintagephoto.com.)

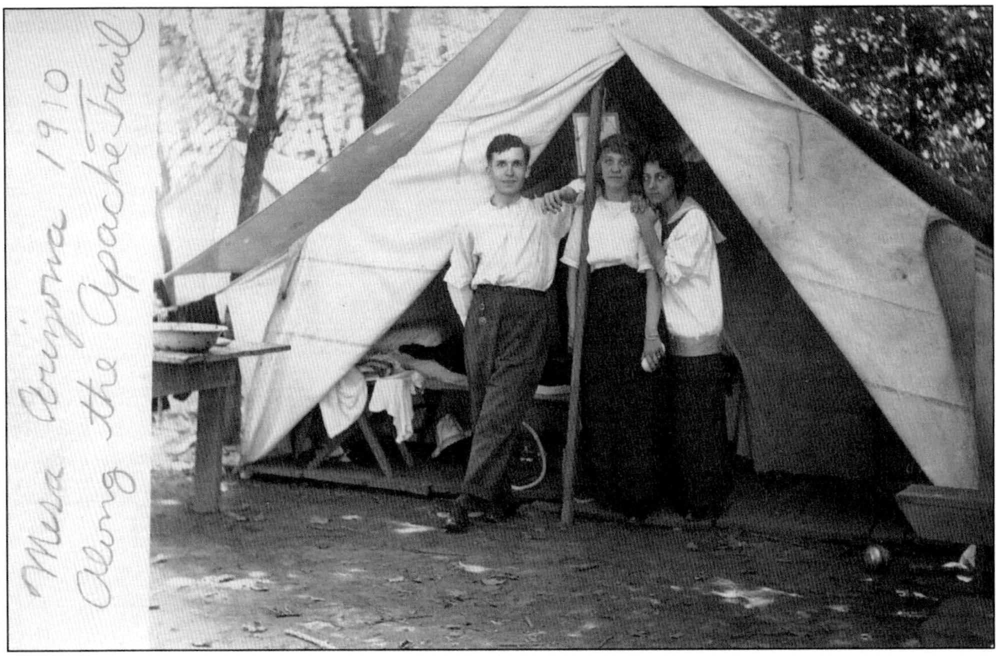

The mild spring and fall climate made camping a popular leisure activity. Young campers pose with their well-outfitted tent along route between Mesa and Roosevelt Lake. (Real photographic postcard, photographer unknown, c. 1910. Collection of the author © vintagephoto.com.)

Ten

1918–1920

Maricopa County continued its explosive growth. In the Eastern Salt River Valley, Chandler grew rapidly since it's founding in 1912. By 1919, Chandler included two banks, two lumber yards, five dry goods stores, one bakery, two hardware stores, three cotton gins, five restaurants, four hotels, two drugstores, three blacksmiths shops, a $25,000 motion picture theater (the Majestic), five churches, and its schools enrolled over 600 students and employed 24 teachers.

In a 1919 commercial history of Arizona, Arizona's first Republican governor, Thomas E. Campbell, focused on the central role that Maricopa County played in the Arizona economy. Campbell referred to Maricopa County as an "Inland Empire" and summarized Phoenix history since 1875: "Phoenix was a small collection of adobe huts [in 1875]. It is now [in 1919] a city of 40,000 with 93 miles of streets (20 miles paved), 80 miles of water mains, 357 fire hydrants, 5,798 water services for dwellings (457 installed the past year), 72 miles of sanitary sewers. Hospitals are "high class and the physicians resident are of a class not usually found in cities five times the population."

Campbell noted that mail routes around Phoenix were 135 miles long. Strong commitment to infrastructure investment was demonstrated by approval of $4 million bonds to pave 250 miles of Maricopa County roads.

Describing the importance of the water and electric power provided by the Roosevelt Dam, Campbell states, "Here water is actually consumed. It is taken by canals to thirsty acres that drink it up to the last drop, that more food and clothing may be furnished to mankind. . . . There will come a time when every farm house in Salt River Valley will be lighted and every barn's machinery operated by electricity."

Also included is a somewhat ironic statement compared with the political climate in Arizona today. Campbell proudly summarized the impact transplants to Arizona had in creating an environment that demonstrated their strong family and cultural values. Campbell highlighted efforts he felt would continue to draw tourists and new citizens, and provide an environment conducive to continued business investment in Maricopa County and the state: "They [these new citizens of Arizona] represent the better element of their former home sections. They abolished gambling and voted to complete prohibition rather earlier than elsewhere, and still earlier suppressed 'gun-toting.' They established schools everywhere and the state's educational advantages are now second to none."

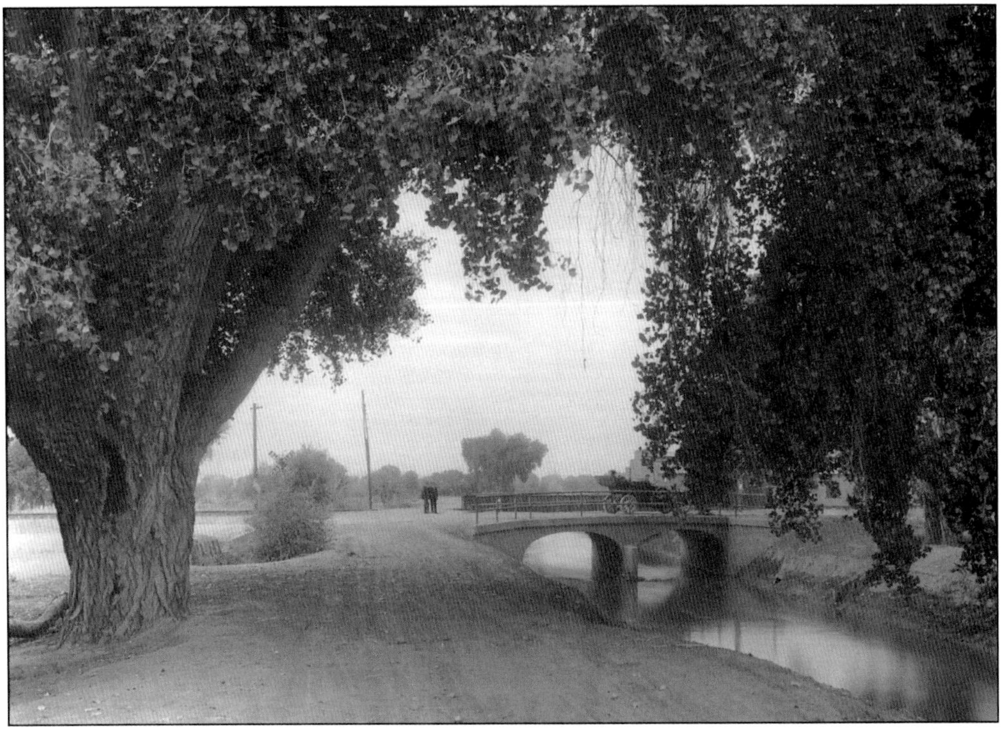

The Crosscut Canal on the north side of the Ash Bridge in Tempe was considered the end point of the Arizona National Reserve Route or Apache Trail. (Hand colored silver print, photographer unknown, *c.* 1918. Collection of the author © vintagephoto.com.)

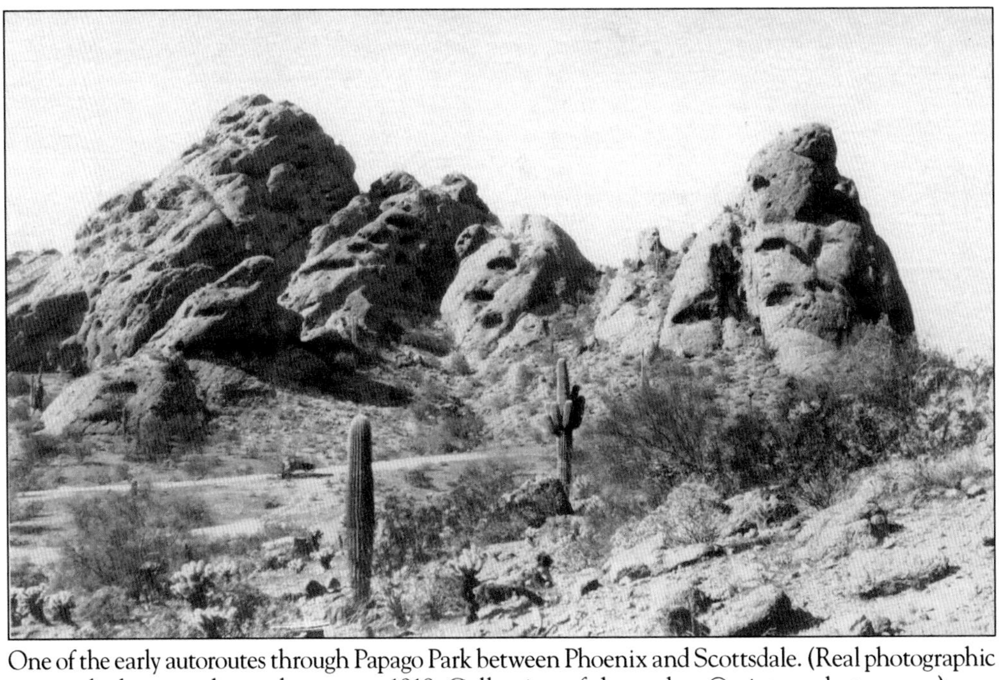

One of the early autoroutes through Papago Park between Phoenix and Scottsdale. (Real photographic postcard, photographer unknown, *c.* 1918. Collection of the author © vintagephoto.com.)

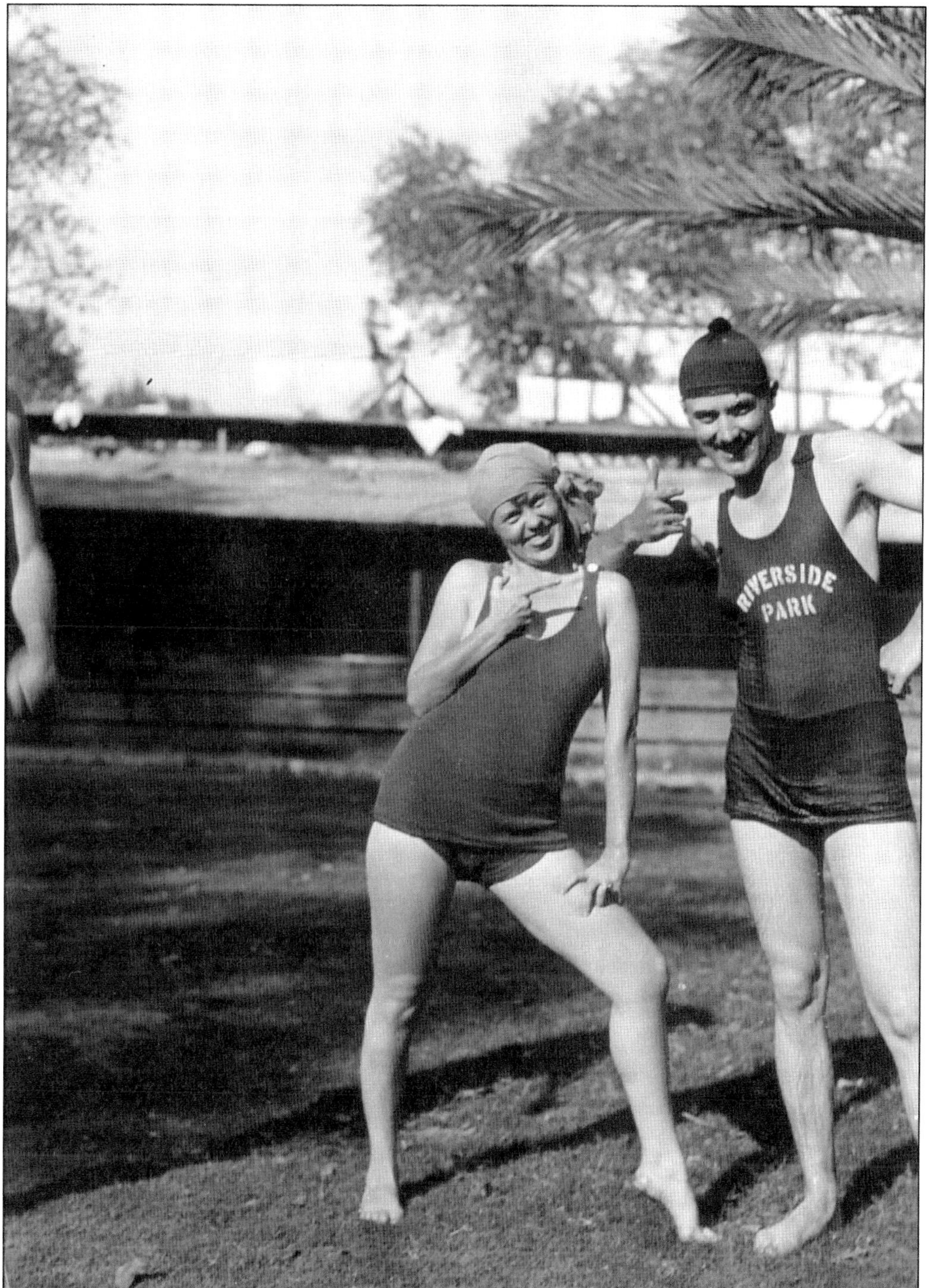

Riverside Park was on the banks of the Salt River near Central Avenue. It was a popular summer recreation site with swimming and an outdoor stadium. The park became the initial home of Spring Training for the Detroit Tigers in 1929. This lifeguard poses with a female patron at Riverside Park c. 1920. (Silver print, photographer unknown. Collection of the author © vintagephoto.com.)

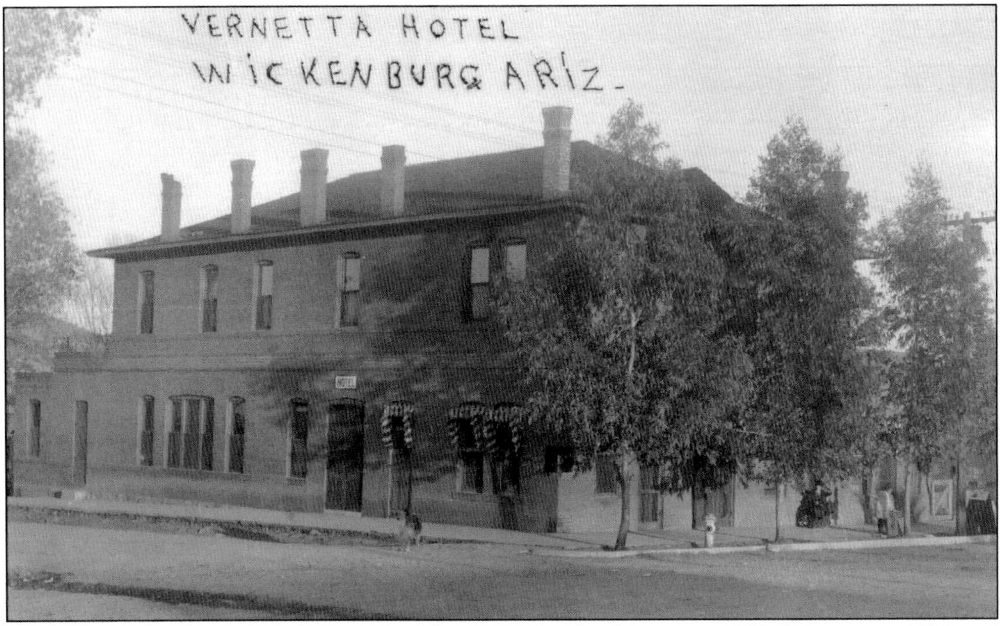

William and Elizabeth Smith, an African American couple, came to Wickenburg in 1897 and operated the Baxter Hotel on Center Street. In 1905, Elizabeth established the Vernetta Hotel on Railroad Street. The Vernetta was soon considered the best hotel in Wickenburg. (Real photographic postcard, c. 1919. Collection of the author © vintagephoto.com.)

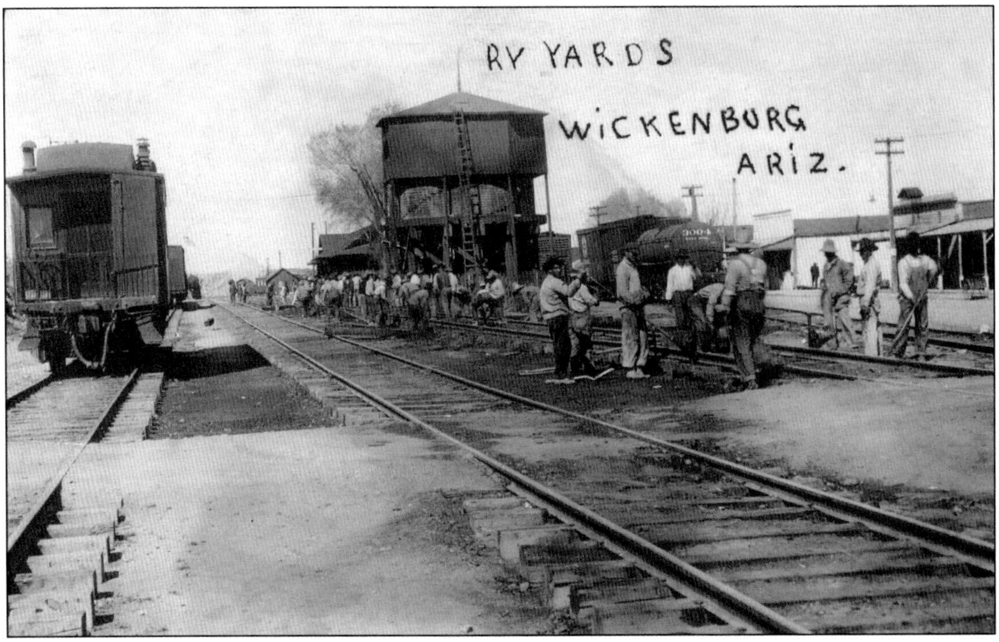

The Santa Fe Prescott and Phoenix railroad reached Wickenburg in 1895. Over the next 15 years, the railroad became central to the community, employing about 10 percent of the population in construction and operations for the SFP&P and Arizona and California railroads by 1910. (Real photographic postcard, c. 1919. Collection of the author © vintagephoto.com.)

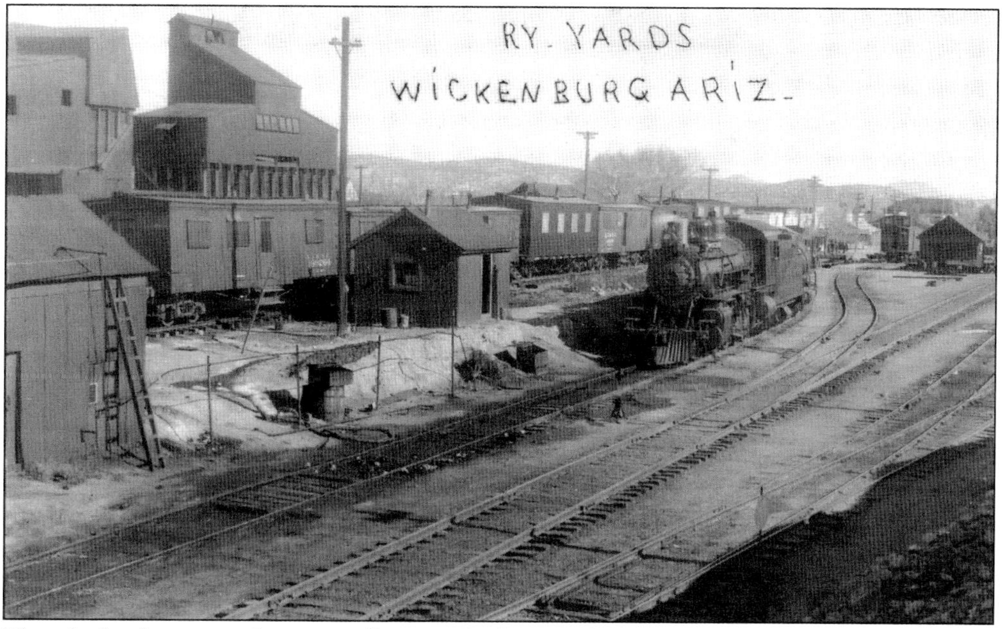

Though the shipping volume initially grew slowly after the arrival of the railroad, Wickenburg's position on the direct rail route from Phoenix to Los Angeles to the west, and link through Ash Fork to the Santa Fe route across Northern Arizona soon justified substantial railroad facilities. (Real photographic postcard, c. 1919. Collection of the author © vintagephoto.com.)

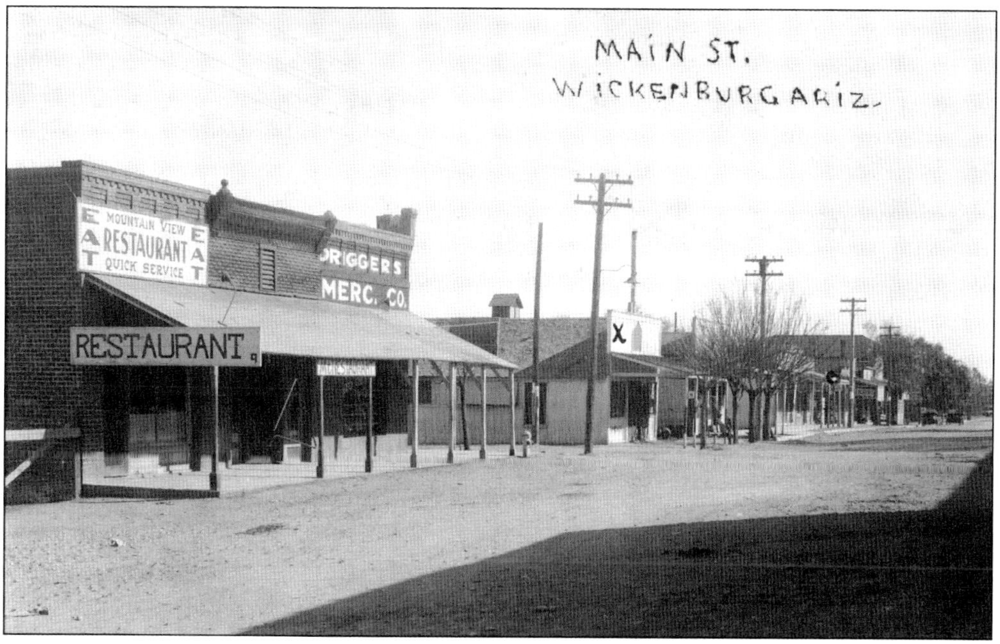

Main Street in Wickenburg developed adjacent the Vernetta Hotel along the railroad. Railroad Street (now Frontier Street) was home for the restaurants, barbershops, groceries, and supply businesses that served the growing community. (Real photographic postcards, c. 1919. Collection of the author © vintagephoto.com.)

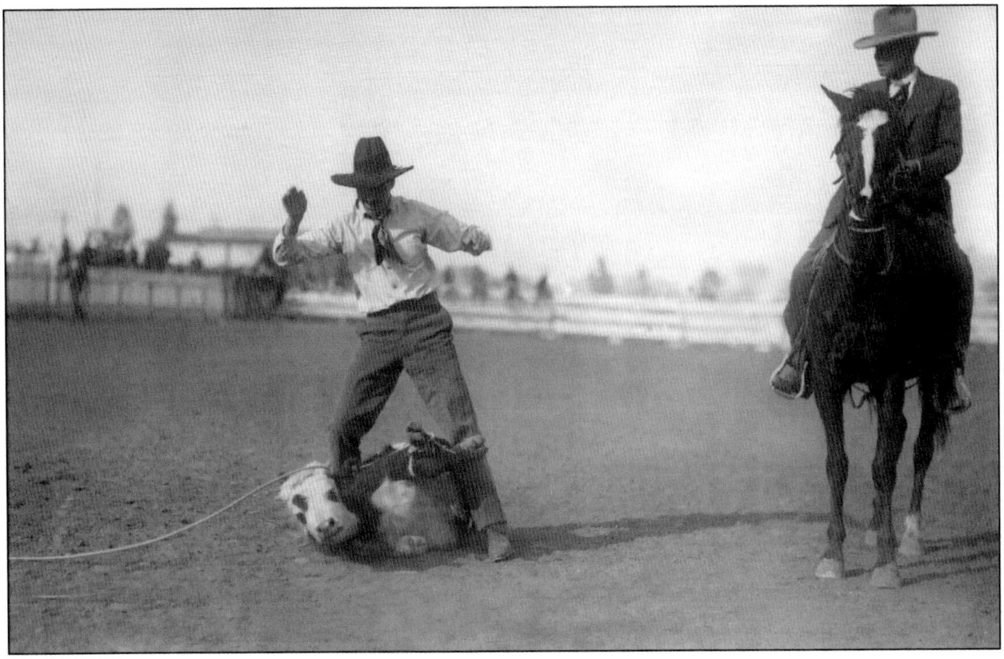

"Count" Jimmy Minotto, owner of V-Bar-V Cattle Ranch and Arizona Politician came to Arizona in 1914. Minotto married into the Swift family and became a banker, businessman, congressman, and rancher. Jimmy entered over 60 rodeos in calf roping and team tying and helped organize the World's Fair rodeo in Chicago in 1933. Here Minotto has just finished roping a calf at the Phoenix Rodeo. (Real photographic postcard, Ralph R Doubleday photographer, c. 1920. Collection of the author © vintagephoto.com.)

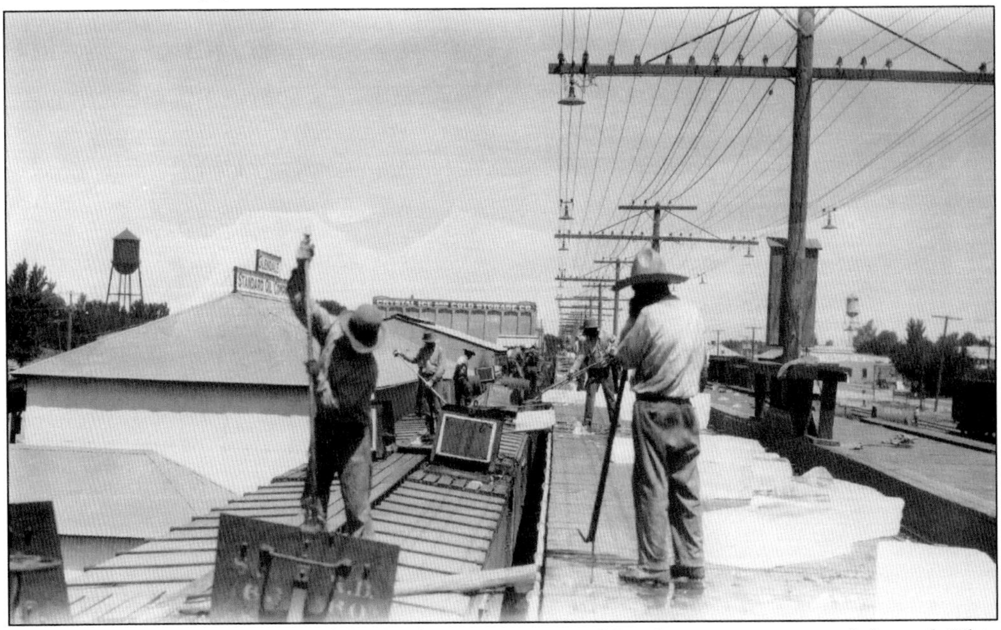

Summer heat made ice essential for food preservation and for shipping many goods by rail. This train loads its freight cars with ice at the Crystal Ice plant. (Silver print, photographer unknown, c. 1920. Collection of the author © vintagephoto.com.)

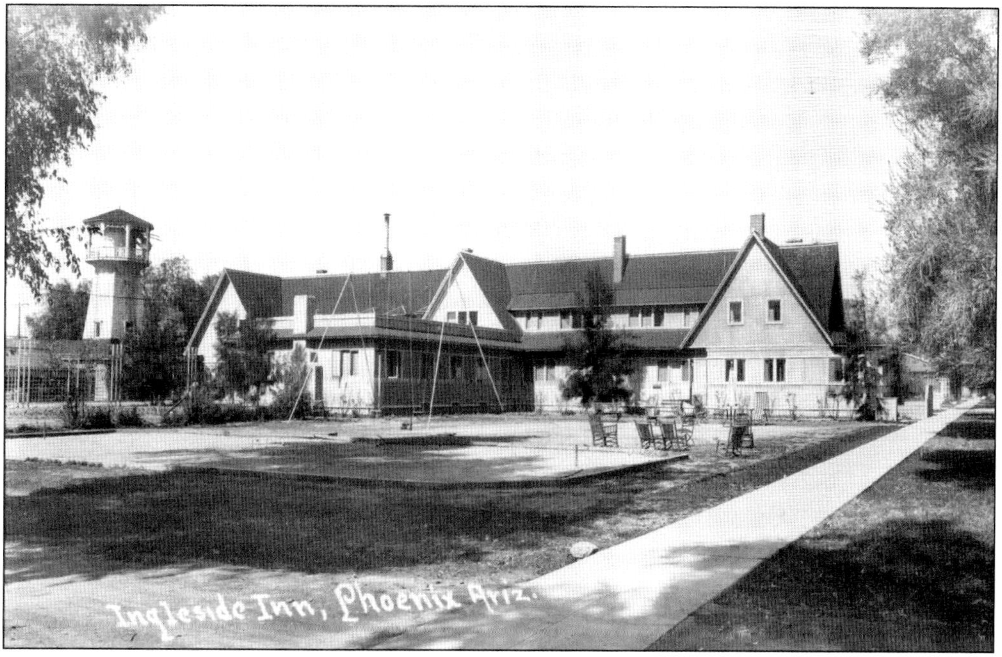

William John Murphy, who had made his fortune constructing the Arizona Canal in the mid-1880s, built the Ingleside club about 1910 east of downtown Phoenix. Originally a private club near Sixty-second Street and Indian School Road, the Ingleside Inn was soon marketed as an upscale health resort open during the prime tourist season from November to May. The Inn was an oasis, offering golf, hiking, camping, and picnics. (Real photographic postcards, photographer unknown, *c.* 1920. Collection of the author © vintagephoto.com.)

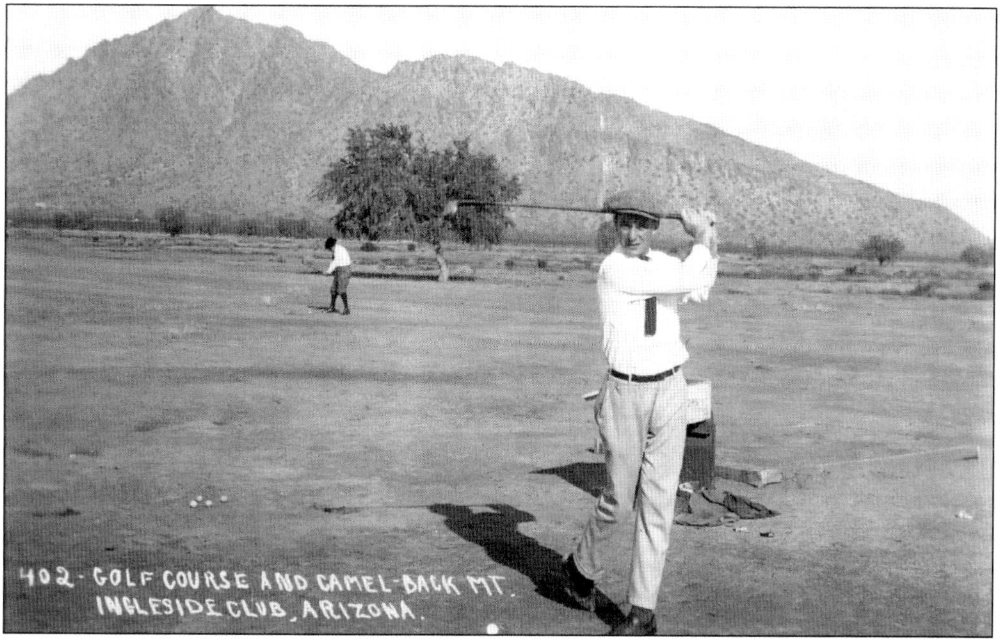

Background on the Photographs

Some of the best links to Arizona's past are the photographs made by the professional photographers and talented amateurs that documented the birth and development of our state. The format of the original image provides important information that can help identify and better understand the photographs. Where it is possible, identifying the photographer that made the original image provides additional information about the image and how it fits into the body of their work.

Though many of the images in this book were originally created for sale, only relatively small numbers were produced. Over the years, many have been lost, damaged, or destroyed. As a result the visual history that we see is largely based on serendipity. It is told by only the images that have survived, been collected and made available, and ultimately been correctly identified by collectors, researchers, museums, and archives. As a result, this history subtly changes over time as new images, and new scholarship about the images, becomes available.

The credits for the photographs that appear in this book when possible, include the format, photographer if known, and approximate date.

Every effort has been made to provide accurate caption information, based on provenance of the image, format, content and any other sources. The caption format requires abbreviated descriptions that hopefully provide sufficient information to help identify, and allow you to further explore these images.

Photographic Format Information

Name	Approximate Image Size	Dates of Popularity
Boudoir cabinet card	5.5 x 8.5	1880s
Cabinet card	6.5 x 4.5	1866–1900s
Carte-de-visite	2.5 x 4	1850s–1900s
Kodak circular images	4.5 x 5.25	1880s–1890s
Stereograph	3.5 x 7 to 5 x 7	1850s–1950s
Real photographic postcard	3.5 x 5.5	1900 to present

The photographs in this book come from the collection of the author, www.vintagephoto.com. The site provides additional information and images of the Salt River Valley, Arizona, and the Southwest.

Maricopa County Towns and Features to around 1920

Agua Caliente
Aguila
Apache Cave
Avondale
Bartlett Dam
Buckeye
Cashion
Cave Creek
Chandler
Desert Station
Dos Palmas
Fish Creek
Gila Bend
Gila Ranch
Gilbert
Gillespie Dam
Gillette
Glendale
Goldfield Mountain
Goodyear
Granite Reef Dam
Guadalupe
Higley
Kyrene
Laveen
Lehi
Litchfield Park
Fort Mc Dowell
Mesa
Morristown
New River
Overton
Papago Park
Paradise Valley
Peoria
Phoenix
Reavis
Salt River
Scottsdale
Sentinel
Tempe
Tolleson
Tortilla Flat
Vulture
Vulture mine
Wickenburg